Wye

Wye

Richard Hayman

Logaston Press

LOGASTON PRESS
Little Logaston, Woonton, Almeley
Herefordshire HR3 6QH
www.logastonpress.co.uk

First published by Logaston Press 2016
Copyright © Richard Hayman 2016

ISBN 978 1 910839 09 6

Typeset in Garamond by Logaston Press
Printed and bound in Poland by www.lfbookservices.co.uk

✤ Contents ✤

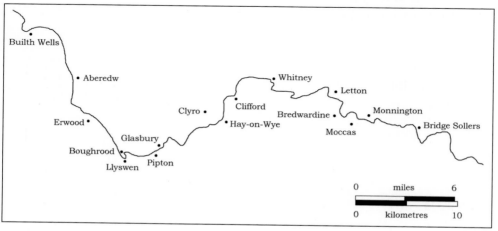

The course of the Wye from the source to Builth Wells (above)
and from Builth Wells to Hereford (below)

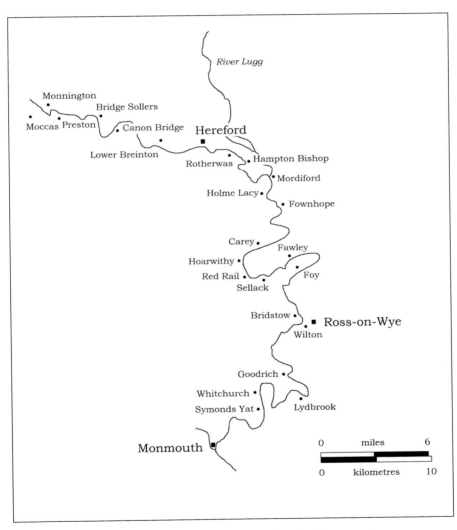

The course of the Wye from Hereford to Monmouth

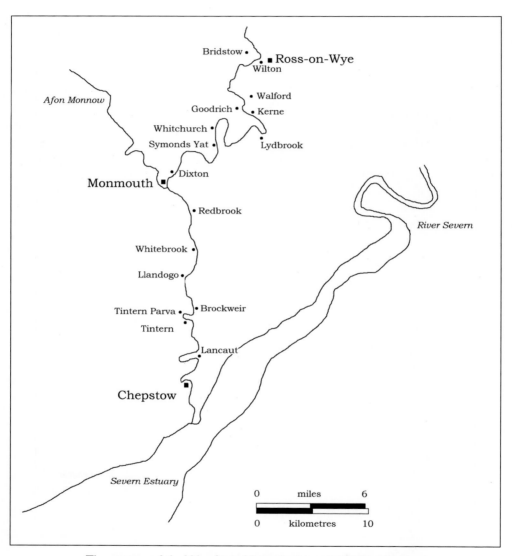

The course of the Wye from Monmouth to the Severn Estuary

❧ Acknowledgements ❧

I am indebted to the staff of several institutions who have helped me in research for this book, and I would like to thank especially the staff at the Cadbury Research Library at Birmingham University, and Tamsin Bapty at the Ironbridge Gorge Museums. Permission to use illustrations has been given by Herefordshire Libraries and IGMT.

❧ 1 ❧
A Noble and Glorious River

Rivers have become part of the background scenery of life. Look at an Ordnance Survey map and notice how much easier it is to follow roads and paths than it is to follow streams and rivers. It was not always like this. At one time the nation was imagined in the form of its river system, which John Leland used to structure his account of England and Wales in the 1530s, one of the earliest attempts to describe the nation. Early maps, like those of Christopher Saxton surveyed in the 16th century, had rivers marked in bold just as modern maps delineate roads. A map of streams and rivers can tell us much more about the lie of the land, and that in turn makes the manner in which people have inhabited and travelled about the Wye valley more comprehensible. From a map of rivers we would learn that rivers rather than roads have determined the infrastructure of our economic and cultural lives.

It is still unusual to view history through the medium of a river, largely because in our society rivers tend to be regarded as natural rather than cultural phenomena. As a result, the regional history of Britain is written in terms of ruins, old buildings and archaeological remains within the context of towns and counties. But if instead of seeing the past through the lens of historical monuments like abbey ruins, we treat a river itself as an historical monument, it offers a fresh and often surprising perspective on our past and why things happened as they did. It also reveals the extent to which our relationship with rivers has changed and how many of the concerns and experiences of past generations have been lost. They are worth making an effort to recover.

The Wye is a major British river, and one of the few that means something beyond its immediate locality, even if it conjures up in many minds merely picturesque scenery or a place for water sports. It has a rich history which can be traced back further than more traditional subjects of historical enquiry like towns and counties. Nor is its history confined to the practical issues of crossing it, navigating it or fishing it, as we will see. The Wye has influenced many aspects of life in the region and we have something to learn from all of them, right down to the history of its name.

The river has three names, two for everyday use and another when we want to talk about it in quasi-sacred terms. The oldest is its Welsh name, Afon Gwy, which was first

The dramatic view of the Wye from Symonds Yat.

The Wye near Coldwell Rocks, as viewed from Symonds Yat.

written down by Nennius in the 8th century. *Gwy* means just 'water' and is a common suffix in Welsh river names such as Conwy, Llugwy, Tywi, Dyfyrdwy and so on. The English name Wye clearly derives from it and was rendered simply as 'Y' in one of the earliest English-language accounts, written in 1478 by William Worcestre. The River Wye of the Welsh-English border is not the only example of the anglicised version of the Welsh word for water. There are rivers called Wye in Kent and Derbyshire, and a River Wey in Surrey. The Latin name for the river was Vaga, apparently from *vagare*, to wander, which is apt, but there is no record of its having been used in Roman Britain. The word was used in the early 13th century by Alexander Neckam in the *distinction tertia* of his *De laudibus divinae sapientiae*, and by William Camden in his *Britannia* of 1586. Poets have often used Vaga for the Wye in the same way that Christianity used Latin and later archaic English to fulfil the need to talk about sacred things in a sacred language. The name Vaga, notably employed by Luke Booker in the 19th century, elevates the river above the utilitarian watercourse that the name 'Wye' may signify.

The Wye is 'a noble and glorious river', in the words of fisherman and cricketer, H.A. Gilbert. George Borrow, the Victorian English traveller, declared it 'the most lovely river, probably, which the world can boast of', while George Bernard Shaw thought its scenery surpassed 'ordinary naturalism and freshness of Nature' to achieve 'a deliberate poetic beauty'. 'Blessed is the eye between Severn and Wye' was once a common saying. The country that borders the Wye is a land of fruits, especially apples and pears, which

Chepstow Castle and Bridge in 1802, one of the chief landmarks on the river.
(Yale Center for British Art, Paul Mellon Collection)

Tintern Abbey is one of the most romantic of medieval monastic ruins
and its fame enhanced the reputation of the river.

The Wye is a rural river, in which a bridge, as here in a painting of Bredwardine
by T.H. Fielding, is a perfect adornment to natural scenery.

further enhances the river's reputation for summery rural bliss. One of the wonders of Britain described by Nennius in the 8th century was the 'apple-bearing ash tree', specimens of which grew on the steep banks of the lower Wye. This was probably the True Service Tree, whose apple-like fruit can be used to make a cider-like drink.

In the 18th century the Wye became one of Britain's first tourist destinations, at a time when it was impossible to journey in Europe in search of the beauties of nature, the Grand Tour through France and Italy that had been so fashionable having become too dangerous thanks to the Napoleonic Wars. Chepstow and Goodrich castles and especially Tintern Abbey were inseparable from the pleasures of river scenery. Over two centuries later the Wye is still for most people primarily a river of leisure and pleasure. The first tourists enjoyed the river by boat, and the tradition has been maintained ever since; rowing gained in popularity in the 19th century and then canoeing became popular in the 20th. Canoes and pleasure cruisers have replaced the old river barges, riverbank walkers now follow the paths of bow haulers, and there are riverside parks instead of timber yards and wharves. The Wye has fared much better than many other rivers in maintaining a post-industrial riverside life. It was one of the first rivers along which there was a recognised long-distance footpath, although it took from 1975 to 2002 for the entire course of the route to be prepared for walkers. And the Wales Coast Path begins in Chepstow below the bridge, a reminder that the Wye is an estuarine river that defines the south-east limit of the Welsh coast.

A river is a natural place of tranquillity and contemplation. Anglers are looking for more than just fish. But the modern world always somehow intervenes. The peace was interrupted as far back as the 19th century when railways were built alongside the river, making use of its relatively flat terrain. Francis Kilvert described an idyllic summer evening by the Wye, when 'the western light shimmered down the broad reach of the Wye and the river flowed softly by, rippling and lapping gently upon the grey shingle beds'. Three men sat on the opposite bank watching Kilvert and his

The Wye is a river of meanders, shown here in dramatic form near Chepstow in 1832 by John Varley. (Yale Center for British Art, Paul Mellon Collection)

The classic view of Hereford, here in a sketch made by W.M. Meredith, c.1905, has long been from the river, with the Wye Bridge in the middle distance and Hereford Cathedral behind it.

father. Then they were all rudely interrupted as 'a luggage train rushed by along the high embankment just across the river, the last gleam of the sun shining upon the engine'.[1]

The Wye is more than the provider of natural tranquillity, a consolation of picturesque scenery. The river has been not just a setting, but an active player in events that have shaped the history of the region, and have been integral to ordinary daily life. It has been a mode of transport, carrying vessels down with the current and upriver with the tide, and once turned the waterwheels of industry. It was also the source of a once abundant supply of delicious and nutritious food, something that allowed early Christian hermits to settle beside it. Many of the chapels they founded became parish churches and are still open for worship. Crossing the river has tested human ingenuity and inspired works of engineering, some of which like the old Chepstow road bridge and Chepstow railway bridge are landmarks in engineering history. The Wye and its tributaries provide water for well over a million people, although in a world where water just comes out of a tap, we tend to take it for granted.

The Wye is one of a minority of British rivers that flow over national borders. Having both a Welsh and an English heritage, it has a special unifying role in British culture, as well as exhibiting some of the classic features of a border. The river has been a psychological barrier separating cultures by language, religion and politics, and a physical barrier separating hostile rivals. By tradition the Wye was the last refuge of Vortigern and of Owain Glyndwr, and down the river floated timber for building the ships that took on the French at Trafalgar. British patriots did not fail to notice that dissolving the

Tintern Abbey by moonlight, in a watercolour by John 'Warwick' Smith.
(Metropolitan Museum of Art, New York)

border was a triumph of the modern nation, and the River Wye distilled the essence of Britishness. (This theme is developed in chapter 14.)

The river is a giver and a taker of life. Its mood can seem to change and darken and the gently flowing waters by day can turn eerie and sinister by night. Rivers are powerful forces of nature and their beauty always comes with the potential for destruction, flooding and drowning. Its flow may be regulated and its threats can be planned for, but the river has never been entirely domesticated and never will be.

⚘ 2 ⚘
The Natural River

There are few more captivating sights in nature than flowing water. A river looks like a finished work of nature from a distance, but look closer and by its movement, the ripples on its surface and the dappled sunlight, it seems to be endlessly recreating itself. Mountain streams give us the added bonus of the sound they make. Water flowing over and occasionally cascading down rocks pleases the ear as much as the eye. It assumes a limitless array of shapes and patterns, and yet the picture it poses is never less than graceful and the flow appears purposeful, as if every drop of water already knows exactly where it is going. Streams are rarely ugly, and a river is always a law unto itself, whether it is a summer trickle or a devastating flood. The strength of water and its continuous rising from the ground is perhaps its most mysterious quality.

A river flows, indifferent to the people who interact with it, but we still like to think of it as a silent witness through the ages. Riverside hermits and ferrymen have traditionally been people of a philosophical cast of mind, the kind of people who look at a river and ruminate on time and the individual's place within it. They simply specialise in thoughts we all engage in from time to time. A river stimulates thoughts like these and is a reminder that the natural world cannot really be separated from culture.

There is more to rivers than quiet reflection, however. A river animates a landscape, distinguishing it from the rock-solid stillness of a mountain. Richard Warner, travelling on the road from Builth to Rhayader in 1797, stopped to admire the scenery on the river bank, made striking by the energy in the water. 'The river appears at our feet, dashing and roaring through a bed of huge, misshapen rocks, and forming, in its struggles, numberless whirlpools, eddies, and small cascades. A bank, rude, abrupt, and bare, rises before us, pleasingly contrasted by the verdant and wooded declivity opposite to it. As the eye roves up the river, it catches softer beauties; the sides become less precipitous, and more thickly clothed with trees. The woods at length descend to the brink of the stream, which, making a quick turn at the distance of a mile, is suddenly lost in a deep mass of shade.'[1]

Rivers have been sought out as places of aesthetic pleasure since at least the 18th century. The nature poets emerged at the same time as the naturalists, those patient

9

observers of nature who laid the foundation of the scientific study of rivers. Early writers about the river, like John Leland in the 1530s, described it in terms of pike, umber and trout, but today's naturalists are just as likely to be talking about reed canary-grass and the white-legged damsel fly. The more we learn about the river the less we take it for granted as a place of nature, and scientific knowledge is the basis of managing its fragile natural habitats. The river is also a vital resource to agriculture and domestic life, and equally a threat when it swells after rain, in response to which we have amassed huge amounts of data about how the river behaves, and what lives in it and beside it.

The Wye is classed as one of Britain's 67 primary rivers, 'primary' meaning that it exceeds 8 metres in breadth at its widest point. The Wye is Britain's sixth biggest river, 215 kilometres (135 miles) long and with a catchment, according to Natural Resources Wales, of 4,171 square kilometres, and it is tidal for about 14 miles, as far up as Bigsweir Bridge. The landscape of the Wye is more diverse than that surrounding some of the other major British rivers such as the Thames and the Trent. Its source is in the mountains of Wales, it flows through rich agricultural plains, then through an extended natural gorge to estuarine conditions at its confluence with the Severn. Around the source of the river in the mountains the annual rainfall is high, averaging 2.2 metres a year on Plynlimon, compared with only 700 millimetres in the area of the lower river. The combination of high rainfall in its headwaters and an underlying geology that is not very permeable means that the river swells very quickly after heavy rainfall,

The river rises on Plynlimon, which has an average annual rainfall of 2.2 metres.

a long-recognised phenomenon known as a fresh, but in a dry period the relative lack of groundwater means that it dries up very quickly too. The Wye has a reputation for being a fast-flowing river, but this impression can be a little deceptive. It is the river with the fifth fastest flow in Britain, but it flows at less than half the rate of the River Tay in Scotland and has only three quarters the flow rate of the Severn, which in many people's eyes is a much more sluggish body of water.[2]

Like all rivers the anatomy of the Wye follows the basic laws of river flow. As it descends toward the sea it slowly brings the mountains down with it, so in its early stages the river is an erosive force, and near the end it receives the sediments carried down by the current. The tendency to see rivers in human terms is difficult to resist, the apparently vigorous flow of the youthful upper reaches in contrast to the ponderous march to the sea at the downstream end, but this is a slightly deceptive impression and one that is certainly confounded by the Wye. Its headwaters, for which fluvial geomorphologists have so far found no more poetic expression than the 'upper section', flow over bedrock, and this is a fast-flowing section of the river because it has the steepest gradient. The river eventually changes character in its 'middle section', flowing through a flood plain, and the river bed is not bedrock but silt, gravel and boulders that the river has itself laid down. Contrary to the impression the eye gives, river flow is higher here than in the upper section, because the channel is wider and deeper, and more water can flow freely without being held back by friction from the river bank and bed. The lower section of the river is similar to the middle section, except that it ceases to be an erosive force and is more subject to deposition.

The young river flows fast over a rocky bed.

The young fast-flowing river as it descends from Plynlimon.

Confluence of the Wye, on the left, with the Tarenig, on the right.

The upper Wye is a small river in an epic landscape,
a consequence of valley enlargement in the Ice Age.

The rocks in the river bed at Rhayader that gave the town its name.

The river at Builth is shallow, with shoals of pebbles visible at times of low water, and flows across a broad floodplain.

The Wye is not at all a typical river, as outlined in this simple model of river flow. Its upper section is unusually long compared with most primary rivers and contrary to expectations, the most dramatic scenery is at the downstream end of the river. The river begins with classic fast-flowing headwaters, cutting deep channels through the thick peat deposits, until it is joined by Afon Tarenig four miles below the source. Very soon the landscape changes markedly in character. The valley is wide, on an epic scale, but this has little to do with the river itself. It is the consequence long ago of glaciers exaggerating the existing land forms that they encountered as they crept southwards. The river continues to flow partially over bedrock as far downstream as Rhayader, immediately upstream of which is a gorge at Nannerth characterised by rocks and overhanging trees which Richard Warner stopped to admire in 1797.

Just below Rhayader the river receives its first major tributary, the Elan River, and becomes a much larger body of water. The landscape now changes again. The Wye is no longer a mountain river, but flows through an alluvial floodplain. There are fewer sections where bedrock resistant to erosion is exposed, and the landscape slowly becomes more conventionally pastoral. From Builth downstream the river acquires water from ever more tributaries – the Ithon, Irfon, Edw, Llynfi – that drain the Welsh uplands. And just below Boughrood the lie of the land forces the river to turn east toward Hereford, unable to continue its southward course because of the Black Mountains.

As the river descends it starts to meander. Once a river reaches its middle section and the gradient is only very slight, the tendency to meander is natural. It has been

The River Wye at the old Nanty mine, in the process of cutting off a meander.

The River Wye at Hampton Bishop below Hereford.

calculated that a river cannot flow in a straight line for much further than ten times its width, the result of a dynamic relationship between the water and the sediment it carries.[3] The Wye is a river of meanders for most of its course between mid Wales and the sea, except where it is affected by other factors. The loops of the river are much more pronounced below Hereford, to the extent that places like Foy are quite peninsular in character. Michael Drayton, writing in the early 17th century, was so struck by the sinuous course of the river as it appeared on Christopher Saxton's map that he declared it unequalled in its 'many turns' and 'crankling nooks'.

As it meanders across the wide plain, the Wye cuts through the middle of Herefordshire before it re-enters the hills in the south-east of the county near Goodrich. The lowlands of Herefordshire represent the basins of the Wye and some of its tributaries, flowing over red marls and sandstones and forming a rich fertile valley of meadow, pasture and orchard, the quintessential Herefordshire landscape. Most of Herefordshire is within the Wye basin as its rivers – the Arrow, Lugg and Frome – all sooner or later deliver their waters to the Wye.

In this section of the river it is not obvious how the topography has been affected by glaciation. During the Ice Age the area of modern Herefordshire was covered in an ice sheet 240 metres thick and the natural landscape was significantly altered in phases over a period of 500,000 years, ending about 10,000 years ago. A huge glacier formed within the Wye valley flowing from west to east across Herefordshire as far as the Wye's confluence with the Lugg. It pushed down and deposited the rubble it carried at its limits, in successive phases of advance and retreat. These deposits, known as moraines, can still be identified in several places, notably at Clyro, Bredwardine and Stretton Sugwas. Before the Ice Age the Wye had been smaller and was effectively a tributary of the River Lugg. The actions of glaciers changed that relationship, since water that once flowed into the Lugg in tributaries was diverted into the River Teme, and so the Lugg was eventually diminished.[4]

One consequence of the scouring effect of glaciers has been to lower the river bed and thereby reduce the gradient of the river, so that it flows at a slower rate than it would have done if there had been no Ice Age. The slower flow has meant that in many places the river is not strong enough to erode the river bank and form loops, but instead forms sequences of pools and riffles (or fords). Islands in the river are another consequence of this process, although islands can also form on the downstream side of bridge piers, where the current is weaker. The river near the England-Wales border is a series of pools and shallows, and many of the pools were known by name, largely because they were sought out by fishermen. Near Clyro Francis Kilvert recorded several of them – Pwll dwrgi (pool of the water dog or water monster), Otter's Pool, Steeple Pool below Hay church, the Moor Water, Stone Pitch and Dole Pitch, the Bychllyn Pool, the Howey and the Bach Howey.[5] Below Hereford it was the shallows that attracted notice, not simply because they impeded river traffic, but also because they could be useful. Where the river was shallow it was easier to build fish weirs, and above Wilton there was a shallow with the self-explanatory name of Sheep Wash. In the section below Ross a survey attributed to Daniel Denell in 1697 identified several shallows – Gotheridge (or Goodrich) Ford, Priory Ford, Lydbrookford and Parkford.[6]

Islands form naturally in shallow rivers especially, as here in Hay,
downstream of bridge piers.

The river changes dramatically below Ross, when the underlying geology changes
from Old Red Sandstone to carboniferous limestone. It cuts through limestone hills to
form a magnificent gorge, with steep valley sides but little valley floor. It then continues
to follow a narrow winding corridor down to Chepstow and its confluence with the
Severn, still meandering as it cuts through the limestone rocks. At Monmouth the
floodplain widens where the Wye is joined by the Monnow and Trothy rivers. Further
downstream the meanders have mini crescent-shaped flood plains on the inner sides of
the loops, and steep cliffs on the outer sides. It is a curious and unusual arrangement to
which several factors have contributed, including the comparative softness of the rock,
a period of glaciation and the fact that the sea was once much higher than it is now. It
is thought that a tongue of ice spread down the valley from Monmouth, about 440,000
years ago, carving a U-shaped profile which is best exhibited between Whitebrook and
Llandogo. The steepest parts of the gorge have flowed over soft limestone rocks and its
meanders have formed steep river cliffs. Once the river flowed at a much higher level,
but a combination of land uplift and sea level fall caused the channel to become incised
through its existing bed with no opportunity for widening. This process created the deep
valleys that we know today. Below Tintern the old U-shaped valley sides remain visible,
through which the river has cut its deeper course.

Like the Severn, part of the Wye's history is concealed on the river bed. There is a
drowned river channel below Chepstow, long since filled up with sediment. The rivers
of South Wales all flowed on over what has since become the Bristol Channel, where
the Severn flowed out to the sea at a point south of modern Ireland. The Wye has been
tidal only for a comparatively short period of time, as a consequence of rising sea levels

The steep-sided wooded valley of the Wye below Symonds Yat.

This view of Chepstow from Wyndcliff, made by John Scarlett Davies in 1834,
shows the steep cliffs that make the meandering lower Wye so dramatic.
(Metropolitan Museum of Art, New York)

since the end of the Ice Age. The sea reached its current level about 2,000 years ago. It means that, officially, the Wye has a short estuary that joins the Severn estuary, with a consequence that the coastline of the Gwent Levels, as far as Portskewett and just short of the Second Severn Crossing, is part of the Wye river system.

The last Ice Age ended about 10,000 years ago so it took the sea level 8,000 years to rise to its current level, and this is the sort of timescale that we usually have in mind when we think about changes in rivers, but there are many examples of change happening in the river quite suddenly. Collapses of river cliffs are the best example. Here, the meanders that cut into the limestone have caused landslips, as at Black Cliff and Wyndcliff, although they are difficult to see now because they are covered with woodland. This kind of change can happen on a small scale too, as Francis Kilvert recorded at Bredwardine after the hard frosts of 1878-79, following which 'a large slice of the Vicarage river bank … has slipped into the river'.[7] Change is not always a slow and steady accumulation; it can be the result of one or more distinct episodes.

In several places the river can be seen to have shifted its course in historical times. One of the characteristic features of the river is that it is quick to rise after heavy rain or a winter thaw. John Duncumb noted in 1804 that by its sudden impetuosity 'large quantities of land are frequently removed from their situations … and new channels have thus been formed in various places'.[8] A meander is only ever a provisional course because the meander itself continues to migrate until a point is reached where flood water cuts it off by creating a new, straighter channel. Study of the Ordnance Survey maps reveals several meanders that have been cut off in the form of classic ox-bow lakes. The old meander at Letton was apparently cut off after a flood in the 19th century.[9] Upstream of Glasbury an old meander can still be seen on the north side of the present river course as an intermittent wide ditch, which has dictated the shape of the fields around it, and on which Grange Farm was built in the 19th century. This channel seems to have been cut off in the Middle Ages and was perhaps the old river course noted in the 1530s by Leland, who said that it was a pool known as 'Henewey', meaning old water or even perhaps Old Wye.[10] By the 16th century the river had taken a more sweeping course south of its present channel, passing Pipton and close to Great House at Aberllynfi, and being shadowed for a distance by the A438 where it passes close to Aberllynfi church. The river had probably adopted its present course by the middle of the 17th century – in 1658 serious floods were said to have endangered the church at Glasbury, the only remedy for which seems to have been to build a new church further from the river.[11]

The Wye is one of the most unspoilt and protected river systems in Britain. The river's entire course, together with some of its tributaries like Afon Tarenig, is a Site of Special Scientific Interest, designated in order to protect the animal and plant species that live in and beside the river. SSSI designation puts a responsibility upon owners to maintain the natural asset and requires them to obtain consent for activities that might cause harm. Designation is also an important factor in determining planning applications that might affect the river in any way.

The Wye is special because it hosts diverse animal and plant communities, its course has not been manipulated artificially and, in comparison with rivers of a similar size, it has only relatively small settlements beside it. The river is a large linear ecosystem which acts as an important wildlife corridor, making it a key migration route and breeding area for several important species. Effective conservation of the upper river is therefore dependant upon conservation of the lower river.

There are also landscapes of national significance found along the course of the river. The Wye gorge is one of the most important areas of semi-natural woodland in Britain, comparable in value with the New Forest and the Caledonian pinewoods. Even the geology is significant, since there are numerous natural caves, of which King Arthur's Cave and Merlin's Cave are the most notable. They retain remains of extinct and former native species like the spotted hyena, mammoth and lemmings that give evidence of the changing climate of the river valley over a long period of time.

The means by which nature conservation is reconciled with the everyday world and our appreciation of it is through designation as an Area of Outstanding Natural Beauty (or AONB). The Lower Wye Valley AONB was designated in 1971 and covers an area 28 miles long from just below the confluence with the River Lugg downstream to Chepstow and is up to seven miles wide. It is one of the few lowland landscapes to enjoy AONB status. The purpose of the designation is to conserve the area and at the same time promote the appreciation and enjoyment of the countryside. It also tries to accommodate conservation principles with the needs of the local economy and its people. An estimated 2 million people visit the lower Wye valley each year, and tourism and other recreational pursuits, like canoeing, therefore make a major contribution to the local economy. The valley is easily accessible from South Wales and from the English Midlands via the M50. People will keep coming, but while much of the appeal of the Wye is its riverside settlements and buildings like Goodrich Castle, Chepstow and especially Tintern, all of them depend upon their natural setting. To retain its natural integrity, the river and its banks therefore need to be carefully managed.

The consequence of steep and inaccessible valley sides and bottoms in the lower river has generally been a happy one for their non-human inhabitants, at least over the past century, but these places are not as devoid of human footprints as they at first look. Riverside woodlands like Ban-y-gor near Chepstow have been pollarded, and the nearby Lancaut limestone beds were quarried for lime burning and for the construction of Avonmouth Docks in the late 19th century. Prisk Wood, on the Welsh side near Monmouth, was once quarried for its quartz conglomerate, which was used to cut millstones. Now they are enclaves of wild nature and designated as nature reserves, the means by which the environment is micro-managed, and they host an impressive range of plant and animal species and rare and delicate habitats.

Salt water washes up the river twice daily, with a result that narrow salt marshes have developed in uninhabited sections such as Lancaut. This fragile habitat is home to rare species like sea aster and sea milkwort. Above it the cliffs and steep banks of ancient woodland are said to provide a habitat for some 350 species of wild flower, with mountain melick and fingered sedge among the rarer species. They include rare species of whitebeam – a tree that does not feature very often in praises of the natural world – and the cliffs offer safe nesting sites to peregrine falcons.

The confluence of Wye and Severn at low tide.
In the distance is the Second Severn crossing of 1995.

Management of the river system goes far beyond identifying and protecting sites within it. The volume of water in the river has to be managed because there are many demands on the Wye and its tributaries, not least for domestic water supply. The Elan Valley reservoirs are key to that strategy, as well as supplying Birmingham with its water. The Wye is a regulated river, which means that if the river level falls below a certain threshold, as measured at Redbrook, then water is released from the reservoirs, although this is partly to ensure sufficient water for other users. The main pressure on water resources comes from agriculture and the prevalence of trickle and spray irrigation. Golf courses use their share too.

Protection of the river ecology is also dependent on the water level. There is a minimum flow necessary to achieve what is deemed a healthy natural river, as well as established levels of the abstraction of water for human use. Certain species are very sensitive to changes in river level, including well-known examples like salmon, twaite shad, lamprey and otters, but also rare species that are important to the ecology of the river but have a low amenity value as far as humans are concerned. These include the pearl mussel and the depressed river mussel, which live on the silty river margins, making them especially vulnerable to excessive abstraction, and a rare diving beetle which is found at Glasbury and Rhayader. Additional abstraction is licensed on a temporary basis according to the level of the river, which can be measured at the Redbrook, Belmont and Erwood gauging stations, as well as gauging stations on the tributary rivers.[12]

The Wye is still essentially a natural river, in that it has been relatively free of straightening, widening or deepening, which is unusual for a major river. However, being now a regulated river, it is far less changeable than it used to be. This is worth bearing in mind when we think about fords, where crossing the river was probably quite straightforward in the summer months, and about navigation. A river might offer free transport but when the Wye was still in a state of nature, barges were often moored for weeks waiting for a fresh to set them on their way downstream. People must once have prayed for rain.

✆ 3 ✇
Plynlimon

The source of all major rivers is always established by travelling backwards – mountain streams give no hint as to whether they will be great rivers or minor tributaries. On the Wye for example, the River Elan looks just as significant as the Wye itself when the rivers join below Rhayader. The same might be said further upstream where the Tarenig joins the Wye four miles below its source, although appearances are deceptive. The Tarenig actually carries a greater volume of water than the Wye. A river is not a single water-course but the main channel in a system with as many branches as the veins in a leaf. We define the main channel not by volume of water or by how far it rises from the mouth, but how high its source is. The source of the river is identified simply by establishing the highest point at which water in the river basin rises. On the River Wye that place is on Plynlimon in the Cambrian Mountains, at an altitude of approximately 680 metres (2,231 feet) above sea level.

Plynlimon has not always been regarded as the river's source, and not every age seems to have been interested in where the river comes from. William Worcestre, writing in the 1470s, first thought that the Wye rose close to the Taff and Usk in the hills above Abergavenny. A year later he described its source as 'in the mountains 10 miles beyond Brecon, almost eight miles high' as if it was too far from civilisation to be of any interest, a 'here be dragons' kind of place.[1] But Plynlimon was known as the source of the Wye to the Welsh author Giraldus Cambrensis in the late 12th century, and it was definitely known to English authors as the source by the 16th century. Of these, John Leland was the first to note that the Wye and Severn rise within two miles of each other in the Welsh mountains and fall into the sea at the same place – a fact that no author has since failed to reiterate.

Plynlimon is a major location in the story of the Wye, although it seems a semi-detached part of the river, given that the Wye has an unusually long mountain section, and also that most people writing about the Wye concentrated on the lower river. Plynlimon – *Pumlumon* (five peaks) – is the mountainous region of western Powys, south of Machynlleth. The name is rather loosely applied, meaning both a group of hills and the single hill – *Pumlumon Fawr* – which is the highest of the group. Several more rivers have their source on Plynlimon, notably the Severn and its tributary the Clywedog, and the Rheidol and its tributaries Hyddgen and Hengwm, which drain to the west coast of Wales. This mountainous region was once also known as Elenid, and Giraldus Cambrensis called it that. Both names appear in the *Mabinogion*. But for Giraldus Plynlimon was a much larger area, and perhaps the notional heartland of Wales, since he identifies it as the source of many other Welsh rivers, including the Tywi, Teifi and Ystwyth.[2]

Welsh hills are never dry, and Plynlimon is no exception. It is defined by water, by the mist and rain in the air, by the streams that hollow out and shape the landscape, and by the groundwater that squelches underfoot. A few hundred yards below the source the river has already picked up a couple of other streams and is too wide to jump across, but even on damp Welsh hills its continual flow, even after a prolonged dry spell, is something of a mystery. In fact the stream, darkened slightly by the peat, changes less than the atmosphere on Plynlimon. A walk that starts in cloudy mist can quickly transform into a sky full of light, and back again.

The source of the Wye is not easy to reach, which is as it should be for a mountain river. There is an official route, the Wye Valley Walk, but it was created before Right-to-Roam legislation was passed, and so its starting point is an elevated position on Cerig y Wyn, nearly a mile below the source (but in view of it on the right day), and initially follows the tributary stream, Nant Iago. There is no path to the source itself, but the

Samuel Ireland's view of the young River Wye on Plynlimon,
showing gentleman and lady travellers with a guide.

unenclosed uplands are now open to anyone to explore on foot. A reasonably fit person can make it up the stream side, but every mile is a hard-won country mile. The journey is an obstacle course of tall moorland grass, unexpected boggy encounters and the challenge of jumping over streamlets. Another way is to follow the ridge of the hill from Hafren Forest to the north. The source is only about 50 metres from the top of the hill, where a fence marks the county boundary.

The source is definitive and quite spectacular insofar as the source of a river can ever be described in that way. A spring issues immediately into a well-cut valley, and is swelled by other springs descending steeply and joining the main stream. It flows down through a broad valley far too wide for such an insignificant body of water, and clearly enlarged by the actions of glaciers. The river descends rapidly. By the time it reaches Pont Rhyd Galed, about 4 miles downstream, it has fallen to 318 metres above sea level, and so has already made more than half of its vertical descent to the sea. Here it is joined by Afon Tarenig, which is about equal in width to the main channel.

Plynlimon is a mountain of the mind, and a Welsh mountain at that. There is a distinction between the English and the Welsh understanding of mountains, as well as a distinction between urban and rural perceptions. In English the word 'mountain' is used to denote something bigger than a hill and often implies a place beyond human habitation, a harsh and inhospitable environment. But the Welsh word *mynydd* means something more and different. It is less concerned with absolute than with relative

Unusually for a river, the source of the Wye is easy to identify because it immediately forms a valley.

altitude, referring to the land above the permanent and even the summer pasture, known as the *ffridd*. Such places are not regarded as wilderness at all. The urban mindset sees the mountain as a place where the ground is traversed in a line to the summit. But the local people inhabit the mountain in a different way, a way that teaches them to avoid the boggy ground and the windy spots. George Borrow recognised this when he walked on Plynlimon with a local shepherd in the mid 19th century. 'My guide walked with a calm and deliberate gait, yet I had considerable difficulty in keeping up with him. ... he was a shepherd walking on his own hill, and having first-rate wind, and knowing every inch of the ground, made great way without seeming to be in the slightest hurry.'[3]

The symbolic importance of Plynlimon should not be underestimated. Mountains are a key element in Welsh national identity. They can be seen as inalienable repositories of Welshness, safe from outside influence, a part of Wales that has never really been conquered by outsiders, whether military generals or mine captains. Attachment to specific places, especially mountains that retain an overwhelming presence, is the essence of Welshness, whether you live in the industrial valleys of the south or in the uplands of the north. Gwyn Jones was born in industrial South Wales in 1907, but the mountains of mid and north Wales were his adult inspiration. He could see Plynlimon from the hill above his home near Aberystwyth, and wrote of it in the 1940s at the same time as he was working on his translation of the *Mabinogion*. From a distance Plynlimon was 'a

As it flows down from the source the river passes through
a combination of moorland and improved pasture.

score of rosy lumps, divagated by green valleys, black woodlands, the silver ribbons of rivers, its fields brown, grey, pink, emerald, until the blunted tops of the five mountains are lost in purple distance half-way to the English border. All this is Wales.' To be Welsh is to live among mountains, and Plynlimon is a quintessentially Welsh mountain range.[4]

We may imagine that these upland landscapes have always been remote and uninhabited places, but if we think that, we are wrong. If the landscape is now a wilderness, it is not because it has never been inhabited, but because it has been abandoned. The Ordnance Survey has been mapping the headwaters of the Wye valley since the early 19th century and has noted every *nant* and *carreg*, with the individual names of hills and outcrops. It is a place that has been intimately known, and not merely in recent times. People travelled across Plynlimon in prehistory, and their legacy of cairns, traditionally places where beacon fires were lit, and standing stones is scattered over the higher ground of Plynlimon.

Plynlimon gained a place in national mythology as a result of Owain Glyndwr's rebellion in the early 15th century, when the link between Welshness and the mountainous stronghold of central Wales was further enhanced. Plynlimon was a stronghold of Owain Glyndwr in the early, invincible part of his rebellion. On Mynydd Hyddgen in 1401 Owain led a small Welsh force to victory over a superior army. The success of the battle was as much political as military – considerable support was attracted to the winning side, who now had access to support from South Wales. The significance

A calm stretch of water, with pebble bed, above Pont Rhyd Galed.

accorded to Owain Glyndwr's exploits on Plynlimon can be measured by the legends
that have attached to the place. Early histories recorded that only 120 Welsh fought
against 1,500 English and Flemish forces. Glyndwr was supposed to have slept, or
perhaps sought refuge, in a cave, possibly the cleft in the rock near Hyddgen known
as Siambr Traws Fynydd. Craig y March (Rock of the Horse) is supposed to bear the
hoof prints of Glyndwr's horse Llwyd y Bacsie. Cwm Gwarchae (Valley of the Siege)
was supposed to have been so-named because Glyndwr fought there. Cerrig Cyfamod
Owain Glyndwr (Stone of Owain Glyndwr's Treaty) is apparently where Glyndwr and
Hugh Mortimer agreed to end hostilities. Y Stablau are caves where Glyndwr's horses
were stabled.[5] Bearing the imprint of these great events, Plynlimon has acquired some of
the glory of Glyndwr's rebellion.

The source of the Wye is almost exactly the boundary between Montgomeryshire
and Ceredigion, between east and west Wales, and it is at the heart of the Cambrian
Mountains between north and south Wales. Plynlimon is also the hill from which three
of the great Welsh rivers flow – Wye, Severn and Rheidol – and many writers have
imagined it as the fountain-head of Wales. The first was the poet Lewis Glyn Cothi who,
by chance, lived as an outlaw on the eastern slopes of Plynlimon after his involvement
on the losing side in the battle of Mortimer's Cross in 1461, a battle in the Wars of the
Roses in which the majority of the blood shed was that of Welshmen. He was one of a
generation of Welsh poets living in the aftermath of the Glyndwr uprising and acutely
aware of his nation's status, or lack of it. Four centuries later George Borrow cited the
most famous of Glyn Cothi's lines when he stood at the source of the Wye:

> From high Plynlimon's shaggy side
> Three streams in three directions glide;
> To thousands at their mouth who tarry,
> Honey, gold and mead they carry.
> Flow also from Plynlimon high
> Three streams of generosity;
> The first a noble stream indeed
> Like rills of Mona runs with mead;
> The second bears from vineyards thick
> Wine to the feeble and the sick;
> The third till time shall be no more
> Mingled with gold shall silver pour.[6]

George Borrow, who can hardly be criticised for failing to immerse himself in the
native culture, sang this song of nationalist pride and drank from each of the three rivers.
It establishes Plynlimon as the fountain-head of Wales, sanctifying the Welsh earth,
although in the long run, as we will see, the greatest influence of these lines would be
on English authors.

In *How Culhwch won Olwen*, a Welsh tale found in the *Red Book of Hergest*, Cai and
Bedwyr sit on the outcrop Garn Gwylathr (the name has not survived) on Plynlimon,

which is exposed to 'the strongest wind in the world'.[7] This is the special symbolic status of Plynlimon. In reality it is far from the highest mountain in Wales, peaking at only 752 metres, well below the summit of Snowdon at 1085 metres and other high mountains like Cadair Idris and the Arans. Its imagined pre-eminent loftiness is well expressed by Michael Drayton's poem *Poly-Olbion*, published in 1613, which was a very different search for the genius loci, in deifying the landscape with female rivers and patriarchal mountains. Plynlimon is eulogised as the source of the great Welsh rivers:

> What once the *Druids* told, how great those floods should bee
> That here (most mightie Hill) derive themselves from thee.
> The Bards with furie rapt, the *British* youth among,
> Unto the charming Harpe thy future honor sang
> In brave and loftie straines; …
> That all the *Cambrian* hills, which high'st their heads doe beare
> With most obsequious showes of lowe subjected feare,
> Should to thy greatnes stoupe: and all the Brooks that be,
> Doe homage to those Floods that issued out of thee:
> To princelie *Severne* first; next to her sister *Wye*,
> Which to her elders Court her course doth still apply.
> But *Rydoll*, young'st, and least, and for the others pride
> Not finding fitteth roomth upon the rising side,
> Alone unto the West directlie takes her way.
> So all the neighbouring hills *Plynillimmon* obey.[8]

Michael Drayton's poem is subtitled 'England's [sic] great variety' and he was one of the first authors to perceive the Anglo-Welsh rivers as a natural expression of British nationhood, only a few decades after the Union of England and Wales in 1536. In *Poly-Olbion*, Drayton deified the rivers with classical nymphs, apparently unaware of the tradition alluded to by William Harrison. Harrison, writing in the 16th century, was the first English author to note that the three rivers on Plynlimon (Wye, Severn, Rheidol) were 'commonlie called the three sisters', although none of the ancient authors – chiefly Nennius, Geoffrey of Monmouth, and the various authors of the *Mabinogion* – mentions it.[9] By the 18th century the original three had been expanded to five, but seems to have been based upon a mistranslation of *Pumlumon* as 'five rivers'. By the early 19th century the tradition formed the basis of Luke Booker's long patriotic poem *The Springs of Plynlimmon*, published in 1834.

Plynlimon became a different kind of place on the cultural map of Britain from the late 18th century onwards, when it was visited and described by travel writers. Few early travellers found picturesque qualities on Plynlimon that were worthy of praise. Benjamin Heath Malkin made strenuous efforts to visit the sources of several major Welsh rivers on his tour of the southern half of Wales in 1803. Although he admired Plynlimon as a vast bed of mountains, 'the ruggedness and inhospitality of its environs is in general so unrelieved, that it affords little for the picturesque enthusiasm'.

Plynlimon is clearly a different proposition close-up. Malkin warned: 'It is the most dangerous mountain in Wales, on account of the frequent bogs, which hold out no warning, concealed as they are under a smooth and apparently firm turf.' His advice was to employ a guide.[10]

Plynlimon was not one of the highlights of the Celtic Grand Tour of the late 18th and early 19th century because it does not have dramatic scenery and is not on a route to or from such scenic thrills. Thomas Pennant, for example, did not visit Plynlimon because he was told that 'it was an uninteresting object, the base most extensive, the top boggy, and the view from it over a dreary and almost uninhabited country'. Pennant's advisor had a point, as anyone who has walked on extensive Welsh moorland on a grey day could testify. George Borrow did visit it and had to admit that Plynlimon 'does not look much of a hill'. Instead 'a mountainous wilderness extended on every side, a waste of russet coloured hills, with here and there a black, craggy summit … The scene would have been cheerless in the extreme had not a bright sun lighted up the landscape.' Today's visitor would enjoy much of what disappointed these early travellers. Leitch Ritchie stood there in 1840 and, although impressed by the majesty of the scene and as conscious of its lack of trees as any modern observer, nevertheless alluded to 'the solitude, the dreariness, the utter desolation of the scene'.[11] For today's visitor that would be an image of beauty. The differences remind us that our idea of natural beauty is not a fixed thing, and it could be said that what we think of today as the beauty of wilderness is beautiful to us because of its contrast with our everyday world.

Some of the accounts of Plynlimon were written by people who never went there, like Michael Drayton, or tried too hard to idealise the landscape, like Louisa Twamley, who wrote in 1839:

> High o'er his mates, how huge Plinlimmon lifts
> His many-beaconed head! – O'er coronalled
> With still and shadowy mist, – or rolling storms
> That speak loud voice to the echoing hills,
> And rouse repeated thunder.

> … dancing onward, like a sportive child,
> A gushing streamlet frolics in the light,
> Gushing from rock to rock, as though its waves
> Were transformed feet of mountain nymph,
> And these her wonted haunts. And even so
> May our fantastic fancy deem her yet –
> That brook is e'ven Plinlimmon's fairest child –
> The peerless Wye.[12]

These conventional sentiments described the source in a way that conformed to how people wanted it to be. Thomas Roscoe was more ambivalent, referring to the 'wild, sterile grandeur' of Plynlimon, but lapsed into cliché as soon as it came to describing

The Plynlimon landscape where the Wye begins is one of upland sheep pasture and a little commercial forestry.

The ruins of an old sheepfold stand by the river, which was once used as a sheepwash.

the river: 'a gay, sportive streamlet, playful as a child, dancing merrily down the glen, frisking about in foam and spray'.[13]

Few of the writers who went to Plynlimon in the 19th century were interested in its prosaic side as a working landscape. In some ways this has remained true of the accounts of their Plynlimon journeys writers have published in the subsequent years, largely because farming around the headwaters has changed very little. There are still sheep and cattle grazing on the upland pastures. A sheepfold on the bank less than a mile below the source shows us that once the Wye stream was a sheepwash, and 'mountain lambs are sweeter' proclaims the road sign outside the farm where Pont Rhyd Galed crosses the Wye, one of the most recognisable sights on the main road from Llangurig to Aberystwyth. But there has been diversification. The most common birds, at least from summer onwards, are now pheasants. Walkers will also encounter the Sweet Lamb Motorsport Complex, which is used for testing as well as rallies. The whine of car engines is not what most people would usually associate with rural diversification, and the complex is serviced by a network of well-maintained tracks, and a bustle of life that would have horrified generations of earlier travellers who came this way expecting desolation and solitude. Solitude can be had here, as well as peace and quiet (when the RAF is not flying), but only in the mile below the source.

Cefn Brwyn, the highest farmstead on the Wye, was shown on the first Ordnance Survey map of the area in 1822 and tenanted by William Jones in 1845. The place name survives on the modern Ordnance Survey maps but the homestead has long been given up and has been erased from the ground. The next farm down was Pont Rhyd Galed and it remains the highest of the Wyeside farms. For the most part the Plynlimon landscape remains a lonely place and, as for T.H. Fielding in 1841, the approach of a farmer may be announced by the sound of a yelping dog, though these days the tell-tale sign may be the sound of an approaching quad bike.

Pont Rhyd Galed, where mountain lambs are sweeter,
one of the abiding modern myths of the harsh upland landscape.

For most naturalists the appeal of the area is its bird life. Thomas Roscoe noticed ravens, herons, cranes, snipe and plover. But these trackless wastes attracted not only curious travellers and naturalists; from the mid 19th century they were also the haunt of mineral prospectors. There was industry at the head of the river, not because a river-side location was essential to these activities, but because the streams cut through the bedrock and exposed veins of ore that were exploited either directly or indirectly by sinking shafts to intercept them. The river water was useful because, instead of steam engines, waterwheels could be used as motive power for pumping and winding, and for crushing the ore on the surface, an initial processing stage to remove waste.

Lead, silver and zinc were mined at various places in the Cambrian Mountains in the 19th century, rarely very profitably, and the upper reaches of the Wye experienced this mini minerals rush in the mid 19th century. Above Cefn Brwyn Farm there were a number of lead mining enterprises beside the river and by one of its tributary streams, Nant y Gwrdy. Beside the latter in 1846 a promising vein was discovered and lead mining began on an ambitious scale. Shaft and adits were employed but, like many of these upland operations, geological problems confounded early promise and mining ceased for about seven years, only to be revived again in 1874, when the Northern Van Mines Ltd and then the Wye Valley Company took it over successively in the same year.

Meanwhile the Wye Lead Mining Company established a mine very close by on the other side of the Wye. By 1869 the mine had a waterwheel for pumping and winding that was 40 feet in diameter. Six men were working at a depth of 40 fathoms, but by 1872 the work had fizzled out for lack of financial backing. Then, optimism again

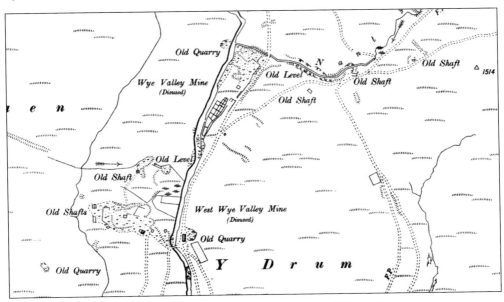

Abandoned mines established by the Wye Lead Mining Company, from the 1903 Ordnance Survey. There were mines still further upstream, at Blaen Wye.

triumphing over experience, a new firm, Kitto & Co, sank a new shaft, erected a new waterwheel and built four cottages. These were not as quaint as they may sound, since they were designed to provide sleeping accommodation for 32 men in addition to the regular tenants. The upper reaches of the Wye have never before or since been so densely inhabited. Needless to say, this venture soon failed, having mined only 360 tons of ore by 1880. The only long-term beneficiary seems to have been the local farmer, who took over the buildings he wanted, although most of them have now gone.

Other lead mines were sunk beside Nant Iago, where waterwheels for winding, pumping and crushing were established in the 1840s. This initial venture quickly failed, was revived briefly in the early 1860s, and enjoyed a fairly successful revival in the years between 1873 and 1888, when investment was made in a new 60-foot diameter water-wheel. An outlier of this operation was a mine at Blaen Wye, the uppermost workings beside the main river channel. The mining historian David Bick interviewed some of the people who worked at Nant Iago when it was revived again in the early 20th century, at which time 12 men worked underground, supported by four men on the surface. Mr Philpott was the head dresser, responsible for crushing the ore to take out some of the waste before it was transported. He worked from Monday to Friday, staying in barracks, and returned to his home near Shrewsbury at the weekend. His shift was from 7am to 4.30pm in winter, and 6am to 3.30pm in the summer. The ore was carted away by two horses driven by Robert Ingram from Llanidloes. The mine closed after the First World War when a government stockpile rendered the Nant Iago ore unsaleable.[14]

Little remains in the area of the mines, although the leats that supplied the water-wheels can still be traced across the hillsides. The waterwheels at Nant Iago mines were supplied by a leat beginning on the main Wye channel. Coming down from the source of the Wye, the first permanent mark of human engagement with the river can be seen in the remnants of an earthen dam that created the small reservoir for the leats. The leat to the Nant Iago mines was over a mile long, with a fall over that distance of only about 5 metres. It is a testament to the surveying skills of the Victorian engineers, and a reminder that the labour of digging and maintaining watercourses was a lot cheaper than purchasing an engine – and of course fuel had to be paid for, whereas rainwater was free.

There are some remains at Blaen Wye lead mine, in the form of a spoil heap, a wheelpit, a plugged shaft and the roofless remains of a former building. They stand in a streamside position, in a steep valley. Once there would have been a network of paths between these sites and the road at Pont Rhyd Galed, but these threads that linked them to the rest of the world and to each other have all vanished, and the ruins are now adrift in the moorland.

The mines may have been abandoned, but Plynlimon still seems like a landscape under threat. Where once there was mining waste, the modern threats are from forests, reservoirs and wind farms. Nant-y-Moch reservoir, completed in 1964 as part of the Rheidol hydro-electricity scheme, now occupies the headwaters of the Rheidol, including Afon Hyddgen. It has the least impact of the various factors that have shaped the landscape in modern times. Forests were planted in the 20th century on farmland that was no longer needed for agriculture, of which Wales has more than its fair share.

An old wheelpit at Blaen Wye mine.

A ruined mine building at Blaen Wye in the deep valley of the stream below the source.

But the most dramatic change has been produced by wind farms, the new pine trees of upland landscapes. They are a good deal more conspicuous than anything that has ever been built on the hills before, being secured to the ground by massive foundations, and because they harness a relatively small amount of power, they have become increasingly resented by local communities.

It was forests that made Plynlimon the site of a major long-term study of river catchments by the Centre for Ecology and Hydrology. In the decades following the Second World War there was growing concern about the sustainability of the nation's water supply at a time when the government was keen to turn many upland landscapes, where land values were low, to commercial forestry. Serious drought in 1959 and the dry winters of 1962-3 and 1963-4 were coupled with rising living standards, population growth, and a consequent demand for more water supplies. A small-scale study of landscapes in north-west England had suggested that, because water evaporated from needles and groundwater was retained by root systems, upland reservoirs would not fill so quickly if their catchments were dominated by forestry, threatening the reliability of water supply. The government set up a Committee on Hydrological Research in 1961, based in Wallingford, Oxfordshire, which was absorbed into the National Environment Research Council in 1965. The study of Plynlimon, one of the most promising locations in Britain for undertaking this kind of research, began in 1967.

Studies of the Wye and Severn headwaters have made it possible to compare open moorland (Wye) with plantation forest (Severn) and to monitor the effect of forestry on river flow. Automatic weather stations measure rainfall, humidity, wind speed and

The Crump weir near Pont Cefn Brwyn.

atmospheric pressure; soil water stations measure soil moisture; and flux stations measure evaporation rates. All of these measuring devices are inconspicuous in the landscape. The most noticeable features are the gauging stations that measure river flow. The lowest of them is the crump weir (a type of concrete weir invented by the fluvial engineer E.S. Crump) at Pont Cefn Brwyn, which was installed in an earlier, smaller project in 1951 and modified in the 1960s with an upstream stilling pool, which measures the river level. Above it are several smaller stations on the main Wye stream and its tributaries, installed in the late 1960s, major components being airlifted in by helicopter. The ultimate aim is to measure rainfall and compare how much is retained in the soil, how much is evaporated and how much is lost in streamflow. The long timescale of the project – over 40 years' worth of measurements – makes it an important international study of catchment science.

The study proved that afforestation would have a negative impact on water supply to reservoirs, and was therefore important in slowing down the haste with which upland wastes were being covered in trees. It is ironic to consider this in the early 21st century, when the problem is how to slow down the flow of water. Another less well-known conclusion was that dense tree cover raised the temperature of stream water, which in turn reduced the optimum time that cold-water fish like the brown trout would spawn there. Since the early days when the questions were all about pine forests, work has continued making measurements of stream flows, the chemical content and acidity of stream water, radioactivity (especially in the wake of the Chernobyl disaster of 1986) and the weather, providing data for research organisations that need it, not least in the

Measuring station below the source, at which point
it has already been joined by several streams.

study of climate change. Even through monitoring the river we are bringing Plynlimon into the modern world.

Today Plynlimon is a lot less well known than it should be, and than it used to be. The reason has nothing to do with forestry or scientific experiments, but is the consequence of a failed campaign to acquire National Park status for the Cambrian Mountains. A proposal was first put forward in 1965, ten years after the first tranche of National Parks, including Snowdonia and the Brecon Beacons, were created. The case for the Cambrian Mountains was compelling. Looking at a contour map of Britain, it is striking that such an extensive upland area, so rich in wildlife and in cultural heritage, has no special protection. In 1972 the Countryside Commission issued a designation order that would have made the Cambrian Mountains the 11th National Park in England and Wales, but opposition from local authorities, farmers and other stakeholders was vocal enough for the Secretary of State for Wales to refuse to confirm the order, and that was that. The lack of any enhanced protection for the Cambrian Mountains is an anomaly and the consequences of this have not been insignificant. The footfall on these uplands is far less than on the neighbouring National Parks, which helps conservation but means that fewer people appreciate them than would do if their attractions were more widely known. The area is also less well protected from development than the National Parks, and the most conspicuous consequence of this is the building of wind farms.

Ultimately, however, the way forward may be not to institutionalize the landscape, but to revive the Plynlimon of the imagination. This is powerfully achieved in the work of Pauline Fisk, who wrote a trilogy of magic-realist novels for young people, *The Children of Plynlimon*, interweaving river landscapes with children's journeys of self-discovery. The trilogy takes liberties with the old myth of the three sister rivers of Plynlimon. In the second of the series, *The Red Judge* (2005), teenager Zachary is exiled to Llangurig and finds himself unwittingly directed to Plynlimon and down the Wye, confronting the Red Judge of Plynlimon, the bogeyman of local children's stories, and his pack of *cwn y whir*, hounds of hell. It is a timely reminder that wild places are brought to life by myths and stories, that we characterise these places not by geology and vegetation, but by the human experiences of farmers, miners, seekers after beauty and solitude, and lovers of myths and stories.

༄ 4 ༈
A River of Churches

The small parish church at Whitchurch, on the right bank of the river near Monmouth, is the ultimate in riverside churches. It has its own landing stage and its churchyard extends right to the water itself. Inside the church, modern representations of the river adorn the walls, including a tapestry made in 1993 showing St Dubricius fishing. The pictures illustrate the intimate connection between churches, saints and rivers. They tell us something about how the church sees itself, a religion rooted in the landscape and building on a pristine world of nature as if the church embodies an organic relationship between nature and religion. It also recognises the importance of the river in the forming of sacred places, which is not specifically a Christian thing. St Dubricius did

Painted panels in the parish church at Whitchurch
depicting the idyllic River Wye setting in which the original church was founded.

Naïve tapestry in Whitchurch parish church, depicting St Dubricius fishing.

not just happen to be by the river. It is a place he sought out. Likewise, no church just happens to be by the river. Churches respect the spiritual, social, political and economic life of the river like no other class of building.

One of the difficult questions regarding riverside religious sites is whether they are sacred places by the river, or whether it is the river itself that was sacred to the people who used the site. Some archaeologists have argued that all rivers were places of deities in pre-Christian societies, and that this was universal across Europe. It is certainly true of some rivers. Julius Caesar, in his conquest of the Rhineland, famously bridged the river and thereby defeated the native river spirits and the German tribes at the same time. Rivers were once associated with specific divinities, especially in Gaul, where Matrona (mother) was goddess of the Marne, Sequana of the Seine, Souconna of the Saone. In England Verbeia was goddess of the River Wharfe, which we know because an altar was set up in her honour at Ilkley. In English the River Dee derives from 'Deva', or goddess; in Welsh *Dyfrdwy* is 'water of a deity'.

But that does not prove that all rivers were sacred, and there is no comparable evidence for the Wye. The dredging of some British rivers has produced evidence, not that rivers were sacred in themselves, but that they were places where deities, or perhaps ancestral spirits, lived. An enormous range of ritual deposits has been discovered, including skulls and valuable ceremonial metalwork (most Iron Age metalwork recovered by archaeologists comprises offerings thrown into water). Rivers flowing eastwards to the North Sea have yielded copious evidence of ritual deposits, especially the (much-dredged) Trent and Thames, but the north-south rivers, and those draining into the Bristol Channel, like the Wye and the Severn, have yielded very little of such material. The discovery of these deposits is of course not necessarily proof that the river was considered sacred. Since rivers are natural boundaries and places of embarcation, objects could have been intentionally sacrificed to the river to seal boundary agreements, or for luck at the outset of a journey.

Prehistoric sacred sites are usually associated with high ground rather than river valleys, but not always. There are some sites close enough to the Wye for the river to have been a factor in their location. One of the larger prehistoric sites, discovered by aerial photography and no longer easily visible on the ground, is a ring ditch on the flood plain at Llangurig. These Neolithic earthwork enclosures were some sort of ceremonial and social centre for dispersed communities, serving a function similar to the more numerous and slightly later henges. Like the ring ditch, henges were also associated with rivers, including a henge by the River Severn near Berriew, and Stonehenge, where the earthwork avenue leads towards the River Avon. However, the class of monument mainly associated with the river is the single standing stone of the later Neolithic and Bronze Age periods. The stones were associated with semi-nomadic people and they could therefore have marked points on routes of seasonal migration, perhaps associated with migration rituals. They are certainly prominent cultural markers in the landscape. There is a lowland standing stone in a field opposite Newbridge, a possible route marker across the Wye valley. Further downstream, in a riverside field opposite Boughrood Court, is the leaning standing stone known as Maen Hir. On the opposite bank a round barrow stands close to the river. Although now a disused railway comes between them, at one time the stone and barrow were intervisible. Were they connected, and was the distance between them a simple earthly journey or a spiritual one?

The best known of Bronze Age stones by the Wye are in fact unworked glacial boulders. The massive stone in the churchyard at Llanwrthwl, which seems almost certainly to have influenced the siting of the church, is by tradition ascribed to the Bronze Age, although it is not typical of the type, which are usually tall stones that have clearly been

The large boulder outside Llanwrthwl church has long been interpreted as a prehistoric standing stone, not least because it influenced the site of the medieval church.

raised upright. The fact that the Llanwrthwl stone is a glacial erratic, one of several that were brought down the Elan Valley by ice sheets, does not preclude a ceremonial or sacred status. Its relationship with the river is compromised slightly by the later road to the east, but at one time the river would have been visible from the stone. Large stones are usually found on high ground but not in fertile valleys, and so it is easy to see why people might have assumed its presence owed something to supernatural powers.

The Queen's Stone, by a bend in the Wye at Huntsham, near Goodrich, is a bit like the Llanwrthwl stone – not a typical tall menhir, but a huge, broad stone that looks like it was left there by a glacier, and with distinctive grooves, probably caused by rain-water. Standing in a field by a bend in the river, it was either too big to break up, or too important to get rid of. Perhaps it was raised upright and venerated as a special stone, or perhaps it marked a route across the Wye valley.

Most evidence of riverside ritual and religion belongs to Christianity. This being border country, for the early history of the Church along the Wye we have to consider the native British Church ('British' because this was before the division into Wales and England), the Anglo-Saxon Church and the Norman Church, in effect three Christian traditions, each with its own identity. One of the sub-plots in this border country is how some of the churches of British origin were taken into the Roman Church and given English names and new Biblical patron saints to supersede their original Celtic dedications.

The early history of churches along the Wye has been well researched, although no one seems to have seen any special significance in their setting by the river. A lot of churches are found by rivers, for a variety of spiritual, practical, economic and perhaps unrecognised reasons. Surprisingly few of the Wye's parish churches were founded to serve existing communities, the default notion of a village church. In almost all cases, especially those of the early churches, it was the other way round: people came to live near the church. In the most obvious example, Tintern village owes its existence to the Cistercian monastery, just as Glasbury and Llangurig villages owe their existence to early Celtic monasteries. But a more intriguing problem is why so many churches were built apparently apart from the landscape of daily life, despite the fact that in a time of relatively low population the landscape was relatively uninhabited. In the case of monastic churches it could be that low-lying, flood-prone land was of little practical value and so was an easy and relatively inexpensive place to establish a community undisturbed. It could also be argued that religious men sought out marginal places because they relished their inherent challenges and because they were suitable to the humble expectations of a religious calling. The other possibility, that the building of churches was determined by sites of pre-Christian veneration of river deities, is attractively romantic, but there is no convincing evidence to support it. It could also be the case that a church in the wilderness had no previous cultural associations and so was a clean break from the past.

One of the common characteristics of Celtic, Anglo-Saxon and Norman traditions is a tendency to build churches by confluences. The most obvious example on the Wye is the chapel on the rock at Beachley, where the Wye joins the Severn. Mordiford is where the Lugg joins the Wye, and its church was close enough to the former to be flooded in 1811. The river is part of its folklore. The east end of the church was formerly adorned with a painting of a green dragon with webbed feet, a monster that terrified the neighbourhood and went down to the river to slake his thirst until he was finally defeated.[1] Glasbury's old church was at the confluence of the Wye and Llynfi and is the best studied of these church sites, partly because the original site has been accessible to archaeological investigation since it was given up in favour of a new church.

The earliest churches on the Wye were Celtic although, as Christianity was founded during the Roman colonisation of Britain, some of them may represent continuation of Christianity rather than its renaissance in the Celtic fringes of Europe in the 5th century. Certainly, however, the foundation of early Wye churches is associated with familiar Celtic traditions of supernatural events associated with local saints and specific places.

The Celtic saints with the strongest River Wye association were St Dubricius and St Oudoceus. St Dubricius, or Dyfrig, was born at Madley near Hereford, but is credited with founding monasteries or churches at several places, including the riverside churches of Whitchurch and Moccas. A life of the saint was included in the 12th-century *Book of Llandaff*, on the basis that he was later Llandaff's bishop, and features a familiar mixture of miracles and innate holiness. Even his birth was marked by miracles. King Pebiau discovered that his daughter Eurddil was pregnant and resolved to have her banished. She was put in a sack and thrown into the Wye, for the river to do with her what it would, but each time she was thrown in, the sack floated back to the bank and the girl emerged safe and sound. Then the king had her thrown onto a bonfire, but on returning the following morning his men found the woman not reduced to ashes, but alive and well and suckling an infant. Trials by water and fire were purification rites but they were clearly not needed because she was already pure. King Pebiau accepted and embraced his daughter and grandson, Dubricius, and then there was another surprise. Having kissed the infant, the king was suddenly cured of a longstanding illness and the child was declared holy.

Destined at birth for a holy life, Dubricius grew up to establish and lead several religious communities. One of them was at Henllan or Hentland, where for seven years he lived in a seminary of the banks of the Wye, probably at the place now called Llanfrother on an eminence above the river. Then he returned home and resided in a place called Ynys Eurddil, or 'Maes Mai Llecheu', which seems to have been an island in the river. It was apparently a place convenient for woodland and fish, the bare minimum to live by, but the site he chose for an oratory, which later became the parish church of Moccas, came to him after a dream. An angel instructed him to go out and look for a white sow and her piglets – *moch* in Welsh means pigs – and to build his oratory where he found them. The site of Moccas church was therefore associated with supernatural events.[2]

Today, Llandogo church is an unremarkable Victorian building, but the original church was also founded upon the supernatural. The story appears in the *Book of Llandaff* in a life of St Oudoceus, who lived in the 6th century and was the third bishop of Llandaff. Bishop Oudoceus was wont to travel humbly about his diocese, and it was while he was living and praying at the Cleddon (Caletan) brook, near the River Wye, that a stag came and rested on his cloak. Unbeknown to Oudoceus, King Einion of Glewyssig had been hunting the stag in the nearby woodlands, but when he saw how the cloak of Oudoceus gave the stag divine protection he immediately desisted. The king and his men apologised to Oudoceus as if they had sinned, then the king granted to Llandaff cathedral, by way of Oudoceus, the entire tract of land over which he had hunted that day. Originally named Llan Einion, Oudoceus built there an oratory and a residence for himself in a place that was ideal for the establishment of a religious community, a place of nature 'abounding with fish and honey'.[3]

One day, Oudoceus and his community received a visit from Welsh monk and erstwhile historian Gildas, in a period of his life when he was living as a hermit. Gildas had gathered timber from a remote riverside woodland and conveyed it across the river in a boat to offer to Oudoceus as building material. Oudoceus protested that the timber was acquired unlawfully and demanded that Gildas seek forgiveness for his act, but he refused. Oudoceus took an axe and in anger struck a blow against a stone, splitting it in two; the divided stone remained by the riverside as a powerful reminder of divine presence.[4]

Churches founded after supernatural events that make their riverside sites divinely chosen are a common characteristic of Celtic hagiographies. Another example is the story of Tewdrig, king of Glywysing (in modern Monmouthshire). Tewdrig had bequeathed his kingdom to his son Meurig, having renounced earthly power and retired to live as a hermit near Tintern. Tewdrig was a formidable and undefeated military leader and he returned to lead his son's army against Saxon invaders, after an angel spoke to him in a dream. The angel informed him that his participation would ensure the rout of the enemy, but that he would himself be mortally wounded by 'Rhyd Tintern', the ford of Tintern. The Christian Britons duly defeated the pagan Saxons and Tewdrig's fate was enough for him to be hailed as a martyr and to be canonised. Wounded, Tewdrig initially refused to depart from the scene, but was persuaded to when two stags pulling a carriage mysteriously arrived to carry him away. They took him downstream to Mathern, just downstream of where the Wye joins the Severn, where he died. On hearing of his father's death Meurig ordered that an oratory be founded on the spot, and gave a stretch of coastline at the end of the Wye to the bishopric of Llandaff. The church of Mathern became the centre of St Tewdrig's cult in the Middle Ages.[5]

In Wales early churches can be identified by place names incorporating *clas*, the word for an early Celtic monastery, or *llan*, a more general word for a religious place. Many of them are dedicated to a founding saint. Glasbury was originally dedicated to St Cynidr, who lived in the 5th century, perhaps following a tradition that he founded the church (there is a Ffynnon Gynydd just over a mile to the north). This early church grew into a monastery and mother church in the neighbourhood and had at least two dependant chapels by the 12th century, at Pipton and Velindre. A village of sorts may have grown up near it, which would explain its place name, an unusual combination of the Celtic *clas* and the Saxon *bury*, or burgh, meaning settlement. Pipton chapel was also built by the Wye, although the course of the river has shifted and the exact site of the chapel is not known. It was probably built by the 11th century but was in ruins by 1811.

The original Glasbury church was on the south bank of the Wye, west of its confluence with the Llynfi. Although the river has shifted its course since early medieval times, the site must always have been prone to flooding because the church was built on a

Llangurig was the site of an early riverside *clas*.
The church arrived first and the village followed.

raised mound. On its south side is a probable earlier curved bank – early churches in Wales were often sites within curvilinear enclosures. It seems to have been an important church too, as it was one of three Celtic monasteries given to Gloucester Abbey by 1088 (who Anglicised it by changing its patron saint to St Peter). The others were Llancarfan in Glamorgan and Llanbadarn Fawr on the outskirts of modern Aberystwyth.

Another important riverside *clas* was at Llangurig, the origin of the present parish church. It is dedicated to St Curig, its supposed founder, who is said to have been bishop of Llanbadarn Fawr and to have travelled to the head of the Wye valley where, at Eisteddfa Gurig (or the seat of Gurig, as it has been known since at least the 15th century) he vowed to found a religious community in the broad valley of the Wye. Llangurig remained a *clas* until the end of the 12th century, when it came under the control of the Cistercian monastery of Strata Florida and came into line with the Roman Church. The present building, which has fabric as early as the 13th century and a tower built in the 15th century, is on a terrace immediately above the river. When it became a parish church from the 12th century it served a dispersed rural community and it must have had a striking appearance in this sparsely populated upland landscape by the river. (A hoard of medieval silver coins was found in the graveyard in 1753, so it was not necessarily as humble as it might have looked.)

An early church site is in the grounds of the Llangoed Hall Hotel near Boughrood. Its cemetery, in which there are 19th-century headstones from a time when it was a private burial ground, extends to the river bank. When the church, originally known as Llan Coit, was founded is unknown, but it was given to Llandaff by Rhydderch ap Iestyn in 1021, a gift confirmed by the Pope in 1119. Foundations of a church building have survived, no more than 30 metres from the river.[6]

St Gwrthwl was the founder of Llanwrthwl church, which stands just over 100 metres from the river, in what again was a more significant relationship than it appears today, now that there has been considerably more development. Although the present church is an indifferent Victorian work, inside the church is a 12th-century font of a type more commonly found in Cornwall. The large rock in the churchyard has long been interpreted as prehistoric and certainly its position suggests that it influenced the location of the church. It could have been a natural stone that was venerated in immediately pre-Christian times, or just a curious large stone that church builders presumed had been venerated in the distant past.

Several churches with *llan* origins are now on the English side of the border or have been given English names. In Gloucestershire is Lancaut, founded as a small monastery by the early 7th century and associated with St Cewydd, a monk from Llancarfan in the Vale of Glamorgan. The fate of this monastery is unknown – its position by the river near Chepstow would have made it vulnerable to Viking raids, and by 956 it belonged to the manor of Tidenham. The surviving building was built in the 12th century, when the church was newly furnished with a decorative lead font, one of six fonts in Gloucestershire churches that were cast from lead, probably in Bristol, and then transported by water to the parishes, all of them on the lower Wye or Severn. The font is now in Gloucester Cathedral.

The ruins of Lancaut church stand above a bend in the river.
It was the site of an early Celtic church.

The position, on steep ground overlooking the Wye, is interesting simply because it seems such an unlikely place to build a church intended to serve a local community. There was a small township here in the Middle Ages, but the population dwindled away, so that there were only five households in 1563, four in 1710 and two inhabited houses in 1750.[7] It is a wonder that the church remained consecrated until 1865.

Several other Wyeside churches have Celtic origins. Dixton church, near Monmouth, is in a lovely setting by the river, but its 19th-century appearance belies much earlier origins. The name is apparently an Anglicisation of Lann Tidiuc, a Celtic

St Michael's chapel, the forerunner of the present Dixton parish church,
is shown here as a typical Celtic hermitage founded in a pristine world of nature.

The medieval churchyard cross at Sellack.

Foy is a church of Celtic origin in an isolated peninsula above Ross,
formed by the acute meandering of the river.

monastery mentioned in Llandaff charters as early as 735.[8] Sellack church is said to be the only church in England dedicated to the Welsh saint Tysilio. Although the building is of 12th-century origin, there was a much earlier church here, granted in the 7th century to the Bishop of Llandaff and known as Llan Sulac (or Syllyg). Foy church stands close to the river and its axis seems to follow the river rather than the traditional east-west. There is no village there and probably never was – just a few individual farms. The oldest part of the church is 12th-century, but the name is derived from the saint Ffwy, which suggests a British rather than a Norman origin. Bridstow was originally known as *Lann San Freit*, or Llansantffraed as it is now commonly spelt, meaning church of St Bride, a common Welsh name. In 1066 Bishop Herewald of Llandaff appointed Guollguinn as priest here. Llansantffraed Cwmdeuddwr is now a suburb of Rhayader but is older than the town and its church of St Bride is perched above the river. The present building is Victorian, replacing the previous church of 1778, which may in turn have superseded a medieval building – although a much earlier *clas* was sited nearby on the Elan river.

The most important of the Saxon foundations on the Wye is the cathedral church at Hereford, founded *c*.676 by Putta, the former bishop of Rochester, making it one of the earliest of Anglo-Saxon cathedrals. It was founded next to an important Roman crossing of the Wye. But perhaps the earliest church at Hereford was the monastery of St Guthlac, south-east of the cathedral on what is now Castle Green. It may have originated as a Welsh *clas*, although excavations have been unable to prove this. The

Hereford Cathedral is a commanding presence by the Wye,
and was founded in the 7th century.

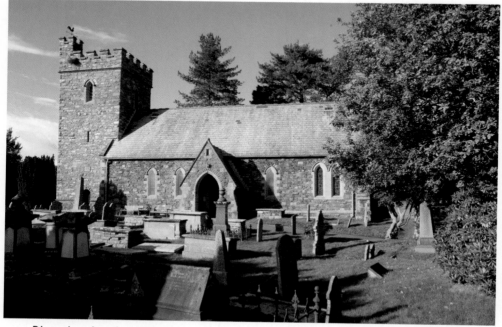

Rhayader church was largely rebuilt in the 19th century but is of medieval origin,
sited close to the castle, and is older than the town it now serves.

community moved after the siege of Hereford in 1138 to a new site north-east of the city, losing its original riverside association as the castle was expanded.

Given the importance of the river crossing, Hereford Cathedral may have superseded an earlier church, but there is no legend of an early foundation and association with a Celtic saint, as is the case with other important British churches along the Wye. In 1061 Hereford had a French bishop, Walter of Lorraine, and under the next incumbent, Robert de Losinga, it quickly became assimilated into the Norman sphere of influence and was rebuilt in the new architectural style. Although it is set well back from the river bank and the bridge, the medieval church was a dominant riverside presence.

The troubled centuries of Celtic, Saxon and Norman conflict made their mark on the building of churches. Rhayader church occupies a commanding position above the Wye and stood close to the castle. It was probably built by the Lord Rhys in the 1170s, close to the castle. Bredwardine is a defensible point where the river could be crossed, and on the south side of the church was a castle standing on a natural hill. The church was clearly of Saxon origin because, when it is first mentioned, in the Domesday survey of 1086, it was ruinous and presumably the castle was too. Despite being burned by Owain Glyndwr's soldiers in 1406, Bredwardine best evokes the rural bliss of the Wye and is associated primarily with Francis Kilvert, the young vicar and diarist who died in 1879 and is buried in the churchyard. Next to Lower Breinton church, near Hereford, is an earthwork overlooking a crossing of the river which is probably military rather than domestic in origin.

In the region of the Wye, monasteries were an important symbol of Norman civilisation, especially potent in the years following the Conquest. Before his death in 1071 William fitz Osbern founded a Benedictine monastery in conjunction with the castle at Chepstow, a statement about the cosmopolitan nature of Norman culture as part of the international Roman Church, at odds with the backward independent Welsh Church. The monastery later became the parish church. Likewise the new fortification begun at Monmouth was followed in 1075 by the founding of a Benedictine Priory, the chief claim to fame of which today is that the great historian of Britain Geoffrey of Monmouth may have entered holy orders there. (It overlooks the Monnow rather than the Wye.) It became the parish church after the Dissolution but was later largely demolished and replaced.

Relatively few important monastic houses (in the reformed version following St Dunstan's adoption of the Benedictine Order at Glastonbury in the mid 10th century) were built on the Wye, perhaps because it was always contested, tense or unstable territory. The Benedictines, the favourite of the Norman orders, were at Chepstow, Monmouth and

Geoffrey of Monmouth, portrayed in the Circle of Legends at Tintern Old Station.

Tintern Abbey was founded in the 1130s, by which time there had been several centuries of monasticism on the Wye. (British Library)

St Guthlac's in Hereford. The reformed version, the Cistercians, eschewed established settlements and built their religious houses in more remote areas. In the Wye river basin these included Abbey Dore, Llanthony, and on the Wye itself Tintern.

Religious communities had been thriving by the river for half a millennium by the time Tintern Abbey was founded in 1131. Like the earlier Celtic monasteries, it does not owe its site to any known previous activity. The site may have been chosen by Walter fitz Richard of Clare, Lord of Chepstow, who endowed the community of Cistercian monks. If the appeal of the site was in its challenging isolation, the monks quickly turned it to their advantage by economic development of the area and by trade on the river. The river meant that Tintern always enjoyed the contradictory status of being an isolated place with excellent communications. It was the second Cistercian foundation in Britain when it was settled by immigrant monks from L'Aumône in northern France, but by the time of the Reformation it was the richest monastic house in Wales, and the presence of the Wye was a contributing factor. Nothing survives of the 12th-century church, but its rebuilding in the 13th and 14th centuries is testament to a religious community thriving in both spiritual and secular worlds.

The *Domesday Book* of 1086 records only 41 settlements in Herefordshire with a church, out of a total of 313 places mentioned.[9] This is surely an underestimate, although

By the 18th century Bredwardine church, seen here in 1794,
was an isolated church by the river. The village is further away.

many churches were associated with estates rather than with villages. In England the system of parishes developed in Norman England but on the borderland those parishes were much slower to emerge, and in fact many of what are now parish churches did not begin as such, but were private chapels associated with manor houses, some of which began as defensive sites like Bredwardine. The church at Moccas, close to the river, became an estate chapel and in the 1130s was rebuilt in a style similar to the famous church at Kilpeck and, it is thought, by the same group of masons. Monnington-on-Wye preserves the relationship of manor and church, although in their present form they are altered from their original medieval appearance. Downstream of Hereford, Fawley has a riverside chapel, 12th-century in its earliest surviving parts, that stands beside a farm and was probably also a private chapel. So too was Rotherwas, a medieval chapel of ease attached to the manor of the De La Barre family. It continued to be a chapel after the Reformation, by which time it had been inherited by the Bodenham family, to whom it owes its notability as a Roman Catholic chapel of the 19th century. But it began as a private estate chapel and is first recorded in 1304.

In some places a medieval church had a village with it, although in numerous cases the village has gone. Lancaut has already been mentioned. Holme Lacy church is set apart from the village, in a low-lying meadow within a loop of the Wye. It is also a long way from the bridge. Earthworks near the church may belong to a deserted medieval village – the one mentioned in Domesday – perhaps cleared when the house was rebuilt. Bredwardine and Preston-on-Wye both have riverside churches serving villages further

Tintern Parva church, 19th-century in its current form but of early medieval origin.

Bridge Sollers church was built close to a wharf on the Wye,
but there was never a village there nor, until the late 19th century, a bridge.

away from the river. Preston church is in an isolated position surrounded by a farm. The story of its foundation is told in the *Book of Llandaff*. At a place called Bolgros near Moccas, Gwrfodw, King of Ergyng, gave 300 acres of land by the Wye to give thanks for a defeat of the Saxons nearby. The bishop came and processed around the boundary of the land, carrying relics and sprinkling holy water, before building a church in the middle of the land.[10]

The economic development of the lower Wye in the Middle Ages was in large part due to Tintern Abbey. Development of the lower Wye valley brought settlement and therefore churches to serve it. The church at Tintern Parva had been built by the mid 14th century, by which time there was probably already trade in the vicinity. It stands by the river beside a longstanding ferry crossing and a medieval wharf. A nearby wayside cross, the original location of which is uncertain, may have been in the churchyard originally. As the river trade developed in the Middle Ages there were new churches built and new reasons to site them close to rivers. Churches were often built by roads and especially by bridges, which are natural focal points. Bridge Sollers church was built in the 12th century close to what was probably a wharf on the river. (It was presumably 'Bridge' Sollers because in early times 'bridge' could also mean 'embarcation point'.)

Other churches continued to be built, the reasons for which are no longer apparent. Llanfaredd and Llanelwedd are close to Builth, although on the opposite bank of the river to the town. The origin of the former is obscure. It was known as Thlannarreyt in its earliest known reference, in 1291. Mariath is an obscure Welsh saint, which may explain why the dedication was changed to the similar-sounding Mary. The building is surrounded by a farm. There seems never to have been a large settlement here. Llanelwedd is a 19th-century church close to the river, but another site, Cae Henllan which is within the Royal Welsh showground and has a suggestive place name, was long thought to be the site of the early-medieval church. This was confirmed by a geophysical survey in 2004 which revealed the plan of the small church and its burial ground. Although at a distance of some 400 metres it is further from the river than the new church, but it stood where the river was the dominant physical presence in the landscape.

Medieval hermits also sought out riverside locations, although in a different tradition from that of the Celtic saints. Hermits who withdrew from society liked places that were wild and difficult to live in – the north European version of the Biblical desert. Stretches of river bank were perhaps unfrequented places where hermits could live in peace and reasonably expect to live in the wild by catching their own fish. That is a romanticised version of the hermit life, however, because in reality a hermit pledged himself to performing charitable works, usually to travellers. This took various forms, including operating ferries, maintaining navigation lights and repairing roads and bridges. They were often seen at rivers. The hermitage on Chapel Rock at Beachley is mentioned in several sources from the 13th century onwards. The chapel was only accessible at low tide across the muddy foreshore and is the only chapel known to have been in the river (both Wye and Severn) rather than on its banks. It was probably dedicated originally to St Tecla, the 8th-century nun who aided Boniface in his missionary work in Germany. In 1290 the chapel was referred to as St Tryak de Betesley, and later St Tryacle or St

Treacle, but since 1830 it has been dedicated to St Twrog.[11] In the 1940s a navigational light was placed beside the ruin, perhaps honouring the original function of the chapel, and around the ruins is a minute island of grass.

In the same tradition, hospitals were established to care for travellers. One such is said to have existed by the river above Dixton, at Chapel Farm. This is variously said to have been a hospital and chapel of St Michael established in the Norman period.

None of the Wye's medieval bridges had a chapel built on it, but in several cases an adjoining church may have performed a similar role, whereby collections were taken from travellers crossing the bridge that were then spent on bridge maintenance, with a clergyman acting as the bridge warden. The position of several churches suggests such a role, like the former St Martin's church by Wye Bridge in Hereford, and St Thomas Becket at Overmonnow, built right by Monnow Bridge by 1186. The dedication here to the archbishop murdered at Canterbury in 1170 is interesting, since his cult was quickly associated with pilgrimage and was an ideal dedication for churches frequented by travellers. Although there is no evidence that proves such a link, the site of the chapel was almost certainly determined by the bridge, still for a century yet constructed of timber until its rebuilding in stone in the late 13th century. Tradition had it that there was a small cell of a Dominican friary close to Rhayader Bridge, which performed the functions of a bridge chapel. The existence of such a cell is disputed, although in the 18th century there was a field and tenement known as Black Friars.[12]

The course of the river is not fixed, and by the 17th century the riverside site of some churches meant nothing but trouble. In 1658 the bishop of St Davids was petitioned about the 'late inundations and violent floods' of the river at Glasbury that had swept away the northern half of the churchyard, including its graves, and warned that one half of the steeple had already been undermined and had fallen into the river.[13] A new site was needed and a church was opened further south in 1664 (replaced by the present Glasbury church in 1837-8). The ruin of the old church is so long forgotten that there is no footpath to it, but the low mound attests to a once important relationship with the river, and also to the river's destructive power. The vicarage in the 19th century stood on the river bank and was described in 1871 as 'a poor tumble-down ramshackle old place and unhealthy I should think, damp and infested by rats'. Today it is lauded as a very rare late-medieval house.[14]

Glasbury is not the only church to have been chased off by the river. Just downstream at Whitney the church was damaged by floods and was rebuilt on its present site in 1740. (It is a problem found not just on the Wye – Carrog church was swept away by the River Dee in the 17th century, and the parishioners of Newtown on the Severn were flooded out in the 19th century). Dixton, near Monmouth, suffered severe losses in the great flood of 1795, when the pulpit, pews and interior paving were destroyed, and the parishioners must have wished they could have rebuilt their church on higher ground.[15]

Not all Wyeside churches are ancient. Newbridge-on-Wye had to wait until 1883 for a church to be built, some time after the bridge was rebuilt and it became an important route and a minor spa town. The isolated inhabitants of Brockweir were ill-served by the church and it was the nonconformist Moravian Church who built a chapel there in

Chapel Rock at Beachley with its ruined chapel. Confluences, here where the Wye joins the Severn, were a favourite place to found places of worship.

The juxtaposition of church and bridge was common in medieval times, and in the Wye valley is best represented by St Thomas church and Monnow Bridge in Monmouth.

1832. The inhabitants were said to be in need of spiritual guidance. At least, that was the opinion of the first minister, who characterised village life as centred on beer houses, skittle alleys and cockfighting arenas, with a result that the waterside community had acquired a reputation as a refuge from decent society.[16]

The Wye churches tell us a story of how the river has been populated in the past two millennia. They document a changing attitude to the river. Once it was sought out as a place of nature, but later it became a place of people and trade, a gradual secularisation that characterises the modern world's relationship with landscape in general. Wyeside villages like Tintern, Glasbury and Llangurig owe their existence to churches. By contrast, Holme Lacy and Lower Breinton churches are the only structure left of the original riverside settlements. Churches were associated with wharves, bridges and castles, often outliving the latter, and must have acted as informal navigational markers. In the Wye above Rhayader the church tower at Llangurig was as significant a landmark as the cathedral tower at Hereford was to the lower river.

Once, fortifications outdid church steeples as the most conspicuous of riverside buildings, but they long ago crumbled into obsolescence. The Wye always had more churches than bridges, and today ancient churches far outnumber ancient bridges, cover a greater time span and extend much further upriver. Churches are the most enduring symbol of civilisation along the River Wye.

❧ 5 ❧
River Crossings

In 1803 Benjamin Malkin visited Rhayader, at that time the site of the most upstream stone bridge on the Wye. The bridge had been built in 1780 for the turnpike road crossing from Herefordshire westwards to Aberystwyth. By Malkin's time this was a well-trodden route for tourists heading for the scenic splendours of Devil's Bridge. Some of them stopped to admire the rocky rapids that gave the town of Rhayader its name, and in doing so noticed the new bridge. 'The arch of the bridge is very elegant, and the picturesque line of the river, furnishes one of the most agreeable' sights on the river.[1] It is a truth widely acknowledged that nothing graces a river like an arched bridge.

Bridges are a comparatively recent innovation and for most of the period that people have been crossing the Wye it has been on foot or on a boat. The need to cross rivers has set a great test of human ingenuity, and it has also engendered a level of sensitivity to the river's flow and its moods, and even the lie of the land beside it. As is true for all rivers, crossing the Wye is easier upstream where it is narrower and shallower, and where the strength of the current is obvious. The trouble is that people tend to inhabit the lower reaches of rivers, where the river is wider and the flow is faster than it looks, and the Wye is no exception.

For the historian, fords are the most elusive of river crossings. Their existence is often implied by *rhyd* or *ford* place names. Pont Rhyd Galed is the uppermost road bridge on the Wye and was a wooden bridge in the late 18th century. Road widening and bridge modernisation have made sure that any traces of a former ford have long vanished. Rhydspence is now best known as a former drovers' inn, but in that context it has little to do with the river, as the drovers' route kept on the north side of the river to Hereford. The name derives from a crossing some 150 yards below the later Whitney bridge, and was perhaps the ford crossed by Owain Glyndwr's men in 1402 when they attacked Hay.[2] Boughrood might have derived its anglicised name from Bach Rhyd, or 'little ford', although that interpretation has fallen from favour in recent years. Other sugges-tive place names include Hereford, Walford, Byford and Mordiford in Herefordshire, but their proximity to Wales offers a cautionary note, as in Welsh *ffordd* means a road. The Welsh name for Hereford, Henffordd, the old way, implies merely a crossing here, even if a ford seems most likely to have been the earliest form of it.

Apart from place names, there are other kinds of evidence for medieval fords. Red Rail, below Hoarwithy, was the site of a ford; excavation in 1969 revealed flagstones scattered in the river that once formed a causeway or stepping stones. A Roman date was suggested.[3] At Newbridge, where there was a bridge as early as the 16th century, the ford, or at least the track leading to it, remains on the downstream side of the present modern bridge. Another example is at Rhayader, where Water Lane runs down to the river. At Bigsweir the natural shallowness of the river allowed for a ford as early as 1445, when a Passage Lane is mentioned.[4] It was probably one of the more important crossing points of the lower Wye in the Middle Ages. The road on the English side led up towards Stowe, which was protected by a castle. The Wye was crossed at Tintern Parva, perhaps as early as Roman times, and on the east bank is a cobbled track that led down to it. On the other side of the river is an early wharf and Tintern Parva church. This is probably the Rhyd Tintern mentioned in the 12th-century *Book of Llandaff*.[5]

Most of the Wye's fords are impossible to date and are as mysterious now as they were at one time unremarkable. In the early 20th century Arthur Lamont recorded the positions of several Herefordshire fords, some of which were used until bridges were built in the late 19th century, at Monnington, Bridge Sollers and Stretton Sugwas. The ford at Lower Breinton near Hereford was still in use in the late 19th century. Many of the old fords, like Clock Mill Ford near Bredwardine and Rowland's Ford near Bridge Sollers, have now disappeared from the Ordnance Survey maps, but the use of fords did not entirely die out with the construction of bridges. Bridges often charged tolls or were out of repair, which encouraged the continued use of older forms of crossing. After the flood of 1795 Newbridge Ford was the only crossing point here for two decades until a

A ford near Pont Rhyd Galed.

new bridge was built; and the ford at Rhydspence was used while repairs were made to Whitney Bridge.

A ford is essentially a local route, since without some knowledge of the river strangers would find it difficult to cross the river in exactly the right place, and the difficulty varies with the season. This lesson was learned in the 1530s by John Leland who arrived near dawn at Hay, but for lack of local knowledge could not find the optimum fording point, which 'did sore troble my horse'.[6] For Captain William Hutcheson Jones, a 26-year-old officer of the 76th regiment, it was fatal, as he drowned while crossing the ford at Sellack in October 1819.[7] John Webb, the Victorian antiquary, reminds us that 'the fords were ways of husbandry as well as highways', often used by farmers who had lands on both sides of the river. 'Where the floor of the ford was too uneven for a wain, the produce of hay or corn harvest was carried over upon the backs of horses.'[8] Herds of animals were once regularly led across the Wye, a practice that continued until at least the end of the 19th century. Apparently a Mr Bennet moved across river from Clehonger Manor Farm near Hereford to a farm in Lower Breinton, and conveyed all his belongings, as well as livestock including cattle and horses, over the Lower Breinton ford.[9] Riders still take their horses through the river below Pont Rhyd Galed and doubtless they still do in other places further downstream.

The ferry as we understand it today is of medieval origin, but there are incidents of more ancient myths surrounding ferries and ferrymen that are found on the Wye as on other British rivers. Ferry crossings are by tradition journeys of transformation, and this applies especially to a story of the earl of Derby, the future Henry IV, crossing by the ferry at Walford/Huntsham in 1386. While the ferryman Pollett was conveying Henry across the river the earl was informed of the birth of his son in Monmouth Castle. The ferry fulfilled its mythical function as a transformative experience – Henry embarked as a man but when he disembarked he was also a father. The incident was good for the ferryman too, since Henry apparently granted the ferry rights in perpetuity to Pollett and his descendants. Never mind whether this was an apocryphal story; it reminds us that ferries had a status beyond the practical.

During the middle ages important crossing points were served by ferries or bridges and, as often as not, were protected by fortifications. Walford ferry operated under the protection of Goodrich Castle. The early history of many of the river crossings is unrecorded and many of them were replaced by bridges in the 18th and 19th centuries. Walford excepted, these ferries generally served local traffic as few important national routes crossed the Wye, and its major towns – Hereford, Monmouth, Chepstow – all had bridges in the Middle Ages. Hoarwithy ferry is first mentioned in 1347.[10] There was a ferry at Hay by 1336, possibly near the Nyport, or Watergate. In 1453 the ferry was out of action because the boat had gone down in a flood, perhaps the flood of 1447-8.[11] By 1629 there was a rival ferry operating from the other, Radnorshire bank of the river. Other recorded ferries were established much later. There was also a ford and/or ferry at Whitney by 1684, which was the means by which the first duke of Beaufort, as Lord President of Wales, reached the town of Hay.[12] There was a ferry at Redbrook by 1718, when it was mentioned by its owner, the duke of Beaufort, and

The medieval cross base marks the position of the old ferry at Wilton.

The Boat Inn at Redbrook, formerly the ferry house.

its position is marked by the surviving Boat Inn.[13]

Ferries continued in regular use into the 20th century although their numbers steadily dwindled from the 18th century onwards as they were replaced by bridges. In some places, however, ferries were established at a relatively late date. Brockweir Ferry is first mentioned in the early 1830s.[14] The aptly-named Waterscross was the site of Lydbrook Ferry, which was probably used mainly by workmen at the nearby iron and tinplate works and is not mentioned until the 1850s. Hunderton Ferry was begun in the early 20th century and owes its existence to the expansion of Hereford.

The operation of a ferry was regulated by landowners, who normally let the rights for a ferry for a certain length of time. In practice the arrangements were regularly renewed and the role of ferryman was in many places passed down through the generations. Thomas Fidoe was operating the Hoarwithy ferry in 1772 and eighty years later it was in the possession of William Fidoe, who had taken it over from Thomas Fidoe, presumably his father. Many of these ferries were operated from public houses, like the Boat Inn at Redbrook and the Hole in the Wall at Foy. At Walford there was a proper ferry house that offered refreshments to tourists.

Many of these ferries seem to have operated on an 'on demand' basis. Typically a bell was rung to summon the ferryman, and the boat was punted across the river. The ferry need be no more than a simple flat-bottomed vessel. To prevent them from being washed downstream ferries were often attached to a fixed point by ropes or, later on, chains. At Huntsham the rope was fixed to posts which had pulleys that could raise the rope to let barges pass under. Walford had a ferry described as being built of substantial oak, with a hull of elm. In 1783 the owners of the ferry, the Misses Clarke of

Hill Court, commissioned Thomas Hudson to build a new, identical boat for £31.[15] Ferries that could carry animals were larger than passenger ferries, but still rudimentary. At Hoarwithy, for example, William Hudson was paid £4 10s for building a new horse boat, and £1 5s for building a new small boat.[16]

A ferry at Dixton, above Monmouth, depicted in 1794.

The Walford ferry below Goodrich Castle in the 1790s. The ferry was hauled across by pulling on a rope fixed to the pole on the river bank.

The landing stage at the Tintern ferry.

The ferry at Symonds Yat, guided across by a wire spanning the river.

Ferry crossings in open boats could be something of a white-knuckle ride, especially for strangers unused to them. When the Reverend Richard Warner of Bath crossed the river at Holme Lacy in 1797 he did so with some trepidation. The ferry was 'long, narrow, flat-bottomed, and worked by a lad, who sits at the stern, and directs it with a paddle. In this little vehicle the passenger is conveyed over a stream always rapid, and frequently, when swollen with rain, extremely agitated and turbulent; thus situated it is absolutely necessary for him to be perfectly motionless, for should he change his position, the cockling boat would inevitably overset, and whelm him in the river, which is here very deep.'[17] And this was in an area that was getting used to ferrying tourists!

For a river with comparatively few important ferry crossings the Wye had an impressive heritage of bridges from the Middle Ages to the 20th century. The possibility that there were Roman bridges spanning the Wye is a tantalising one but, although archaeologists have taken some interest in the subject, they have not been convinced by eyewitness accounts of the river at low water. Wooden posts were apparently seen in the river in 1911 at Chepstow and the site of another bridge has been suggested at Kenchester where, in 1880, it was claimed that 'the remains of the pier foundations' were visible when the river level was low.[18] Roman roads certainly crossed the Wye at these places, and at Hereford, but the earliest known bridges on the Wye belong to the medieval period, the economy, and with it the transport infrastructure, of England having developed after the Norman Conquest.

There were few medieval bridges spanning the Wye and only one of them survived into the modern period, testament in part to the destructive power of the river. As we will see, it is the smaller tributary rivers that retain their medieval crossings. Place names are of little help in determining the site of early bridges, since the name 'bridge' can imply merely a wharf. Neither Bridge Sollers nor Canon Bridge had a bridge, much like Slimbridge on the Severn. John Leland travelled along much of the course of the Wye in the 1530s and recorded only five bridges. Four of them, at Chepstow, Monmouth, Wilton and Builth were of timber, and only one of them, at Hereford, was built of stone.[19] Further upstream the existence of bridges can only be guessed at. Christopher Saxton's map of 1610 indicates a bridge at Newbridge, perhaps the same bridge that was destroyed in the great flood of 1795.

On the English section of the river bridges were generally free of tolls because the king's highway was open and free of charges. The problem was that bridges were expensive to maintain and the old Anglo-Saxon idea that there was a feudal obligation to repair them had run its course by the 13th century – in fact a clause in Magna Carta of 1215 rescinded such obligations. One of the answers to the problem of bridge maintenance was pontage, a system of grants that allowed a town or parish to charge bridge tolls for a stipulated length of time in order to raise funds for bridge repairs. Hereford was awarded pontage for three years in 1334 and for ten years in 1383, when the bridge was considered dangerous to cross after it had been damaged by a flood, while Chepstow was granted pontage for five years from 1399.[20] Tolls payable on bridges under these conditions tended to be standardised. From 1383 tolls were charged on all kinds of merchandise crossing Hereford Bridge, from a farthing for things like a horseload of grain, a bundle of fine cloth or hundredweight of alum or verdigris, rising to a penny for a cask of ale or wine, or ten pigs or sheep brought to market.[21]

Hereford also drew on other sources of revenue for bridge repairs. In 1329, 1380 and 1383 the people of the city were allowed to take stone from one of the king's quarries, presumably to build the abutments as it was a timber bridge at this time, and in 1329 they were also allowed to take 12 oaks from the king's forest. Grants of timber for the bridge's repair were also made in the reign of Edward I (1272-1307) and in the reign of Richard III (1483-5). In 1383 Richard II, in addition to granting pontage, permitted the city to acquire 30 oaks from the neighbouring Haywood forest.[22]

Timber might seem a flimsy material for bridge building, but the longevity of Chepstow and similar bridges on other South Wales rivers, prove it to have been a durable material. The best known medieval timber bridge, although not the earliest, was at Chepstow, which made an unforgettable sight as it strode 'like a spider o'er the Wye', in Robert Bloomfield's phrase. A crossing of the Wye near its confluence with the Severn was an important route from England to Wales. Its strategic importance was acknowledged in the building of Chepstow Castle so soon after the Conquest, and implies a regular land route. The early date of the crossing of the Severn from Aust to Beachley, known as the Old Passage, is evident in the cluster of medieval chapels along this section of the Severn, almost certainly inhabited by ferrymen or keepers of lights. The early origin of the Old Passage only makes sense if there was a corresponding crossing of the

Chepstow Bridge portrayed by William Coxe. The river is a busy scene with flat-bottom boats on the water and barrels landed on a small quay.

Wye. There is no evidence of a ferry at Chepstow, but there was a bridge there by 1234-35, when 50 oaks from the Forest of Dean were felled to build or rebuild it.[23]

The bridge was probably temporarily unusable by the 1530s. Leland refers to it twice, once as a ruin and once as a former bridge.[24] However, it seems to have been under reconstruction in 1545, and was repaired at the time of the Commonwealth, when four oaks from Park Grove, Tidenham, were cut down for the bridge.[25] These appear to have

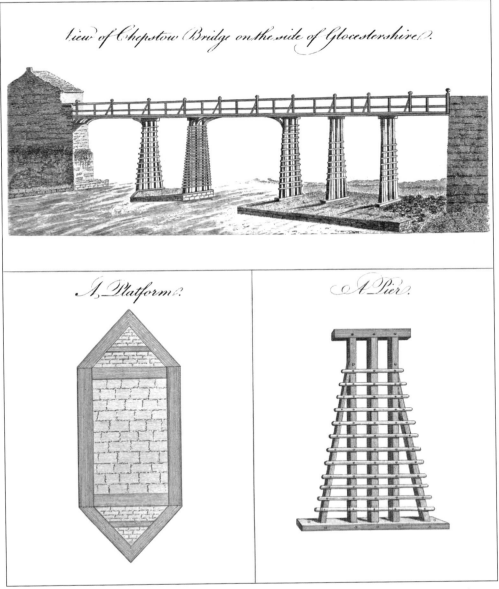

A drawing of the trestles making up Chepstow Bridge. Although they were drawn by William Coxe and published in 1801, the design is considered to be a medieval one.

been repairs as opposed to a re-design, and the bridge in its medieval form survived until the early 19th century. It was very similar in construction to the bridge over the Usk at Newport and there is no reason to doubt that the design we know of, if not the actual timbers, is a medieval one. Its appearance is well known because it appears in a series of watercolours and sketches made by artists at the end of the 18th century when the Wye Tour had become popular. It was constructed in timber and looked like a long trestle table across the river. At some time in the 18th century the centre was defined by a stone pier, which marked the boundary between Monmouthshire and Gloucestershire, and defined the halves of the bridge for which the respective counties were responsible. In the 1780s the Monmouthshire side was improved by building masonry piers for all of the spans. By this time, however, cast iron was proving itself to be technically superior to timber and the bridge was replaced in 1816.

The last half century of its existence was one of several phases of repair, which offers an insight into the maintenance of the bridge over the many centuries that preceded it. Chepstow was hardly the easiest place to build a bridge. The river is far too wide to cross in one span, and it has the added disadvantage of a very high tidal reach (consider that the lowest bridge on the Severn was a long way upstream at Gloucester). Construction of a timber instead of a masonry bridge had its advantages. Floods and the action of the tide inevitably meant that the bridge would need regular repairs, and timber repairs were cheaper than masonry. There was logic in having thin timber trestles, as opposed to broad stone piers, because they presented only a narrow obstacle to the current. In times of war a timber bridge is also easier to defend as spans can be dismantled with little effort compared to a masonry bridge. Due to the exceptionally high tides the planks laid out as the deck were not firmly fixed, meaning that they rose and fell when the tide was at its peak.

The construction of the bridge, very similar to Newport and Caerleon bridges on the Usk, consisted of trestles rather than stone piers, constructed of three posts strengthened by horizontal braces and outer diagonal shores, and set into a horizontal sole plate. Each of these trestles was set into a platform, much like the wooden platforms, or starlings, around the piers of masonry bridges, and with V-shaped cutwaters to smooth the flow of water past them both upstream and downstream. Excavations at Monnow Bridge in Monmouth revealed that the 12th-century precursor to the surviving stone bridge was also of timber construction and probably had trestles similar to those portrayed in the late 18th century at Newport and Chepstow. Chepstow is perhaps one of the best recorded examples of medieval timber bridge construction, and was a super-sized version of a technology of bridge construction that was found across Britain regularly on a smaller scale for the bridges of castle moats.

The earliest documented bridge over the Wye was built of timber at Hereford, probably in the early 12th century. There was no mention of a bridge there in 1055 when Earl Ralph crossed the Wye to battle Aelfgar and Gruffudd ap Llywelyn. The timber bridge was replaced by a new stone bridge with a fortified gate c.1490. The present appearance of Hereford's Wye Bridge documents the ensuing five centuries of repair and improvement. Four of the six spans are basically of the 15th century. One span that

Wye Bridge in Hereford is the oldest surviving bridge on the Wye.

had been destroyed in 1645 during the Civil War rebuilt in 1684-5, and the arch at the south end was probably built in the 18th century but supports an arch a century older. On top (or more accurately to the side) of this the bridge was repaired and widened by John Gethin in 1826, which makes the earlier masonry difficult to see.

Little is known about the other medieval timber Wye bridges. Wilton Bridge, just outside Ross-on-Wye, was replaced in stone in 1597, and Monmouth Bridge was rebuilt in stone with pointed arches in 1615, rebuilt again in the 17th century, and widened in the late 1870s by Edwin Seward of Cardiff. Builth had a new bridge in 1779 after the previous one had been damaged by floods, although a ferry also operated just downstream.[26]

There are other significant medieval stone bridges on tributary rivers close to their confluences with the Wye. The best known, and arguably the finest surviving medieval bridge in Britain, is Monnow Bridge in Monmouth, a classic medieval bridge with a church on the bank at one end and fortified gate on one of the piers. But it all came together in a piecemeal fashion. The church of St Thomas is of 12th-century origin (inside is a fine chancel arch and mid 12th-century font) and it seems very unlikely that a church would have been built there unless there was already an important crossing. The original timber bridge was rebuilt in stone in the 13th century, probably c.1272. The fortified gate came slightly later, after 1297 when the town received a murage grant, which enabled the town authorities to raise money to erect a town wall, of which the gatehouse was an integral component. Originally the gatehouse walls were embattled – the hipped roof it now has was built in the 18th century. After 1705 the gatehouse was converted to a house, and an extension was added on the downstream side that projected out over the river, supported on a masonry pier. This gave it a very medieval appearance, since some bridges had been inhabited in medieval times, although none of those on the Wye were, as far as is known. The extension lasted long enough to be

Monnow Bridge in Monmouth is one of the finest surviving medieval bridges in Britain, and the only one to retain its gatehouse on the bridge.

Mordiford Bridge, with a pointed arch of about 1352, and a round arch of the 16th century.

depicted by artists of the Wye tour, and was finally taken down in 1815.[27] During the 18th century the gatehouse became the town lock-up. Monnow Bridge and Wye Bridge at Monmouth were both host to public whippings from the time of the 1530 Whipping Act, a law that was intended to deter vagrancy, until the 19th century. Vagrants and petty criminals were tied to the back of a cart and whipped as the cart was drawn slowly to the centre of the town. As the bridges stood at the entrances to the town they were chosen as the starting point of this painful journey.

Another notable medieval bridge, at Mordiford, dates from the 14th century and is on the Lugg above its confluence with the Wye. There was a tradition that the family who held the manor did so on condition that they presented the king with a pair of gilt spurs every time he crossed the bridge.[28] The original structure of the bridge is uncertain. Corbels on the piers have led to a suggestion that it once had stone piers, but a timber deck carried on diagonal struts fixed to a beam carried by the corbels.[29] Numerous medieval bridges were of a similar stone and timber construction. The bridge was then rebuilt in stone with pointed arches, one of which has survived and was constructed by 1352. The other, round arch was rebuilt in the 16th century and flood arches were added in the 18th century.

Wilton Bridge was built in the period 1597-1600 and is in style a medieval bridge. One of the arches was destroyed during the Civil War. Wilton Bridge was widened in 1939 on the upstream side. It has six arches with stout stone piers and massive cutwaters

Wilton Bridge, built in 1597. The sundial was added in the 18th century.

that rise to the parapet and form refuges, a reminder that bridges were not merely points of transit, but on a busy river places to stop and watch the world go by. As if to emphasis the point, the central refuge has a sundial of 1718, with an inscription, which is eroded, but is clearly aimed at dawdlers on the bridge:

> Esteem thy precious time
> Which pass so swift away
> Prepare then for eternity
> And do not make delay.

It may have reminded loafers to get a move on, but to our generation it suggests a time when the river was more central to daily life. Few people now loiter on bridges to contemplate the river flow, just one of the ways in which our relationship with the river and our sense of the pace of life has changed.

There was a transport revolution in the 18th century, a great age of turnpike roads and bridge building. However, for several decades yet the transport infrastructure in Wales and Herefordshire was notoriously poor. The Wye was an impediment to traffic, often served by ferries and fords that had a poor reputation for safety. A correspondent to the *Gentleman's Magazine* in 1819 pointed out that 'communication is most grievously interrupted by the Wye. There are only three bridges for forty miles, from Ross to Chepstow, where for the purposes of commerce, there ought to be twenty'.[30] Anecdotal evidence suggests that more lives were lost on the Wye than on the busy River Tyne. The hazards of the Wye were worth pointing out because tourists who saw it in summer had no idea how the river swelled and changed character in the winter.

Ferries were inadequate to the nature and volume of traffic. There were horse ferries and smaller passenger ferries, but nothing larger. 'The conveyance of carriages is … from causes well known to the natives, exceedingly rare, because excessively inconvenient and troublesome. Nocturnal passage by carriages, horses or men, is not quite as rare, but studiously and prudently shunned.' Between Bridge Sollers and Byford there was by the mid 19th century a ferry capacious enough to convey horses and their carriages across the river. Such ferries could be dangerous. 'If a horse is unaccustomed to enter the boat, he is sometimes so restive, as to jerk his rider overboard by a sudden pull of the bridle, as he is being driven from the bank into the boat; and, as to foot passengers and ferrymen, they are often drowned by the stream forcing the boat from the rope.' And again: 'In short, the river as it now is, through want of bridges, is hurtful to life and property, which it ill becomes an enlightened age to endure patiently.'[31]

Slowly, new roads were laid and several new Wye bridges were constructed. Many of them were or became toll bridges – Bigsweir, Boughrood and Bredwardine all have surviving toll houses, a class of building for which no one seems to have found an ideal re-use. Simple solidity was the order of the day for most of these rural bridges. Bredwardine Bridge was built after 1759, replacing two ferries. It is the finest of the Georgian bridges on the Wye and, although of traditional construction comprising arches on piers with cutwaters and refuges, it is built of brick. Most Wye bridges were still built of stone or timber into the 19th century. The Walford ferry was finally replaced when Kerne Bridge, designed by D.B. Jones, was built in 1828, a severe looking five-span

Bredwardine is arguably the finest of the 18th-century bridges on the Wye, a rare example of the use of brick.

stone bridge with solid parapet, shunning the neo-classical pretensions that characterise British town bridges of the period.

Glasbury Bridge was and remains an important crossing of the Wye between Leominster and Brecon. According to Theophilus Jones the first bridge was replaced by another timber one after 1738, and this was superseded when a stone bridge was constructed in 1777 by the son of the great bridge builder William Edwards of Pontypridd. Benjamin Malkin in 1803 described it as a light, elegant bridge: 'The arches are small segments of large circles on high piers, as best adapted to facilitate the passage of floods under the bridge, and travellers over it.'[32] Malkin was unfortunately mistaken

The toll house at Bigsweir Bridge,
built in 1829-35 for the St Arvan's-Redbrook Turnpike Trust.

Boughrood has one of several surviving toll houses.
This one was built in 1843 by T.H. Wyatt and David Brandon.

when he described the bridge in the present tense, however. Samuel Ireland had made a sketch of Glasbury Bridge in August 1794, but by the time he came to publish it the drawing was only a memorial of what was now 'little more than a wreck; every arch of it having been blown up by the torrent of ice, which poured down ... after the long frost in the beginning of 1795'.[33] The stone bridge that was destroyed in February 1795 was replaced by another timber bridge, part rebuilt in stone in 1850, which remained until 1877 when it was part-replaced in iron; this was demolished in 1922 to make way for a reinforced concrete bridge designed by the county surveyor of Breconshire, W.L. Harpur.[34]

The former toll house built for Brynwern Bridge, near Newbridge, in 1885.

The toll house at Bredwardine was built after the flood of 1770 that damaged the bridge.

Kerne Bridge, the last of the major stone bridges on the Wye, completed in 1828 and replacing the Walford ferry below Goodrich Castle.

After the 1795 flood Whitney Bridge was rebuilt, retaining the outer stone arches, but with three timber spans between them.

The bridge at Whitney, first promoted in 1774, was conceived as a replacement for the ferry, which operated about 150 yards downstream. The bridge, by James Mathias of Pembrokeshire, was not completed until 1780 because it had been difficult to establish firm foundations on the shifting gravel. This would prove its undoing. It was undermined and badly damaged in the flood of February 1795. Originally of five stone arches, only the smaller, outer spans were retained, and in 1802 it was given three lighter timber spans in the centre. It is still a mainly timber bridge and is still a toll bridge.

The first bridge at Hay, which had five stone arches, was completed in 1763. Like the bridges at Whitney and Glasbury, it was crippled by the flood of 1795. The new bridge had timber spans in the middle of the channel, like Whitney, but was in a dilapidated condition by 1838 and was damaged by a flood in 1855, although it had withstood the more serious flood of 1852. In 1865 the *Hereford Times* described it as 'a crazy old structure, spliced, propped and patched in all directions, with dangerous approaches on each side with a short steep pitch with a tramroad crossing at the bottom'.[35]

The maintenance of Hay Bridge was funded by tolls. A toll board of 1847 (now in the Brecknock Museum) lists the rates in force at the time, which included fourpence for each drawing beast, one penny for horses not drawing, a halfpenny for passengers, and no charge for carriages with lime, or for children in arms and under three years of age.[36] In 1779 an inscription was fixed in the gallery of Hay church: 'that the commissioners by an Act of Parliament 29 Geo II granted the Wye bridge a lease of the toll thereof for 98 years from 1 October 1763 and after the expiration thereof the bridge is to be free from toll'. The trouble was that this had no legal force, and tolls were the only

T.H. Fielding's mid 19th-century view of the bridge at Hay
shows its timber superstructure on stone piers.

The bridge at Builth, built in 1779 to replace an older timber bridge.

Boughrood Bridge was built in 1842 by T.H. Wyatt for the Maesllwch Estate.

way of raising money for the upkeep of the bridge. On the day when the lease expired in 1861 a crowd of about 300 people from Hay and Clyro gathered at either end of the bridge in preparation for a celebratory mass walk-over. Fireworks heightened the sense of occasion. But the gate-keeper refused to open the gates and the angry crowd tore them down and threw them in the river. It was subsequently established that the Bridge Commissioners retained the right to charge tolls and the gates were recovered and re-erected. As it happened, the expiry of the lease coincided with the approach of the railway to Hay, and Thomas Savin, who was contracted to build a rail bridge nearby, built a new lattice-girder road bridge that allowed the railway line to pass underneath. This was completed in 1864, and tolls were collected until 1933. Savin's bridge was replaced by the present bridge in 1958.[37]

The timber bridge at Builth, of medieval origin, was damaged in 1740 and replaced in 1779 by a fine arched bridge of six spans, sturdy and relatively simple, designed by James Parry of Hay-on-Wye. But for its rounded rather than pointed segmental arches, it is little different to a medieval bridge, and the same is true of Boughrood Bridge, built in 1842 to replace the ferry owned by Walter Wilkins of Maesllwch Castle. Builth is the first substantial bridge on the Wye, since the upstream bridges are all of a single span. As well as the bridge at Rhayader, there was a bridge at Llangurig by 1713 and by 1794 a wooden bridge at Pont Rhyd Galed on the main route between Llangurig and Aberystwyth.[38]

Timber remained a favoured building material until the mid 19th century. Road improvements at Hoarwithy needed a bridge to do them justice, but it was a long time

The toll house and central pier are all that survives of the bridge built at Hoarwithy in 1855. The original deck was timber.

Chepstow Bridge at low tide, showing the stone piers and starlings.

Bigsweir Bridge, built in 1825 to carry the new turnpike road between Chepstow and Monmouth, and the first iron bridge on the Wye to cross the river in a single span.

coming. A design by Joseph Gwilt, exhibited at the Royal Academy in 1813, was for a timber bridge of five spans, but it was never built. In 1855 an Act was passed for the building of a toll bridge, which was of three timber arches on stone piers. Constructed using local chestnut, the bridge was in constant need of repair, and the boatman who passed under it in 1875 had no idea how recently it had been built when he described it as 'a very dilapidated old wooden bridge'.[39] Hoarwithy Bridge was rebuilt with iron girders in 1876, and this was in turn replaced in 1990. The original toll house still stands.

In the 19th century iron and steel began to replace timber and stone. The use of cast iron began at Coalbrookdale and the bridge built over the Severn in 1779; and for the next half century investment was made in several iron bridges over the Severn. The Wye valley enjoyed less investment in its bridges, a sign that it was poorer than the Severn valley and was forced to use cheaper materials. But the most important of the Wye crossings, at Chepstow, was a notable engineering achievement and saw the arrival of the first iron bridge on the river.

Chepstow Bridge was designed by John Rennie and cast by Rastrick and Hazledine of Bridgnorth. The components were presumably transported to Chepstow by river, and construction of the new bridge was completed in 1816. The lattice-work in the arches – five spans in all – was typical of the period, as was the segmental arch as the basic structural component. The bridge still stood on high masonry piers, however, in order to accommodate the exceptional tidal range of the lower river. Other iron bridges followed. Bigsweir Bridge near Llandogo, built in 1825 on the turnpike road from Chepstow to Monmouth, shows how fast bridge technology was developing; it is a single-span bridge, designed by Charles Hollis. It is often said to have been cast in Merthyr Tydfil, with the exception of the outer flood arches which were added later in the century, but according to Nicholson's *Cambrian Traveller's Guide*, published in 1840, the bridge parts were cast by Bough & Smith of Enfield and the cost of the bridge was £5,982.[40]

Many sections of the rural Wye were not bridged until later in the 19th century, and the iron and steel bridges of this period were much inferior to those built at Chepstow and Bigsweir. In 1885 Maynard & Cooke built a road bridge to Huntsham, a hamlet near Goodrich, in the typical lattice-girder style (it was rebuilt in 1982). An iron bridge was built at Bridge Sollers in 1896, designed by the Rhayader architect S.W. Williams; it was rebuilt in 2003 by Halcrow Group Ltd.

The Wye's most egregious road bridge was built at Brockweir, proof that not everything on the Wye is beautiful. It was built by Finch of Chepstow in 1905-6 and promoted by wealthy incomers to link with the road on the Welsh side of the river. (Until then the village had been quite cut off.) The ferryman, Edwin Dibden, tried unsuccessfully to stop the building of the bridge on the grounds that it would put him out of business (which it did). He might have been better arguing that the bridge was an offence against good taste. The promoters decided on a mediocre railway bridge design and seem to have acquired the bridge components – girders standing on cylindrical steel piers – off the shelf. That would explain why the bridge is so ill-fitting, set down on the Brockweir side in a brutal manner in front of the fine Elizabethan manor house. The promoters would

Brockweir Bridge, the ugliest bridge on the Wye.

Brunel's railway viaduct built in 1852 for the South Wales Railway, the first railway bridge
over the Wye. Its tubular suspension-bridge design influenced his later Saltash Bridge.
(Ironbridge Gorge Museum Trust)

have done better to contract the firm of L.G. Mouchel, one of whose functional and elegant concrete road bridges was built at Newbridge in 1911 (but replaced in 1981).

Iron and steel bridge construction is more often associated with railway bridges. Railways brought their own, more spectacular bridges to the Wye. Railway bridges need a flat deck, which makes girder construction well suited to the task, but they have a less intimate relationship with the river than a road bridge because they often soar over a river valley where a road would wind down to its banks.

Isambard Kingdom Brunel's Chepstow railway bridge, built in 1852 for the South Wales Railway, was the first to span the Wye and surpasses all subsequent railway bridges, in technical and probably in aesthetic terms too. Bridging the Wye at Chepstow would prove a special challenge because the ground level on the English side is much higher than it is on the Welsh side, and thus a high-level bridge was called for. The technology of the suspension bridge was already established for this type of topography, but its moving deck made it unsuitable to carry a railway. Brunel set about creating a design that would overcome this problem. He achieved it by erecting iron tubes between the bridge piers, from which chains were attached like a conventional suspension bridge, but the roadway was kept stable by means of girders. The concept was to ensure that weight was distributed evenly over the bridge while the train passed over. Instead of masonry piers it has cast-iron cylinders sunk to a depth of 48 feet into solid limestone, and filled with concrete. These cylinders provided the stable footing to which tubes were attached. The design worked well, and Brunel's Saltash Bridge of 1859 is a larger, improved version that owed much to the Chepstow prototype. The bridge remained in use in its original form until 1962, by which time it was deemed unstable for fast trains. The tubes were therefore taken down and the bridge acquired the steel sub-structure which remains in use today.[41]

The modified Chepstow railway bridge after the original bridge
was deemed unsafe for modern rail traffic.

Chepstow's railway bridge set a standard of design that was impossible to live up to, and the remainder of the Wye's railway bridges are generally undistinguished. The Victorian railway boom did not reach the Wye until the 1850s. After the South Wales Railway came the Newport, Abergavenny and Hereford Railway, which opened in 1854. The Hereford, Hay & Brecon Railway was built in 1862-4; the Wye Valley Railway from Chepstow to Monmouth was opened in 1876, and included a branch to Tintern

Kerne railway bridge, on the former Wye Valley Railway between Ross and Monmouth, in the early 20th century. The line closed in 1959 and the bridge was taken down.

The Duke of Beaufort railway bridge near Monmouth, retaining its original girders.

Wireworks that incorporated a bridge; the Coleford, Monmouth, Usk and Pontypridd Railway opened in 1857, although it did not cross the Wye, at Monmouth Viaduct, until 1861; the Mid Wales Railway opened from Llanidloes to Three Cocks Junction, near Glasbury, in 1864; the Central Wales Railway opened in 1864; and the Ross and Monmouth Railway opened in 1874. Today, a century and a half after the railway boom, only the Chepstow bridge and the bridge near Builth Road station (just outside Builth Wells) of the former Central Wales Railway still carry trains.

Some of the old railway bridges have survived, either in disused form or converted for pedestrians and cyclists. Hunderton Bridge in Hereford, built in 1853 for the Newport, Abergavenny & Hereford Railway, originally had three segmental arches, but they were replaced by steel girders in 1912, and the bridge is now a cycle path. A three-span viaduct of the Wye Valley Railway which crosses the river at Tintern was built in about 1865 to connect with the local wireworks. It has iron trusses on stone piers. Iron bridges abounded on the Wye, mostly of a girder design. Those at Lydbrook and Troy and the Duke of Beaufort Bridge near Monmouth, manufactured by Edward Finch of Chepstow with novel bowstring trusses, are now footbridges. The Wye Valley Railway bridge at Redbrook (1876) is also a footbridge but the same railway's Troy bridge was partly taken down when the line closed in 1964. The approach viaduct has survived but the iron spans across the river have been removed. Monmouth Viaduct, designed by Christopher Firbank and built by Kennards of Crumlin in 1861, is also constructed as a stone viaduct of 22 arches across the floodplain, but the lattice girder span across the river has been removed.

The approach to the river of Monmouth Viaduct.
The girders spanning the river have been removed.

Sellack Bridge, built in 1895 to replace the ferry
and to connect with Kings Caple on the opposite bank.

Foy Bridge was built in 1921 to replace an earlier bridge.

By the end of the 19th century suspension bridges began to appear on the Wye. Many were footbridges – Sellack in 1895, Victoria Bridge in Hereford in 1898, Foy in 1921, and later bridges at Cwmcoch (1967) and Dernol (1975). The single-carriageway Llanstephan bridge, built in 1922, is a rare suspension bridge for vehicular traffic. The bridges at Foy and Sellack connected the two halves of each parish, which were only previously connected by ferries.

The iron bridge at Chepstow became secondary when the high-level A48 bridge was built to sail imperiously over the Wye as the twin of Brunel's revamped railway bridge. It overcomes well the difficulty of standing next to a revered 19th-century structure. With its cylindrical concrete piers it consciously follows the spirit of the old bridge, but is a much simpler design with smoother lines. It will never enjoy the attention focused on the railway bridge, partly because it was built after the heroic age of bridge building had passed, and it has been surpassed, at least in terms of traffic flow, by the Wye Bridge which opened in 1966. The motorway viaduct over the Wye at Chepstow is very much secondary to the great Severn Bridge spanning the mile-wide Severn estuary, and most motorists remain unaware that they are crossing two rivers. But it is a fine cable-stayed bridge and a fitting structure to mark the boundary between England and Wales.

If the designers of the Wye Bridge, Freeman, Fox & Partners, are little known, that shows the diminished place of bridge building in today's society. Once, building a bridge was the most important investment made by a community, after the parish church. Into the 19th century building bridges was a sign of prosperity and ambition, and during the railway boom years it was the ultimate expression of new engineering technology. Crowds turned out to watch the erection of the iron span of Monmouth Viaduct in 1861, but nothing like that would happen now. Bridges are no longer written up in newspapers and crowds no longer gather at openings, now that crossing the river is taken for granted. The heroic age is over. Most of the 20th-century replacements of earlier bridges are unworthy of special notice and new bridges have few fans, perhaps with the exception of Bridstow Bridge on the M50, designed by Scott Wilson, Kirkpatrick & Partners, which opened in 1960. And yet bridges are so much part of the story of human engagement with the river. For a major waterway, the Wye is lucky to retain two bridges earlier than 1600, with others on its tributaries. The story of its Chepstow bridges, from wooden trestles to iron arches, from tubular suspension bridge to cable-stayed bridge, is one of the best examples in Britain of how bridge technology has advanced over the past five

The road and rail bridges at Chepstow.

centuries. Upstream, the story is different. The timber trestles of Whitney and the brick arches of Bredwardine, both crossing some of the more tranquil stretches of the Wye, grace the river in ways that never fail to please us.

Wye Bridge, which carries the M48 over the Wye below Chepstow, is a cable-stayed bridge designed by Freeman, Fox & Partners.

✎ 6 ✎
Frontier and Battleground

One of the earliest written descriptions of the River Wye ('Aque Y'), written in 1479 by William Worcestre, defined it as a kind of frontier, a river of castles. 'It flows first through the town of Builth Castle, belonging to the Earl of Warwick … then by Pains Castle of the Earl of Warwick … then it flows straight to Hay Castle … and passes by Monnington Castle of Lord Audley … Thence it goes to the king's castle at Hereford … to Wilton Castle, belonging to Lord Reginald Grey. And from Wilton Castle it flows to Goodrich Castle … to Monmouth Castle … [and finally] to Chepstow Castle'.[1]

The character of the Wye valley now seems so peaceful that it is perhaps hard to believe that it was once contested territory. By the late 15th century the border was relatively settled and it has remained so, but in the preceding thousand years the Wye was witness to several episodes of conflict. The most tangible surviving evidence of this belongs to the decades following the Norman Conquest. Marcher lordships created by the English Crown covered the course of the Wye up to and beyond Builth, and Marcher lords maintained and expressed their power by building the castles, many of them beside the Wye, that William Worcestre catalogued in 1479. But defensive structures on the Wye cover a span of time from the coastal forts of prehistory to the Second World War tank traps by the river at Chepstow.

A river is a natural frontier, a barrier that offers sanctuary and protection, and a line across which rivals can face off. As a waterway connected to the sea it is also a means of attack, at least in the form of a raid if not an invasion. In places the Wye is still a boundary between England and Wales – in a stretch of a couple of miles between Hay and Rhydspence, and a shorter stretch below Symonds Yat and above Monmouth. Further downstream it is the border from Redbrook to the end of the river below Chepstow. In south-west Herefordshire is the district of Archenfield, or 'Herefordshire in Wales', the eastern boundary of which was the Wye. In the medieval period Archenfield was in Welsh ecclesiastical territory as part of the diocese of St David's, a status that persisted until the 19th century. The old division has endured in the language of place. Look at the map and it becomes apparent that the river was a cultural boundary with Welsh names in Archenfield like Kilforge, Tryseck, Llanfrother,

Concrete tank traps by the river at Chepstow,
defence against possible German incursion in 1940.

The parapet of the iron bridge at Chepstow marks the mid-stream boundary between
Monmouthshire and Gloucestershire.

with English names on the east side of the river like Brampton Abbots, Brockhampton and Fawley.

As a long navigable river it is perhaps not surprising that fortifications were built to protect various stretches of it. The Iron Age hillfort is the classic military site of later prehistory, although whether they were the pre-Roman equivalent of medieval castles is rather doubtful. Some seem to have been densely settled and to have been villages with defensive earthworks. Others that were not permanently occupied seem to have been gathering places for communities across a wider landscape. There are many of these hillforts along the course of the Wye, although the extent to which they were directly associated with the river, rather than being built to serve or command a wider territory, is debatable. On the Monmouthshire coast is the Bulwarks, just below Chepstow, which would certainly have defended entry to the river from the Severn estuary, the most strategically important position on the Wye. There are other Iron Age hillforts on the lower river that look down on its course and could watch over incursions from the sea. The two defended sites at Piercefield, Piercefield Camp and Pierce Wood Camp, are both perched safely on the top of the cliffs overlooking a loop in the river, though in a position where the inhabitants would have been unable to use the resources that the river offered. Upstream from there, what makes Symonds Yat one of the finest viewpoints in England also made it ideal for the construction of a defensive enclosure. From its vantage point it commands views over the winding river eastwards and south-westwards. It has impressive earthwork defences and an elaborate entrance of a type thought to be as much a status symbol as a defensive device.

The Romans used the Wye valley in their early campaigns in Wales under Ostorius Scapula (AD 48-78). The valleys offered greater mobility for the Roman army than the native hilltop strongholds, which were essentially of a static, defensive nature (although for a short period the Roman army used Credenhill Camp as a supply base). The earliest Roman fort built in what is now modern Wales seems to have been the one near the confluence of the Wye and Monnow at Monmouth, a forward base for the imperial army's attack on the Silures of South Wales. Known as *Blestium* in the Antonine Itinerary, it remained under military control for far longer than the military garrisons built further upstream. For the Romans, the upper river was in hostile territory on the border between the Ordovices and Silures, although the Wye seems to have been garrisoned only for a short period. A fort overlooking the river was built at Clyro, perhaps overlooking an important crossing point, but it was apparently abandoned by AD 69. Another fort, presumably of a similar nature, has been identified at Clifford.

It was after the Romans left that the landscape of the lower Wye was fought over. Much of what we know about this period was written centuries later in histories that modern historians would not consider as authoritative. Even if the details are unreliable, however, the overview makes it clear that the lower Wye valley was an area where the Britons and the Saxons clashed, making conflict one of the defining characteristics of the Wye between the 6th and 9th centuries. The *Book of Llandaff* was compiled in the 12th century from assorted documents relating to the history of the diocese, and including hagiographies of its early bishops. The diocese held estates which extended

Tewdrig in the Circle of Legends
at Tintern Old Station.

eastwards as far as the Wye valley. 'Be it known that great tribulations and plunderings happened in the time of Teithfallt and Ithael, kings of Wales, which were committed by the most treacherous Saxon nation, and principally on the borders of Wales and England' as far upstream as Hereford, 'and especially about the River Wye'. It mentions frequent night and day skirmishes by the river, leaving owners dispossessed and forcing the people to flee. It was in this period that St Tewdrig, formerly king of Glywysing, fought off the Saxons at Tintern (see p.44).[2]

The Wye is also associated with the legend of the British king Vortigern, largely thanks to Geoffrey of Monmouth. The story of Vortigern was told by several early historians, including Nennius, Robert Wace and Bede, but Geoffrey's account became the best-known, and was repeated by William Worcestre among others. The real Vortigern (Gwrtheyrn in Welsh tradition) was probably one of the men who rose to power following the demise of Roman administration in the 5th century, and was probably a native of the border region, which served as his power base. It might also be true that he recruited German mercenary soldiers to help defend his territory against the threat posed by the Picts. But later historians had their own agenda, and by the 12th century, when Geoffrey was writing, Vortigern was a figurehead for treachery. He was blamed for welcoming the Saxon immigrants Hengist and Horsa (and lusting after Hengist's daughter) and, in consequence, was allowed to go free from the notorious massacre of the Britons at Stonehenge. From there he fled back into Wales and summoned his magicians, Merlin prominent among them, to ask what he should do next. They told him to construct a fortress, and it was in this fortress that he perished when the castle was besieged and burned to the ground by his successor as king of the Britons, Aurelius Ambrosius. Confusingly, when Geoffrey describes the building of the castle he places it in Snowdonia, usually taken to be the castle at Dinas Emrys. However, in his account of Vortigern's end Geoffrey makes it clear that the castle, called Genoreu, was situated beside the Wye in Ergyng (part of Archenfield) on a hill then called Cloartius, known today as Little Doward.[3] Geoffrey's account perpetuates the idea of the River Wye as a frontier, a meeting of different cultures. A few other places have also laid claim to the legends of Vortigern. William Camden, following the account by Nennius, saw him escape the blaze that destroyed his castle, from where he travelled alone to the upper

Wye valley, which provided a safe place of refuge, at least until he met his end in a lightning strike.[4]

The other persistent myth of the Wye of the Dark Ages is that the border was defined by a long bank in the time of King Offa of Mercia, who reigned between 757 and 796. There is an earthwork between the Severn at Sedbury cliffs and Tallard's Marsh on the Wye that was constructed in the age of Offa and is traditionally said to be the southern end of Offa's Dyke. Further north the intermittent sections of bank running parallel with the Wye were once confidently assumed to belong to the 8th century. Recent archaeological work has cast doubt on that, however, and Offa's Dyke is now considered to have terminated at Rushock Hill near Kington, which is well north of the Wye in Herefordshire. So Offa's Dyke was never really associated with the Wye. The lower Wye seems like a logical border, and means that the river and its resources were shared by both Mercians and Britons.

King Offa in the Circle of Legends at Tintern Old Station. Offa may not be part of the events of Wye history, but he is part of its mythology.

By the 9th century the Saxons and Welsh had a common enemy in the shape of Danish longships. Hereford was fortified at the time of the Danish invasions and became a Saxon *burh*, one of the fortified settlements that offered refuge in times of invasion and later became the centres of local government. The Danes' natural territory was water, so they preferred to stage their attacks by sea or by river. In the 9th century most Viking raids were carried out on the east coast of England, but they managed to penetrate the kingdom of Mercia by sailing up the Severn and Wye rivers. The reign of King Burgred of Mercia, from 852 to 874, was dogged and eventually curtailed by Viking attacks by land and water. By the 10th century the Vikings had established bases for themselves in northern France and the western side of Britain was in the sights of landless pirates. It left the lower reaches of major rivers, including the Wye, especially vulnerable. The Celtic monastery at Lancaut may have been destroyed by invaders at this time. The *Anglo-Saxon Chronicles* record that in the second decade of the 10th century (918 in the Worcester Chronicle and 914 in the Parker Chronicle) Archenfield was attacked by Danish pirates based in Brittany, who had sailed unopposed up the River Wye. The assault was led by two jarls, Ohtor and Hroald, and was successful in seizing Cyfeiliog, bishop of Archenfield. Seizures of this kind were commonplace and the Danes had their desired reward – a ransom of £40 was paid to release the bishop. The second time the Danes tried this tactic in Archenfield, however, the men of Hereford and Gloucester were ready for them and Ohtor and Hroald were both killed.[5]

The building of defences along the river in the century before the Norman Conquest shows that there were still Anglo-Welsh tensions and occasional violent episodes along the river. Ralph, made earl of Hereford in 1046, had built a castle at Hereford by 1052. Three years later the earl met Aelfgar of Mercia in battle. Aelfgar was the son of Leofric, earl of Mercia (and possibly the son of Lady Godiva), but had been exiled in 1055 through the machinations of the Godwine family. Aelfgar responded by assembling a small army with the help of Gruffudd ap Llywelyn, the powerful Welsh leader who had previously defeated Aelfgar's father Leofric in a battle on the Severn in 1039. Gruffudd had his own agenda, of course. He saw an opportunity to repossess lands that he thought rightfully Welsh, and perhaps saw Aelfgar as a useful ally in his ambition to become established as the ruler of all Wales. When the rebel army was approaching Hereford Earl Ralph left his castle stronghold, crossed the river and met with Aelfgar's army in battle. The rebels were victorious and, as Earl Ralph retreated, the victors did with Hereford as they pleased, probably destroying the castle. According to the chronicler Florence of Worcester, its monastery and cathedral were burned. Harold Godwinson refortified the city immediately, but it was never again to be attacked by the Welsh. Gruffudd was not hunted down and killed until 1063.

With the arrival of the Norman Marcher lords, a series of castles were constructed in western Herefordshire as defence against Welsh attacks, including near the banks of the Wye. Between the major castles of Hereford and Clifford these included a site at Lower Breinton (above) which overlooks the ford on the Wye, and from the 12th century was the site of the country house of the Treasurer of Hereford Cathedral, but was abandoned in the later Middle Ages. There was also a castle at Bredwardine, mentioned in the Domesday Book and presumably the site that was re-fortified in the 12th century.

A new generation of fortifications was built after the Norman Conquest. The Normans were thoroughbred colonisers, having established themselves in northern France at the beginning of the 10th century, where the Duchy of Normandy was created, and taking over the crown of England via Canute in 1016. Memories of Gruffudd ap Llywelyn's incursions were still fresh and William I reigned over a period of new military reinforcement along the border, proof that he was not really interested in an all-out conquest of Wales.

As a first line of defence against attack from the west, William established Marcher lordships, by which means Norman barons controlled large areas of border territory on their own terms. The most important fortifications were built on the lower section of the river between Hereford and Chepstow; the Norman castles further upriver were less grand.

Soon after his coronation on Christmas Day in 1066 William granted the Welsh kingdom of Gwent, to be known as the Marcher lordship of Striguil, to William fitz Osbern, newly ennobled as the first earl of Hereford. The lordship was known as Striguil, after the Welsh *ystraigyl*, meaning the bend in the river. Fitz Osbern built many fortifications between Clifford and the sea, but his immediate priority was to secure the lowest defensible point of the Wye, on a cliff top at a bend in the river at Chepstow. The keep at Chepstow was the first masonry castle built by the Norman conquerors. Stone was transported by river from Portskewett and Caldicot and the stone keep, in style a bit

The wall of the lower bailey at Chepstow Castle, looking towards Marten's Tower.

In this view of Chepstow Castle by Hendrik Frans de Cort, made *c.*1795, the craggy hilltop site of Chepstow Castle is exaggerated but shows how the castle commanded the river. (Yale Center for British Art, Paul Mellon Collection)

like a Roman fortress, was erected before fitz Osbern's death in 1071. The importance of Chepstow was manifold. The castle was built on the Welsh side, easier than building on the steeper English bank, which allowed control of the river as a means of communication. The castle looks most impregnable from the river, which would have daunted any sea-borne invaders. Below the castle it was possible to cross the river, perhaps only by ferry, and the re-use of Roman material in the original castle keep suggests that the Romans had indeed crossed the river here on a road between Caerwent and Gloucester. By building on the Welsh side of the river the new earl of Hereford was able to defend the river and the crossing, and had a bridgehead that allowed him to launch incursions into Welsh territory if necessary.

Upstream the next important strategic point was at Monmouth, where the Monnow joins the Wye. This was obviously an important strategic position, and the Romans built a fort here. The earl of Hereford began a new castle here in 1067. Initially only an earthen motte and bailey castle, it was later rebuilt and enlarged in stone and stands over a loop in the River Monnow rather than overlooking the Wye itself. The surviving structures belong to the 13th century, probably the period after 1267, and built by Edmund Crouchback. Its principal claim to fame is that Henry V was born there in 1387.

Chepstow Castle in 1850, from an early Bradshaw's Guide, looking downstream.
(Yale Center for British Art, Paul Mellon Collection)

Hereford Castle was strengthened and extended by the earl of Hereford, and was one of a minority of castles that witnessed conflict in the Middle Ages. A new motte and bailey was built about 1100 on what is now Castle Hill, but it was not until the mid 13th century that it was completed as a stone castle, by Henry III. Hereford was caught up in the conflict of King Stephen's reign and in 1138 was held against the king, for which it was besieged; during the Anarchy, substantial parts of the city, including the bridge, were burned down. The castle acquired a keep in the 13th century.

Further upstream William fitz Osbern built another castle at Clifford, begun in 1069 and standing on a hill overlooking a bend in the Wye, which at this point is still the boundary between England and Wales. The surviving masonry remains belong to the 13th century and later, when the castle belonged to the Clifford family. A small settlement grew up close by, indicative of peaceful periods in this part of the medieval border. Only a few miles to the west, and on the same side of the river, is Hay Castle. Fitz Osbern may have built the first fortification, a simple motte and bailey (no longer in evidence) which was replaced by a stone castle commanding the river and protecting the town, consolidating the Norman gains in the region. This castle was built by William de Braose, of the family that dominated Hay until the mid 13th century.

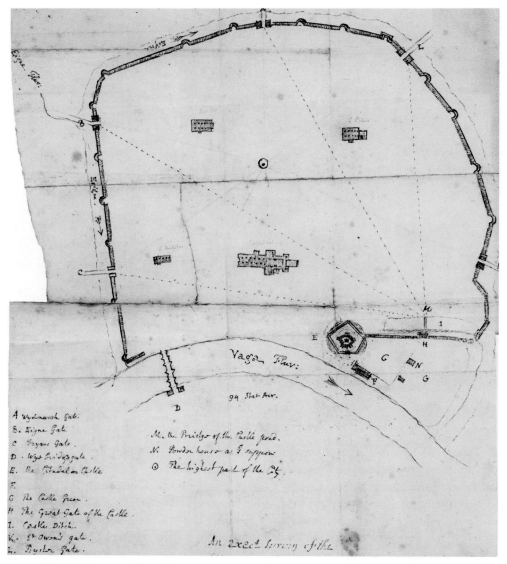

This outline map from 'An exact survey of the city of Hereford in 1716' shows
the medieval defences, in the form of the town wall and the castle by the riverside.

Other castles were built in the Wye valley, most of them constructed of timber
defences on a tall mound, or motte, such as Bredwardine, Clyro and Glasbury. According
to Domesday, the district around Goodrich was the property of Godric Mappeson, and
the first Godric's Castle is mentioned in 1101. The castle as it now stands is largely the
work of the de Clare family in the 12th century and William de Valence from the 1260s
onwards, when oak from the Forest of Dean was floated upriver.[6] Goodrich Castle has
a dramatic setting overlooking the river, where there was also a well-established ferry

Samuel Ireland's view of Clifford Castle in the late 18th century,
commanding by this time a quiet stretch of river on the England-Wales border.

By the 18th century Hay Castle had been converted to a house.
It was one of two defended sites by the river here.

crossing. However, we cannot really be sure whether the castle was built to protect the river crossing, or whether the ford and ferry became established because it was a safe place to cross.

99

Part of Goodrich Castle, drawn by Horace Jones (1819-1887) in 1842.
(Yale Center for British Art, Paul Mellon Collection)

Wilton Castle was rebuilt in stone in the early 14th century by Reginald de Grey.

Wilton Castle overlooked the river where it was crossed in the approach to Ross, first by a ferry, then a timber bridge, and finally, at the end of the 16th century, a stone bridge. The Norman castle was of the motte and bailey type, with timber palisades and keep, but was rebuilt in stone in the early 14th century by Reginald de Grey. The strategic importance of Wilton declined over time, and in the final quarter of the 16th century it was partly converted to a house.

Beyond Hereford and into modern Wales, the castles were built in more hostile territory. They include Aberedw Castle, in existence as a motte by 1093 when the Normans launched an invasion into Welsh territory. The first castle at Builth was built by Philip de Breos, also in about 1093, but was destroyed when the Lord Rhys invaded the area in 1168. A new castle was begun in the early 13th century and changed hands several times before it was destroyed in a siege in 1260.

After the conquest of Wales in 1277 some castles were rebuilt in places where they were no longer really needed. One such example was Aberedw Castle, built on a spur above the confluence of the Edw and Wye. Llywelyn ap Gruffudd, recognised by Edward I as the Prince of Wales but ousted from his fortress at Dolforwyn on the Severn, was said to have stayed at the castle in 1282, before he was caught up in a skirmish near the Wye at Cefn y Bedd near Builth, at which he was killed. A new castle, perhaps better described as a fortified house, was begun at Aberedw to consolidate the new power over Wales, but it was redundant in military terms as there were no hostilities in the region for over a century, until the rebellion of Owain Glyndwr. Builth Castle was rebuilt again after 1277, but was never finished.

The castle at Rhayader was built by the Lord Rhys of Deheubarth in 1177, but at the end of the 12th century it was taken first by Maelgwyn and Hywel, sons of Cadwallon ap Madog of the neighbouring kingdom of Maelienydd, then almost immediately by English forces, before it was regained by the Lord Rhys. In effect it was a disputed frontier for only a short period and the castle was redundant by the 14th century.

The upper Wye enjoyed a century of relative peace following the death of Llywelyn ap Gruffudd in 1282, until the rising of Owain Glyndwr in 1400. The rising started in north-east Wales but Glyndwr was active across large parts of Wales in the earlier, more successful years of his campaign. The Wye seems to have become important only after Glyndwr fled to the mountains in 1413 and was never heard of again. Tradition claims that he died in 1415 at Monnington, which is not an outrageous suggestion given that it was the home of his daughter Alys Scudamore. In the 19th century his grave was presumed to be by the porch, marked by 'a flat stone of whitish grey shaped like a rude obelisk figure, sunk deep into the ground in the middle of an oblong patch of earth from which the turf has been pared away, and, alas, smashed into several fragments'.[7]

The most prolonged war to be fought in the vicinity of the Wye was the Civil War between 1642 and 1648. In the king's long struggle to assert his control over the nation, Parliament's forces held London and Charles I therefore based his campaign to defeat them in western England and Wales. Although the Wye was never the front line, it was in Royalist territory that had to be captured by Parliament, which it duly did in stages following the decisive defeat of the Royalists at the Battle of Naseby in June 1645.

Throughout the conflict Parliament had a stronghold at Gloucester on the Severn, from where raids were launched against Royalist strongholds, which included those that stood by the Wye, using the river as a protective barrier. The Wye only became a significant factor in the fighting as Parliament's forces began to prevail. The most sensitive points along the river were the bridges, since attacking forces were necessarily funnelled to those access points, which could be defended effectively by removing one of the spans and replacing it with a wooden drawbridge.

Many of the events on the lower Wye are known in detail from an account written by John Corbet, chaplain to Colonel Massey, the governor of Gloucester, although obviously it covers events only from Parliament's perspective. Likewise the fall of Hereford is known in large part due to the military memoir of Colonel John Birch, the Roundhead leader who became the governor the city after the Royalists had been ousted.

Throughout the Civil War Chepstow and the confluence of the Wye and Severn was an important strategic position. River and coastal traffic was vital for transporting supplies, and the crossings of the Severn and Wye needed protection in order to link Royalist forces in Bristol with those in South Wales. From 1644 this area was contested in a number of naval and field skirmishes. In 1644 Parliament's garrison at Gloucester built a 'friggot' to make mischief on the river. According to John Corbet, 'the friggot was sent down Seavern manned with sea-men and a party of souldiers, for whatsoever attempt sudden opportunity should offer; and arriving at Chepstow, our musketeers hasted ashore, and entered the town', launching a surprise attack. The royalist garrison under Colonel O'Neill was largely stood down, and a Captain Carvine was killed as he supped in the George Inn. On the quayside 'another prize fell into their hands, where they took a vessel laden from Bristoll with oyle, wine, sugar and other commodities' bound for Worcester.[8]

The Royalists responded by augmenting their naval strength in the estuary and fortifying the headland around Beachley. Prince Rupert, the king's German nephew and his most illustrious ally, took a party of 500 men and began to fortify the ground between the Severn and Wye with a defensive line, part ditch and part hedge, which allowed his forces to guard the entrance to the rivers. Parliament's forces resolved to launch an attack against the headland from the landward side to the north. It was not possible to attack from the river because the Royalist navy presence was too strong. Ships guarded the rivers, but they also had big guns that could fend off attacks by land, and supply ordnance and men as required during an assault. The only snag was the very high tidal reach of the lower Wye and Severn, of which the Roundhead forces took full advantage. Parliament's forces encountered a small advance force of cavalry from Chepstow, capturing some and driving others back into the river, but waited for low tide before they launched an attack on Prince Rupert's defensive works. At low tide the naval ships had to retreat to a point where their guns were no longer in range and they could not reach the shore to deliver reinforcements or rescue their retreating comrades. According to Corbet, the Parliamentary action was so successful it looked 'more like the pomp of a triumph than the confused face of a fight'. Some of the defenders were killed, some taken prisoner. Others fled into the water where many drowned, although a few reached the safety of the Royalist vessels offshore. To make the victory sweeter for Parliament, 'it was performed in full view of a multitude on Chepstow side'.[9]

Such was the strength of the Royalist forces in the area that they quickly re-took Beachley, and set about improving the defences by erecting palisades in addition to the ditches and hedges. To the Roundheads it was a formidable defence, 'the pinnaces riding in each river with ordnance to play upon us, and the line so strongly guarded with hammer guns, and murtherers placed on the flanks at either end, that it seemed impossible to storme the same by day without apparent great losse'. Parliament's tactic was the same as before. It waited for low tide, which coincided with daybreak, and on the morning of 14 October 1644 launched an attack without the fear of a naval bombardment. Even though they were in range of the artillery on the Welsh bank of the river the Parliamentary forces successfully stormed the defences and forced the Royalists back to the water. Famously this is where the hated Royalist Sir John Winter, the leading Royalist figure in the Forest of Dean, was able to make his escape. Although 'they forced Sir John Winter downe the clift into the river', it was 'where a little boate lay to receive him, and convey him thence into the ships'. The cliff is still known as Winter's Leap. The other troops were not so lucky, realising that the water was their only escape route. 'Many tooke the water, some whereof were drowned, and others saved themselves by recovering the boates'. The hedges and palisades were cut down as, in the short term, Parliament was not strong enough to hold the headland, but it put an end to Royalist fortification of it.[10]

After the first successful raid on Beachley the Parliamentary force led by Colonel Massey had set its sights on taking Monmouth. Monmouth was well protected by its two rivers and a castle. Massey's troops approached from the Forest of Dean, meaning that the river lay between them and the town. They feigned a retreat, disappearing back into the forest to give the impression to the garrison at Monmouth that they had returned to barracks in Gloucester. Then they played a trick, whereby Colonel Kyrle, a Royalist turncoat, took an advance party to the town gate at Wye Bridge and persuaded the garrison to lower the drawbridge and let his party into the town, claiming they were mainly prisoners. Massey's men took advantage and stormed the entrance and secured the bridge. The small garrison was quickly overwhelmed with little bloodshed. But Parliament failed to hold it, partly because Massey had too many other targets in his sights. Massey was persuaded to turn his attention to the renewed defences at Beachley and his remaining small garrison at Monmouth was vulnerable and was duly successfully attacked after Massey had been diverted to Oxfordshire. The town was back in Royalist hands. Then Colonel Massey decided to attack an outpost of the Monmouth garrison at Pembridge Castle (near Welsh Newton) but, on reaching Ross, found the river to be an impenetrable barrier. The bridge (or at least one span of it) was taken down, boats were sunk on the opposite bank to impede an army landing on it, and it was protected by a small Royalist force.[11] Monmouth was not taken permanently until October 1645.

The Royalists, led by Sir John Winter, took another step to strengthen their hold on the lower Wye in 1645 by establishing another passage at Lancaut, which they intended to fortify. A small party of troops advanced from Chepstow by frigate and landed at Lancaut, where they met the Parliamentary forces. Rivers are a fine form of defence if they are in front of you but become a trap when they are behind you. The Royalists were routed and were forced back to the river. About 80 were slain, but 'of the residue some adventured the river to recover the frigate; many were drowned ... but Sir John Winter and his brother with some few besides escaped'.[12] Details of the victory reached Parliament in a hastily written letter of 18 February proclaiming 'A great victory obtained by Colonel Massey' in which Sir John Winter's house had been stormed (truth here a casualty of war) and 60 men were drowned and some of their boats were sunk.[13]

Chepstow saw plenty of fighting during the Civil War. It was briefly evacuated in April 1643 when Sir William Waller's Parliamentarians advanced towards it, and in October 1645 Parliamentarians overran the town, besieging and bombarding the castle. The 64 Royalists who had not fled surrendered. But when fighting flared up again in 1648 Chepstow was taken back under Royalist control under Sir Nicholas Kemeys. Cromwell's men gained back control of the town but the garrison in the castle was more stubborn in its resistance and by May was under siege. The castle was bombarded and then stormed, and most of the garrison, including Kemeys himself, perished.

Ross saw some action in the Civil War too. Parliament was able to take it but not consolidate its gain, so that it continued to be fought over. The bridge was stoutly defended but was not impregnable. The difficulty was not simply securing a bridge, but securing it intact. In 1644, when Wilton Bridge was being guarded by the Royalist Captain Cassie with the help of 30 musketeers from Goodrich Castle, a small Parliamentary force seized the bridge. Parliament had two cannon but it is not clear whether they were needed, or whether the defenders destroyed one of the bridge spans themselves. In May the river was low enough for Massey's forces to ford the river and mount a surprise attack from a new front, in which the wounded captain was captured.[14] The small force could not hold Wilton Bridge but it took the opportunity to proselytise in the area, with the intention of allaying local fears and distrust of Parliament.

Hereford was in a strongly Royalist area and as a medieval walled town was ideal for defence. There were Parliamentary campaigns in 1642 and 1643 that were briefly successful in taking the city, but as the surrounding area remained loyal to the king it could not be held and the Parliamentary forces drew back. To protect the city from attack by river Viscount Scudamore of Holme Lacy in 1643 urged that a breastwork should be erected on either side of the bridge, and another by the Castle Mill. Hereford was secure enough for Charles to take refuge there after his defeat at Naseby in June 1645. The king had appointed the viscount's brother, Colonel Barnabas Scudamore, as the city's governor, and he immediately prepared for the inevitable siege, implementing recommendations made by Sir Richard Cave in 1644 for strengthening the city's defences. A siege began when a 12,000 strong Scots army arrived at the end of July, but it was not successful.

A letter sent by Barnabas Scudamore gives an insight into the role played by the river in the siege. The Royalists controlled the bridge, from where they could send out small raiding parties of 20 cavalry to attack the Scots and then retreat hastily. Access to the city from the bridge was protected by a gatehouse, and it was to this that the Scottish artillery turned its attention. After two days of assault it was rendered useless, 'yet our men stopt it up with Wooll-sacks and Timber, and for our greater assurance of eluding their attempt, we brake an Arch [of the bridge, replacing it with a rising timber span], and raised a very strong Worke behind it'.[15] The position of the broken arch is easy enough to determine, as it can be seen today that one span is of a different build to the others. The battered gatehouse was not demolished until 1782.[16] Then the Scots sought to batter the town wall by the river, near the old Greyfriars, and after that was unsuccessful built their own temporary bridge across the Wye in order to strike the city from a new angle. This was a sophisticated wooden bridge carried on two trestles sunk into the river bed.[17]

Colonel Birch finally took Hereford on a frozen December day in 1645, with little resistance, and held it for the rest of the war. In the event the city's defences were superfluous. The enemy gained access to Hereford by deceit when a gang of men appeared at the bridge dressed as labourers, with a constable bearing a warrant for them to work in the town on breaking the ice in the river and city ditches. Once the guards had been overpowered the main forces went in by the undefended gate. But several important Royalists escaped, among them Scudamore and Sir Henry Lingen, who were able to bypass the bridge and cross the river on the ice.[18]

Goodrich Castle had been an important strategic position as its ferry was one of the most established crossing points on the river. By 1646, however, it was garrisoned because it was a formidable stronghold, rather than for its river connections. In July 1646 the decisive campaign took place, and Colonel Birch's Parliamentarian army bombarded

Wilton Castle was burned down during the Civil War
and by the 18th century its ruins were part of a garden.

Henry Marten, the Parliamentarian and regicide imprisoned in Chepstow Castle between 1668 until his death in 1680.

the castle. Sir Henry Lingen had found refuge and reinforcements here after he had escaped from the fall of Hereford. The brutal siege of Goodrich lasted six weeks, notable mainly for the use of a super-sized piece of artillery known as Roaring Meg which tore into the castle walls.

Capture by Parliament usually meant that the old military strongholds of the Marcher lords were 'slighted' to ensure that they were never again garrisoned against Parliament. Goodrich was slighted first, followed by Monmouth Castle in 1647. Hereford Castle was taken down and a century later became Castle Green, a promenade and gardens on the riverside. The fate of Wilton Castle was altogether different. It had been converted to a mansion in the 16th century but it was garrisoned in 1643 to defend the bridge. It was burned in 1645 on the orders of Sir Barnabas Scudamore because its owner, Sir John Brydges, refused to give up his neutrality. The tactic backfired because Brydges immediately took revenge by siding with Parliament. After the Civil Wars the castle was ruinous. Thomas Roscoe visited it in the mid 19th century, by which time 'the area of the castle serves as garden ground, and flaunting dahlias flourish luxuriantly among the strangely-abused memories of former days'.[19] It was a melancholy place and led Roscoe to thinking, not of the bad old days of tyranny, but how monuments that tell 'many a stern truth' should be preserved.

Unlike the other castles, Chepstow was in the possession of Oliver Cromwell and its defences were strengthened during the Commonwealth between 1648 and 1660. In the event it saw no further military action beyond its role as a prison. Chepstow is best remembered in the Restoration years as the place where Henry Marten, one of the Members of Parliament who signed Charles I's death warrant, was imprisoned between 1668 and his death in 1680. Although he was an ardent Republican, there were several mitigating factors that spared him from a sentence of execution. He voluntarily surrendered himself after the Restoration of Charles II in 1660, his quarrel had been with the monarch only, and he was known to have treated Royalists with restraint while Parliament was in the ascendant. The tower in which he was imprisoned has since been known as the Marten Tower, but it was not a medieval-style incarceration. He was apparently not closely guarded and was occasionally allowed out into the town to dine.[20] In the circumstances, Henry Marten was very lucky.

❧ 7 ❧
Industry

Industry on the River Wye sounds like a contradiction in terms, and it is true that of all Britain's major rivers the Wye can now claim to be the least industrialised, but that was not always the case. The novelist Harry Fletcher, reflecting on the relatively unspoilt landscapes of the Wye, thought that 'for some reason there are districts where industry does not fit in, and when it is made to fit the union is never quite stable and does not last. View this as objectively and as unsentimentally as you like, some places belong to the country and cannot turn into a busy manufacturing area.'[1] The Wye was a prime example of this, but when Fletcher was writing in the 1960s he had in mind the industrialisation of the 19th century and all its connotations of coalfields, smoke and scale. Industry has had a much longer history and wherever there is a body of water, especially when it is a navigable river, there has been industry. Perhaps the Wye has merely been a lucky river, industrial at a time when it operated on a small scale in buildings that were built using traditional local materials – i.e. before the mid 19th century when the landscapes of industry changed radically.

Water mills were a medieval phenomenon and there were once many of them along the course of the Wye, although not necessarily drawing water directly from the river. Waterwheels could be placed on river banks to be turned by the flow of the river. To offset the unreliability of the river level, most mills were served by ponds that were created by building weirs across all or part of the river channel. The problem with this kind of mill is twofold. Firstly, weirs block river channels and annoy other river users in the process if there is no bypass channel or vessels can only pass over the weir at times when the river level is high. Secondly, riverside mills can only effectively power undershot wheels, where the wheel is turned at the base by the flow of the water. Waterwheels derive more power more efficiently if the water can be channelled to the top of the wheel, where it falls in buckets, turning the wheel by the force of gravity. The gradient of the Wye is so low that if overshot waterwheels were to be used, the river would have to be dammed a long way upstream and then the water conveyed to a waterwheel on a raised, probably wooden, water launder (trough), which would have been impractical. The Wye's tributary streams and rivers, however, have a steeper gradient and are much easier to exploit for powering overshot waterwheels. Although the mills powered directly from the river are probably the earliest type, most mills by the Wye drew their water from tributary streams rather than the main channel.

Waterwheels were the primary source of power for industry until the 19th century. Places that are ideal for exploiting it were generally discovered in the Middle Ages and in many cases saw a succession of water-powered industries. When an existing lease expired it was often taken over by another concern. For example, where ironworks were established at places like Tintern and Carey Mills, they were preceded and succeeded by corn mills. Most of the water-powered industrial sites on the Wye were corn mills. Other applications included fulling (or tucking) mills for cleaning cloth, which was an important part of the woollen industry, furnaces and forges of the iron industry, paper mills and, to a small extent, the generation of hydro-electric power in recent times.

There is no surviving evidence of mills built on the river bank to exploit the flow of the river, but we know they existed. In 1680 a list of mills and weirs was drawn up that identified obstructions to the Wye navigation. Some were also mentioned in a survey of the river in 1697. The densest concentration of mills seems to have been between Ross and Hereford. The lowest of the these were the two at Wilton, then Gulston Mill, Carey Mill and Hancock's Mill near Fownhope, which was 'decayed and beyond repair' in 1697, unlike the nearby Fownhope Mill which was still in good condition at that time. During the dry summer of 1984 part of the weir at Carey Mill, upstream of Hoarwithy, became visible, constructed as a series of walls between natural islands in the river.[2] At Hereford, below the bridge, were three corn mills and three tucking mills.

Some of these mills were established early – the two mills at Wilton and Fownhope Mill were mentioned in the Domesday Book of 1086. The mills at Ross were both fulling mills in 1324. Carey Mill was first mentioned in 1250 when it belonged to St Guthlac's Priory in Hereford. The mills at Hereford were rebuilt in 1555 after they had been destroyed in 1538 on the orders of Henry VIII. In 1555 the destroyed mills were described as having been there 'tyme out of mynde'. The fulling mills were important to Hereford's economy, and before 1538 'so beneficiall for thinhabitantes of the said Citie, that thereby Clothemaking was there greatly encreased, and verie much people there inhabiting sett on worck, as Weavers Fullers Walkers Spyners & Carders, whereby the said Citie was well occupied, & thinhabitantes thereof then very Welthye and Riche'.[3]

Above Hereford there were riverside mills at Stretton Sugwas and Monnington, as well as one at Bridge Sollers.[4] The mills below Hereford ceased to be viable after their weirs were removed following the Rivers Wye and Lugg Navigation Act of 1695, and very little evidence of their former existence has survived. However, one small riverside mill survived on the Wye until at least the late 19th century. It was built in a loop of the river at Boughrood, where a weir was built along the left bank of the river, sufficient to allow a small reservoir to be created without affecting the whole river. This mill was flooded in 1795, forcing the miller and his family to flee to safety.[5]

The best known of the riverside mills was at New Weir, near Symonds Yat. The earliest documented reference to the New Weir, in 1454, implies that there was an

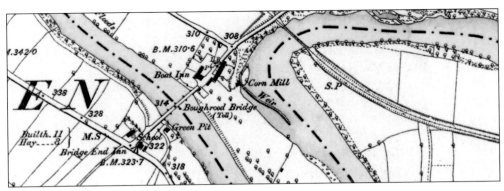

The riverside corn mill at Boughrood,
marked on a late 19th-century Ordnance Survey map.

older weir, and in 1697 'Old Weir' was described as being two miles further upstream, although little of it was then visible. The New Weir was almost certainly built originally to serve some form of agricultural mill before it was leased for ironworking in the 16th century. But the weir across the river seems always to have been controversial. It was apparently attacked in 1589 in connection with a dispute between landowners.[6] The river below Monmouth was the busiest part of the river navigation and it was mainly river users who complained of the inconvenience of the weir. One of the provisions of the 1695 Rivers Wye and Lugg Navigation Act was that the landowner was responsible for building and maintaining a lock, since an existing lock was in disrepair.[7]

Toward the upper end of the river there was no commercial traffic, the watercourse was narrower and it was therefore easier to build a dam across the river. Llangurig Mill, perhaps better known as Felin Fawr, was known as Magwr y Graig Velen in 1692. A weir was built across the Wye, and from this water was channelled into a leat to the mill, from where a tail race returned the water to the river.[8] The river has a shallow gradient here and it seems unlikely that the mill was powered by anything other than an undershot waterwheel. The mill remained in use until at least the end of the 19th century.

Most of the Wyeside mills were supplied from tributary streams, although often channelling the waste water directly into the Wye. The mill furthest upstream is Bidno Mill, where there was a Tyddyn Pwll y Melin (Cottage by the mill pool) in 1692, implying a corn mill. In the 19th century there was a woollen mill on the site, set well back from the Wye on the Bidno stream.[9]

At Rhayader, the ruins of Cwmdeuddwr Mill stand in the small village across the river from the town. The mill stood opposite Rhayader castle on the Nant Gwynllyn, fed by a leat and pond. It was clearly a going concern in the 19th century, since all the machinery that was recorded at the site was installed after 1850, including two waterwheels, one dated 1868 and the other 1901.[10] The mill is the lowest of a succession of mills on Nant Gwynllyn as it flows down to the Wye. Further downstream on the Wye is Llanwrthwl Mill, now converted to a house, which stands close to the Wye but was supplied with water from the adjacent Dulas Brook. Not far down on the opposite bank of the river is Argoed Mill, on the Doldowlod Estate founded by the engineer James Watt. Taking its water from Nant Treflyn, just above its confluence with the Wye, Argoed Mill was rebuilt as late as 1878, continuing to work until the 1930s (before a turbine was installed for generating electricity for the Doldowlod Estate). Just below Builth was Aberduhonw Mill, which took its water from the Duhonw brook. A much larger mill was built further downstream in the early 19th century by the Glanusk Estate at Trericket; it is a three-storey brick building and is the largest industrial building on the Welsh section of the Wye. These mills supported typical rural industries, grinding wheat, rye and barley for domestic and agricultural use.

Castle Mills in Hereford was probably founded by St Guthlac's Priory before the community was moved away from the river in the mid 12th century. The mill is first recorded in 1219, situated on the river bank by the outfall of the town ditch, but was burned down in the siege of Hereford in 1265 and then rebuilt. By the early 19th century it was still a corn mill, although in 1695-6 there had been plans to use the waterwheels to pump water to the city centre. When the mill was advertised in 1811 it had four pairs of French stones worked by two waterwheels. French stones, or burrs, were imported by mills in Britain at this period because they were capable of milling a very fine white flour. The days of the mill were numbered, however. The mill pond was a notorious health hazard in the city and it was infilled after the Hereford Improvement Act came into force in 1854. The mill itself was demolished.

The catalogue of tributary mills continues along the rural parts of the Herefordshire Wye. Clock Mills, on the Bach Brook in Clifford, was working until the 1920s and was then converted to a house. Fields Mill in Madley, which is of 17th-century origin, has also been converted into a house. Downstream from Hoarwithy most streams seem to have attracted a mill: Hoarwithy Mill was on the Wriggle Brook, Mordiford Mill on the Pentaloe Brook, How Caple Mill on Totnor Brook, Tarrs Mill on Tars brook at Holme Lacy and Nupend Mill on the Tan Brook at Fownhope.[11]

The Wriggle Brook had a succession of mills leading down to the Wye, of which Hoarwithy was the lowest, and in the early 19th century included a paper mill at Tresseck, supplied by rags delivered to Hoarwithy by river. In 1810 four hundredweight of paper was despatched to Bristol.[12] At Walford Mill, on the Castle Brook, corn was ground until 1946 but the buildings had mainly been converted to a sawmill, in the 1860s.

Some of the mills mentioned in Domesday appear to have been tributary mills, including Brampton Abbots and How Caple. Brampton Abbots Mill was on the Rudhall Brook. Sellack Mill, near the church, is first mentioned in 1268, and the two mills at Eaton Tregoz were first mentioned in 1369; all of these were fed by streams rather than the Wye itself.

Corn mills served a regional market, so the river navigation was not essential to their business. This was also true of some of the other medieval industries on the Wye. In the woollen industry water mills were needed for cleaning the cloth, but otherwise woollen manufacture was not a riverside industry on the Wye. A specialised branch of the woollen industry was cap-making in Monmouth, even earning a name check in

Shakespeare's *Henry V*, in which Fluellen describes Welshmen 'wearing leeks in their Monmouth caps'. Rhayader and Hay-on-Wye were also woollen-manufacturing towns in the 18th and 19th centuries. Ross was at one time known as a town of iron manufacture and leather working, before those industries grew in scale and shifted toward the coalfields in the 18th century.

The river was important in all of the larger industries that emerged after the Middle Ages, like paper mills and especially ironworks. The Wye has an impressive ironmaking heritage that is often underestimated. The iron-industry heritage of the Severn is much better known but covers the period from the 18th century onwards when coal was the fuel used in the industry and it was centred upon the coalfields. The iron-industry heritage of the Wye is generally earlier, and belongs to the period when the industry was fuelled by charcoal, most of it the produce of Wyeside woodlands, a rich resource that gave landowners an incentive to invest in ironmaking.

There was a small amount of iron smelting close to the Wye during the Roman occupation of Britain. At Monmouth the iron-rich slag from the smelting process was piled high close to the banks of both the Wye and Monnow, and this proved a boon when the iron industry expanded in the 17th century and there was an easily accessible source of iron-rich material that could be sold to new furnaces more efficient at extracting the iron from the rock. There is still a Cinderhill Street in Overmonnow. In 1769 the Cock Alehouse, close to the quay on the Wye, was sold with its 'iron cinder mine', a clear indication that this Roman slag heap was worth having.[13]

The iron industry expanded in Britain in the 16th century, partly because of government initiatives to drag Britain's antiquated metals industries into the modern world, and partly because improvements in the capacity of the industry stimulated a search for sites where water power was available – the same places that had been colonised by corn mills for centuries in some cases. In Roman times iron was smelted in a small furnace called a bloomery, kept up to temperature by manually-operated bellows and shaped by hand-held hammers. Water power was gradually introduced to the industry in the Middle Ages in order to increase the capacity of bellows, which resulted in significant rises in bloomery output. By the end of the Middle Ages new iron-industry technology divided the industry into two separate processes at separate places, the furnace and the forge. First the iron ore was smelted in a blast furnace, producing pig iron that had a carbon content of between 3 and 4 per cent. In order to convert it to malleable iron it needed to be worked in a separate hearth at a forge. Both processes consumed considerable amounts of charcoal and both needed water power for the working of large bellows. Forges now also used heavy, mechanically operated hammers powered by waterwheels. Furnace and forge were rarely situated in the same place, and did not need to be as long as there was a reliable means of transporting semi-finished iron between the different works – hence the importance of the Wye.

The source of some of the highest-quality iron ores in Britain is a region centred on the Forest of Dean, but extending to encompass part of the Wye valley. Some of the early blast furnaces were built in the late 16th and early 17th centuries on the site of earlier bloomeries. An example is at Bishopswood on the Gloucester-Herefordshire border, where Robert Devereux built one, perhaps two, blast furnaces that were working briefly from the 1590s until by 1617 they were apparently in ruins. Of the two furnaces, one had been built on the Dry brook, while the other, on the Lodge brook, was brought back into production by 1674 and continued working until 1751, when a new blast furnace was built. The latter survived long enough for Wye tourists to notice it in passing in the late 18th century, although the economic downturn for the iron industry that came with peace with France in 1815 was its death knell. In its later years the ironworks relied for its raw materials on iron ore from the Furness district of Cumbria, which was imported by river.

A blast furnace also seems to have been built on the bank of the Wye at New Weir. The site was well known to 18th-century tourists as a forge, but excavations at the site in 2009-10 unearthed waste from the blast furnace smelting, which was quite unexpected.[14] By 1575 there was also a blast furnace on the site of an earlier bloomery at nearby Whitchurch, sometimes called Old Forge, where iron was smelted until 1750. Further downstream, Coed Ithel blast furnace was built in Bargain Wood, close to Llandogo, and was in operation in the 17th century, until the 1660s. It is one of the few ironworks of the period with substantial upstanding remains.

Ironworking began at Tintern in the 16th century. William Humfrey was hired to establish a wireworks at Tintern in 1567-8, initially to produce brass. He was previously Assay Master at the Royal Mint and was a shareholder in the Company of Mineral and Battery Works, one of two metals-industry monopolies created by Elizabeth I with the aim of improving home production of iron and brass wire. Wire was an important component of wool cards and was associated with one of Britain's leading industries. To make a success of his Wyeside enterprise, Humfrey employed expert workmen from Germany. Given how close the wireworks stood to the former abbey, it seems likely that there was a mill here in the Middle Ages and that the site had already proved its suitability for industry.

Later, a succession of furnaces, forges and wireworks were built in the Angidy valley upstream of the confluence, supplied by iron from the local blast furnace but also from further afield in the Forest of Dean. By the end of the 18th century iron was also imported by river from Furness.[15] A short-lived furnace was built by the earl of Worcester in 1633 by the river, and is said to have derived its motive power from a tidal waterwheel. It was superseded around the time of the Restoration in 1660 by a new blast furnace a mile upstream of the confluence, which continued working until c.1820, another casualty of the downturn in the iron trade that followed peace in 1815. Samuel Ireland took a detour up the valley in about 1794 to watch the blast furnace at work, noting how the blast was delivered by massive cylinder pumps (no longer the old-fashioned bellows), and then he visited the forge where the pure metal was separated from the dross under the water-powered hammers.[16] Wire was a specialist industry conducted in only a few places until production expanded in the 19th century and the industry drifted to the coalfields. The wire works closed in the early 19th century, as did the forge, at a time when iron was ceasing to be predominantly a riverside industry but was shifting to the coalfields and the use of steam power.

Outflow of a reservoir on the Angidy Brook that served the furnaces,
forges and mills at Tintern.

Blast furnace at Tintern on the Angidy Brook.

Tintern forge in 1798, by Thomas Hearne. The forge attracted the attention of artists because of its proximity to the abbey. (Yale Center for British Art, Paul Mellon Collection)

Tintern wireworks in 1807. The works had been established in the 16th century by William Humfrey. (Yale Center for British Art, Paul Mellon Collection)

The Abbey Mill at Tintern with its gigantic waterwheel fed by the Angidy Brook,
pictured by Joseph Powell, c.1801. (Victoria & Albert Museum)

When the Tintern wireworks closed it was converted again to a corn mill and became known as Abbey Mill. Exactly the same thing had happened much earlier at Carey Mill. In 1629 an iron forge was constructed there on a disused but well-established mill site. Records of its construction are interesting because they indicate how unreliable a means of transportation the River Wye was at this time. Hammers and anvils were delivered to the works from Bewdley, the transport hub on the Severn, but most of it was transported overland from the Severn. When the Wye navigation was used it was only possible to deliver the goods as far as Huntsham, from where it was an overland journey. Carey Mill remained a forge for only half a century at the most, and was a corn mill again by 1679, probably using the same waterwheel that powered the bellows and hammers of the forge.[17]

There was a forge at New Weir by the end of the 16th century, replacing the earlier blast furnace, and perhaps supplied by the blast furnace at Whitchurch. In the first decade of the 18th century a slitting mill was added, in which flat plates were slit into thin rods of square section for making nails or to be drawn into wire. Thomas Whately described the forge in 1770 and, although his words betray a lack of understanding of the technicalities, he gives an impression of a self-contained industrial enclave on the river: the forge was 'covered in a black cloud of smoak, and surrounded with half-burned ore, with coal [i.e. charcoal], and with cinders; the fuel for it is brought down a path, worn into steps narrow and steep, and winding among precipices; and near it is an open space of barren moor, about which are scattered the huts of the workmen.'

The New Weir Ironworks, a watercolour by Hereford artist James Wathen.
On the hill to the right are the workmen's cottages.

The waterwheel at Abbey Mill in Tintern,
documenting several centuries of water power drawn from the Angidy Brook.

He remembered too the 'sullen sound, at stated intervals, from the strokes of the great hammers in the forge'.[18]

There were ironworks on the Forest of Dean bank of the Wye at Lydbrook and Redbrook. A forge was built at Lower Lydbrook in the 1590s, about 200 yards from the Wye, following the building of two other forges further up the valley. It was probably previously a corn mill. By 1815, the Lydbrook forges had been combined into a tinplate works, which was then a regional specialism whereby iron was rolled into thin sheets and then dipped in molten tin. The works continued in production throughout the 19th century and limped on a little after 1900, long after which the industry was dominated by the South Wales coalfield. The former lower forge, meanwhile, became a corn mill again and continued as such until 1976.

In 1691 a copper works was built at Lower Redbrook, importing copper ore from Cornwall by river. By 1771 it had become a tinplate works, perhaps only slowly super-seding copper smelting and probably using the same rolling mills. Production of tinplate, latterly using steel imported from Belgium, continued on a small scale until 1961, the longest-surviving concern of the industrial revolution period on the Wye, and long after the Wye and water power had ceased to be a significant factor in its location.

Paper mills were built in the Wye valley for the same reason that iron forges were built there – the need for water power close to an effective means of transportation for bulky wares. In addition, clean water was an essential ingredient in paper making. Paper was made from rags, which were washed, fermented and then reduced to a pulp under hammers, before the pulp was knitted on to a wire and compressed to form a sheet of paper. Tresseck Mill has already been mentioned. The copper works at Lower Redbrook was also previously a paper mill. Along the Whitebrook, a tributary of the Wye near Llandogo, a succession of industrial enterprises operated from the first decade of the 17th century when a branch of the Tintern Wireworks was built. By 1760 ironworking was finished and the aptly named Clearwater Paper Mill was built, followed in the 19th century by the Glynn Paper Mill, Bridget's Mills, Sunnyside Mill and Fernside Mill, all of them in the beautiful wooded valley, a reminder that paper making was essentially a rural industry.[19]

The natural resources of the riverside include the growing of withies, used for basket making. Willow setts apparently also helped preserve the river bank. The industry had a long history above Ross-on-Wye. In 1634 Thomas Earsley and Isaac Deverox, basket makers of Fownhope, leased stretches of the river banks for planting willow setts.[20] Tanneries and breweries were often sited by rivers because they needed copious amounts of water although, apart from public houses, these industries have left little trace. Stone has always been one of the Wye valley's chief resources. The Wye is a rocky river and in places there has been quarrying close to the water's edge. The quarries at Capler are well known because the stone was used to rebuild the west front of Hereford Cathedral after its partial collapse in 1786, but there were others on this stretch of river at Ballingham, Bridstow, Sellack and Hoarwithy. Quarries on the right bank above Lydbrook were exploited to build Bristol Bridge, one of the advantages of the river quarry being that the stone could be transported by water. In the 19th century lime became an important component of both industry and agriculture. Lime kilns for burning limestone were often set up close to riverside sites, from where the burnt lime could easily be transported away, and there are remains of this small-scale industry still to be seen at Tintern and Symonds Yat. In the late 19th century, only large-scale quarrying was really profitable. Stone was quarried from the gorge above Chepstow, effectively by shaving off the cliffs that face the river, the kind of industrial exploitation that quickly blends in with the scenery and remains unnoticed unless looked for, but in the 19th century it made an impression on water-borne travellers: 'The hand of the destroyer is however at work here, the rock being quarried, and immense quantities of stone sent off in barges, which come and go with every tide.'[21] The stone was used to build Avonmouth Docks.

By the 18th century it was common to bemoan the state of the Wye navigation and to cite it as the reason for industrial decline, especially in Herefordshire. The old medieval industries had certainly declined. The expense of fuel was given as a reason why manufactories of gloves and woollens had dwindled, although poor communications and a shift toward regional specialisation in industry also played a part. The cost of rectifying the problems of the river navigation was prohibitive, and much of the Wye valley had to wait for the coming of the railway to improve its economic prospects. But industry never came to the Wye valley in any significant way in the 19th and 20th centuries, and what industry there was had little to do with the river; the Wye was not a determining factor even for those industries that were established close to it, like the Rotherwas Munitions Factory near Hereford. The industrial revolution shifted the focus of industry to the major coalfields, and for that reason the Wye has become a river of countryside and not of industrial towns.

✎ 8 ✎
The Working River

It is natural that rivers should be a conduit of trade, and for much of its course the Wye, and its main tributary the Lugg, was once navigable for commercial traffic. The Wye had the added advantage that it joins the Severn at its mouth and so had access to the Severn ports and the open sea. As a general rule, the volume of traffic decreased in an upstream direction. The lower river benefited not only from proximity to the sea, but also from carrying the produce of the Forest of Dean and the monastic estates of Tintern, the most economically advanced regions of the Wye in the Middle Ages. In the 17th century John Taylor remarked that no town on a navigable river was poor, and that there were no prosperous towns and cities that did not stand by a river or the sea. That statement was more or less true of the River Wye.

Next to the Anchor Inn at Tintern is the medieval Watergate, the main entrance to the abbey precinct from the river.

There may have been a wharf at Kenchester in Roman times, and one at Monmouth where there was ironmaking by the Wye and the Monnow, but regional trade on the river really began in medieval times. The most flourishing area in the Middle Ages and after was the tidal river; Chepstow was the chief port, but trade with coastal vessels extended further upstream to wharves at Brockweir and as far as Monmouth.

The mouth of the Severn was a busy commercial waterway, with major ports at Bristol on the Avon, Gloucester on the Severn and Chepstow on the Wye. Chepstow could anchor large ocean-going ships to serve the sheep, wool, cattle and leather trades of Wales, which were staples of medieval industry. Chepstow traded with the Severn and South Wales ports, but also further afield by the end of the Middle Ages, principally with the Breton and Gascon ports of France and Iberia. As early as 1314 the *Shorham*, under the command of John Hart of Chepstow, was wrecked off Cornwall.

Johannes Kip's bird's eye view of Chepstow Bridge, published in 1712, also shows the barges and other vessels moored at what was then a busy sea and river port.

A decade later the port had four ships over 40 tons burden for ocean-going voyages. Most of the imports were of wine. In 1372, for example, the *Katherine* arrived in Chepstow with 111 tuns of wine from Bordeaux, and the *Salvador* arrived from the same port with 50 tuns. The ships got bigger with time. By the 1440s the *George* was bringing 125 tuns, the *Trinity* 128 tuns, the *Elenour* 135 tuns and the *Christopher* 93 tuns. On their outward journeys these ships carried wheat, beans and malt. For example, in 1517 John Boet of Bordeaux shipped wine from Bordeaux, and returned with a cargo of 38 weys of wheat and 35 weys of beans (a wey or weight was about 40 bushels or 320 gallons in volume).[1]

Chepstow was a transhipment point where ocean-going ships could transfer their cargoes to coastal vessels or river trows and barges. Before railways, coastal vessels were the most effective means of transportation, like having a river around the whole country, and there was a regular trade between the ports of South Wales and north Somerset and Devon.

Chepstow became one of the biggest towns in Wales. By the early 14th century it already had a population of about 1,500 and, despite the Black Death the population continued to rise to about 2,000 by the end of the century, roughly the same population that lived there in 1800. In the intervening centuries it experienced phases of growth and decline, much of it down to reliance on the Gascon wine trade. Chepstow might have been a small town by English standards, but it had an international character. It was common to hear French and Spanish spoken in the taverns and on the streets. On the quayside were salt houses, a 'longe cellar' by 1555 and a wine yard by 1573, to complement the usual range of buildings – there were 20 taverns by the

Chepstow at high tide, with the masts of trows, barges and fishing boats, as depicted in the late 18th century by Samuel Ireland.

Red Rocks below Chepstow was one of the lowest landing places on the river.

1530s and in 1637 it was claimed that there were 16 major taverns offering superior accommodation.

Chepstow was small compared with Bristol – in 1535-36 its imports of wine were a mere 6 per cent of the trade to Bristol – but it had distinct advantages as a sea port. The Crown had no jurisdiction over the Marches of Wales and therefore could not set the customs rates for the port. Chepstow made the most of this: in many cases customs payable in Chepstow were a fraction of those payable at ports under the English Crown. In 1535-36 the duty paid at Chepstow on wine was threepence per tun, wheat threepence per wey, tanned leather threepence per dicker (i.e. 10 hides), and fruit threepence per ton. The equivalent figures for Bristol in the period 1533-42 were 3 shillings per tun on wine, 1 shilling per wey of wheat, on tanned leather 3 shillings and 4 pence per dicker plus a further 8 pence custom, and 2 shillings per ton for fruit.

It was therefore profitable for merchants to land cargo in Chepstow for transhipment to English ports. Needless to say the Crown did not like it and tried to put pressure on the Marcher Lords of Striguil to fall into line with English practices. In 1392 the Crown complained that 'a great number of merchants who ought to come to the port of Bristol, there unlade wine, and pay such prises and customs, draw to the port of Chepstow in Wales, where they pay but 3d upon every tun, there and elsewhere along the sea coast unlade it in smaller ships and bring it after for sale in Bristol and elsewhere'.[2] This remained a widespread practice into the 16th century. In 1526 John Gurbey and John Coke, Bristol merchants, made a contract to buy 40 tuns of wine from Bordeaux, which was delivered by trows from Chepstow. The transhipments at Chepstow of wine bound for Bristol reached its peak in 1492-93, when over 29,000 gallons of wine were transferred to trows and lighters. A consequence of transhipment was smuggling, since it was all too easy for transhipped cargoes to be unloaded on the pills of the lower Severn and the creeks of south-west England.

Chepstow's low tariffs also made it attractive to the wool trade. As early as 1345 the government of Bruges in Flanders submitted a request to Edward III to release a ship detained at Chepstow. Rather than taking their wool to the Severn ports, merchants had been taking a longer route to Chepstow to reduce the customs rates payable. Bruges was at that time a major destination of wool exported from England and Wales. By way of a charter granted to Chepstow in 1524 the port clung to its privileges until the 1560s, some time after the Union of England and Wales in 1536, when the Marcher lordship was replaced by the county of Monmouth.

Bristol vessels traded on the Wye as far up as Monmouth from an early date. When in 1315 the earl of Gloucester built a weir in Trellech lordship (south of Monmouth) people in Gloucestershire and Herefordshire complained that it blocked the river, and that ships had from time out of mind navigated the river with all manner of merchandise. Monmouth was often the termination of transport by river. The obstructions further upstream made it easier to unload there and make the rest of the journey by road.

Brockweir is situated midway between Chepstow and Monmouth but, more importantly, the river is tidal here, allowing sea-going vessels to dock. It was an important transhipment point where goods brought down in barges from Herefordshire were

The quay at Brockweir.

A medieval building in Brockweir, traditionally said to have been constructed by the monks of Tintern, and the oldest surviving building associated with the river trade at Brockweir.

transferred to larger trows of 60-80 tons for carriage to Bristol. It also conveyed timber and iron from the Forest of Dean. The 'prettily situated and populous little hamlet' was easier to reach by water than by road, until the bridge opened in 1906. By the end of the Middle Ages there was a grange belonging to Tintern Abbey at Brockweir and it was probably under the initiative of the abbey that a port developed there. Brockweir is a tight cluster of buildings close to the wharf, a village whose economy was dominated by the river as late as the 19th century. There are two buildings in Brockweir that retain fabric from the monastic era, chief of which is the building later used as a malthouse and a pottery, but which was built in the Tudor period and stands close to the river.

Hereford is mentioned as a port in the *Anglo-Saxon Chronicles* and the *Domesday Book*. Trade on the river helped in the economic growth of places like Hereford and Ross, but the river navigation was not without its problems. The Wye is a shallow river, which in effect made it unusable for long periods while the barge crews waited for a sudden rise in the river level, known as a fresh or a freshet, to ensure a sufficient volume of water to keep the barges afloat as they navigated downstream. Traffic on the Wye could, in extreme conditions, be suspended for several months for lack of water.

For a river to flourish it also needs to be free of obstacles, and this was not the case on the Wye. Above Monmouth there were various weirs that impeded traffic, for example at Hereford, and further upriver at Stretton Sugwas and Monnington. At Monnington a windlass was used to haul vessels over the weir. Despite these difficulties, there was commercial traffic as far upstream as Hay on Wye until the 1860s. Not all of it went to or from the sea ports, however. Some cargoes, like timber and building stone, were often traded quite locally.

Some of the problems of the navigation were encountered by John Taylor (1578-1653) who is best known as the 'Thames water poet', but who was a native of Gloucester and a strong advocate of river transport. In 1641 he made a journey on the five chief commercial rivers in Britain – the Severn, Thames, Wye and the two Avons – in order to investigate the state of the nation's waterways. He left Bristol on 19 August and reached Hereford exactly a week later, by which time he seems to have had enough of the Wye and considered selling his boat and returning by land. However, he took to the water again, and the downstream journey was at least quicker. Travel on the Wye was generally very slow, partly because the river meandered in such an unhelpful way between Monmouth and Ross. Taylor complained of leaving Monmouth in the morning, when he was 12 miles from Hereford, and arriving in Lydbrook by evening, still 12 miles from his destination. On the return journey he stopped again at Lydbrook, where his host Mr Mosse 'understanding and knowing the passage down Wye and up Severne to be very long and dangerous (especially if stormye weather should arise, the boate being split, torne and shaken that she did leake very much) these things considered, and that I was within five miles of Severne by land to Newnham, and that by water thither there was no lesse than 50 miles, I hired a wayne from Lidbrook to Newnham.'[3] The land route between Wye and Severn was much quicker than the river route and Taylor was not the only person to take it, bypassing the tidal river altogether.

There were many initiatives to improve the reliability of the Wye navigation, chiefly by means of Wye and Lugg Navigation Acts, the first of which was passed by Parliament in 1662. The 1662 Act made provision for a towpath for bow haulers and the building of locks at the New Weir near Symonds Yat, although the New Weir lock was not particularly successful and was apparently decayed by 1696, after which a new lock was built. A second Act of 1695 ushered in more substantive changes, including removal of weirs from mills such as Carey Mills, the Dean & Chapter's mills at Hereford, and the mill at Stretton Sugwas. Some of the numerous shallows were dredged and trees were cut from the river bank.

In the wake of the 1695 Act there was evidently an upturn in trade at Hereford, where a new wharf was built on the site of the old castle barbican in 1725, but as soon as canals came to be built from the middle of the 18th century the Wye looked distinctly unfit for purpose. The problem was exacerbated by the poor state of the roads serving the river, although it was partly alleviated in the 18th and early 19th century by the construction of turnpike roads. Robert Whitlock, formerly assistant to the canal engineer James Brindley, carried out a survey of the Wye in 1779 from Hereford to Tintern. His solution was predictable enough – that sections of the Wye should be canalised – which was fine in theory but not matched by any enthusiasm from potential investors. The other more contentious issue put forward to improve the navigation was to provide a horse towing path. The task of hauling vessels upriver against the current had long

James Wathen's view of the quay on the north bank at Hereford in 1794.

been performed by bow haulers, men who were proud of their independence and naturally resisted a measure that would put them out of work. However, the towpath came into being and the section from Hereford to Lydbrook was opened in 1811. Because the towpath switched sides from time to time (known as roving) it was necessary to provide new horse ferries at Putson, Bullingham Road, Hoarwithy and How Caple.

The most notorious obstacle on the river was the New Weir near Symonds Yat, despite the provision of a lock. The only way to manoeuvre the barge in and out of the lock was to pull it through the current. In 1763 Isaac Taylor, a Herefordshire surveyor, noted that every barge owner kept a large cable rope on board, and a crew would need additional help for both haulage and managing the capstan when negotiating the lock. Wye tourists like to watch barges and their own boats passing through it. When the lock chamber had filled, 'young and old, boys and girls, fly to the rope and, with the zeal of the most hearty, soon deliver the vessel from her otherwise stationary situation, to the current of the river'.[4] Not until 1826 was the New Weir demolished, and by that time the railways were only a few decades away.

The cargo carried on the Wye tended in general to comprise raw materials and semi-finished wares downstream, and stone, coal and luxury goods upstream. The same is true generally of the port of Chepstow. The value of the imported goods was higher than the value of exported goods. In one respect at least the Wye was an indispensable means of transportation – when it came to carrying bulky, low-value cargoes like stone, wood and coal. Timber was transported downstream on the river on barges, but from medieval times it was also transported by tying tree trunks together to form a raft, or 'float', on which the crew travelled, doing their best to steer the raft out of trouble. Floats on the

Hereford in the 1790s, by Samuel Ireland, with a barge, fishing boat and pleasure boat.

Wye and on other rivers had an unimpressive health-and-safety record, although their passage down the Wye was made easier by the comparative lack of bridges on the river below Hereford until the 19th century. As late as December 1806 it was reported that five men were conveying a float down river, at a time when the level was very high, when it struck Wilton Bridge and threw three of the men overboard, all of whom drowned. Robert Crompton, from a well-known family of watermen in Hereford, died while assembling a float at Hereford in 1846.[5]

An important by-product of the timber trade was bark, one of the bulk products shipped down the Wye, destined for use in the tanning industry, and shipped as far afield as Ireland. The bark was stripped from the trees in spring and taken to several bark houses along the river between Tintern and Fownhope. Large ricks of bark were a common sight on the river bank, as William Coxe noted at Monmouth in 1801. Here, bark shipped from the upper Wye was dumped on to the banks where it was cleaned and chopped, ready for further shipment: 'I observed on the side of the river numerous piles of this commodity, as large as hay-ricks, from fifty to one hundred tons; and noticed with pleasure the expedition and facility with which the operations of cleaning and piling are performed.'[6] By the end of the 18th century about 6,000 tons of bark were exported annually from Chepstow.

Coal became a near-universal domestic fuel after the railway boom of the mid 19th century, but some towns, where coal could be shipped by river, were early adopters. Hereford was one of them, and shares that distinction with the main Severnside towns. Improvements to the navigation in the 18th century enabled barges to deliver coal from collieries in the Forest of Dean. Lydbrook wharf was already a thriving industrial port

A grain warehouse built in 1883 on Gwynne Street, near the river in Hereford and a throwback to the day when the river was the focus of trade.

when Thomas Whateley visited it in 1770, and sent its barges to wharves at Hereford and then elsewhere on the Wye and Lugg. However, the difficulty of transporting bulky items is illustrated by a number of accidents involving coal shipments. For example, coal barges sank near the same spot near Fownhope on two occasions, in 1817 and 1819, and on the second occasion a family who had gone out to visit the spot lost their boat on the return journey, all of them except the father drowning.

The Wye being a rural river, large amounts of cereal grains, grass seed, potatoes and peas were shipped on barges, but the best known export was cider. Although it was mainly produced for local consumption, it had become fashionable in major cities such as London and Bristol and became a significant export commodity carried on the river from the beginning of the 18th century, with several riverside warehouses where the large hogsheads were stacked ready. (Cider, like timber stacked on the river banks, was particularly vulnerable in times of floods, when it was often seen floating downstream, invariably having been contaminated by the dirty water.)

Cargoes imported upriver were generally of a higher value than those taken downstream. So as cider went down river, wines and spirits came up river, imported mainly via Chepstow, from which Wyeside towns enjoyed wines from Portugal and Spain, claret and brandy from France, and rum from the West Indies. Sugar came from the same source and other luxury items like soap were also carried. A visitor in the early 19th century watched the ships moored at Chepstow unloading wine from Portugal, as well as timber, hemp, flax, pitch and tar from as far afield as Norway and Russia.[7]

All kinds of vessels are shown in this engraving of Llandogo, a ferry to the left, a larger barge, and a pleasure boat on the right. Nearly all of the vessels that worked the river were built on the river.

Coracle man William Dew demonstrating how the coracle
was carried like a shell on the fisherman's back.
(By kind permission of Herefordshire Libraries)

Occasionally there were people on board, notably in 1740 when Thomas Prosser carried a group of men and women convicts from Hereford gaol to Bristol, from where they were transported to America.[8]

Boat-building was carried out in several places on the Wye, and on the tidal section at Chepstow and Brockweir for river and sea-going vessels. It was said to have been the most important industry at Brockweir by the 1830s, and records show that commercial vessels were built on the river as far upstream as Hay. Wye barges had flat hulls, by which means they were adapted to suit the conditions of the river. But the river craft most notably adapted to local conditions were the coracles used by fishermen.

Coracles, also known on the Wye as truckles, were found in all parts of the river where men were out fishing. Wye tourists mentioned them frequently, enjoying their apparent primitiveness. They saw coracles as the most basic form of river craft, giving the onlooker a glimpse back to the dawn of river navigation. Robert Bloomfield compared them to the bark canoes of savage chiefs and expected to see on board a primitive native of the New World instead of a modern Wyeside fisherman. As Bloomfield journeyed downriver in a pleasure boat with his friends he noticed that anglers 'skulk'd in the alder shade' from where they cast their rods for salmon. The coracle was light and portable too:

> And o'er his back, in gallant trim,
> Swung the light shell that carried him;
> Then down again his burden threw,
> And launch'd his whirling bowl anew;
> Displaying in his bow'ry station,
> The infancy of navigation.[9]

The last coracle made on the Wye was built in 1910 by William Dew and is in Hereford Museum. One of the reasons that coracles were once common on the river is that they were simple enough to be constructed by fishermen themselves. Essentially a coracle is a small tub boat without a keel, propelled by a single paddle held in two hands. They were constructed of the best available materials, usually willow and ash laths, covered originally with animal hides, and latterly by calico stretched over the frame and made waterproof by coating it with a mixture of pitch and coal tar. The coracles that Samuel Ireland saw in the 1790s were 'ribbed with laths or split twigs, and ... covered with a strong, pitched canvas, to prevent its leaking,' and were 'about five feet and a half long and four broad'.[10] It is well known that different rivers saw slight variations in the shape and dimensions of coracles, but there were also local variations that are now difficult to elucidate since at one time there were many makers of them. The coracle was usually fitted with a leather strap and was light enough for a man (traditionally it was only men who paddled out in them) to carry it on his back, and then hang it up on the door of his cottage.

Coracles were used by salmon fishers and looked 'in the distance like walnut-shells set floating by fairies'.[11] The coracle was best suited to smooth water. Mark Willett watched salmon fishermen at Lydbrook, where he saw that 'on a smooth part of the river you may see him gliding gently down with the current; on approaching a cataract or a weir, he paddles to the shore, and like a tortoise, with his shell upon his back, passes the interrupted navigation, and anon he is seen again on the water below'.[12] In times of flood coracles could become a lifeline, as small and agile craft were needed to rescue flood victims or deliver essential supplies. The most ambitious, and easily the craziest, coracle adventure was undertaken by Luke Hughes in the 18th century. Hughes was from a barge-owning family in Wilton and ventured out into the Bristol Channel in his coracle. There are two versions of his story. William Gilpin heard that he had navigated (or drifted) as far as Lundy Island in the Bristol Channel, but according to a later version by Charles Heath he navigated as far as the Bristol Channel, where a 'ship of war' found his craft drifting, took him on board and cheered him up with some refreshments, then put him back on the water and guided him into the Avon on the flood tide, where he paddled as far as Bristol.

Most of the commercial vessels that worked the Wye navigation were built on the Wye, and most of what we know about boat and ship building on the river comes from the latter half of the 18th century and the first half of the 19th, the final century of the river's commercial usefulness. Most of the commercial vessels used on the river were classed as barges, which were smaller than the trows that operated on the lower river and in the Bristol Channel. Because the river was so shallow, barges and trows were flat-bottomed vessels and had no rudder. Trows could have a temporary rudder fitted for coastal sailing, although they were notoriously unstable in sea-going conditions. Barges

White-sailed trows navigate the river near its confluence with the Severn.
On the right is a shipyard below Chepstow town.

In Peter de Wint's view of Chepstow bridge and castle of the early 19th century,
a trow prepares to lower its mast to pass under the bridge.

A barge, with its sail unfurled, makes its way toward Ross.

A barge makes its way downstream in T.H. Fielding's view of Chepstow.

Parker's Steamer in 1894, moored at Belmont, where the passengers enjoyed a picnic.
Steam boats were built on the Wye from the 1830s.
(By kind permission of Herefordshire Libraries)

and trows had masts which could be lowered to pass under bridges, but the opportunities to unfurl their sails were limited. Although the natural instinct of artists was to portray the barges in full sail, the impression they give is probably misleading.

In 1791, Edward Phillips of Monmouth had two trows of 60 and 80 tons burden respectively, and barges of 28, 24 and 20 tons. Added to this was a smaller vessel known as a boat, of only 3 tons. He therefore had a 'set' of vessels which could be used, depending upon the volume of water in the river. His trows were docked at Brockweir and his barges at Monmouth. The *Valiant*, built at Hereford in 1790, was a typical 28-ton barge, 50 feet long and 30 feet wide, and with a draught when fully laden of 2 feet and 9 inches.[13] The notional capacity of a barge was not always reached, however, largely because they carried lighter loads when the river level was lower. According to John Duncumb, at the beginning of the 19th century barges of anything between 18 and 30 tons burden traded with Hereford.[14] When William Jessop made his survey of the river in 1805 he suggested that it was feasible to maintain a constant depth of 20 inches in summer, a depth that would allow barges to carry cargo of about 13-16 tons, even though they were built to carry 20-30 tons.

Hay-on-Wye had active boatyards constructing barges including the *Penelope*, built by Thomas Thomas in 1807, and the *Liberty*, built by James Prout in 1824. The barge *Sally* was built at Rhydspence in 1780 and was 56 feet 8 inches long, by 12 feet 6 inches wide. There were several Herefordshire boat builders, including Richard Lewis, Thomas Maund, George Crompton, Joseph Thomas and Thomas Mann. Joseph Thomas built the *Martha* at Holme Lacy in 1824 and the *Mary and Elizabeth* at Bullingham in 1828. Hereford boatyards also had the capacity to build larger vessels, including brigs (two masts) and sloops (one mast, known locally as snows). The *Pomona* was a brig of 108 tons launched in 1823, when it was taken down river to be rigged.[15]

Vessels built on the tidal stretch of the river were mainly concerned with coastal shipping. At Brockweir John Easton of Hereford began to build sea-going vessels in about 1826, mainly brigs and schooners. A decade later his yard closed but another was opened by the Swift family, formerly timber-merchants, and during the next decade they built brigs, schooners, barques and sloops, as well as trows for the river trade. Thereafter only smaller boats seem to have been built there until the end of the 19th century.[16]

Chepstow was a deep harbour by virtue of the high tides. In 1697 it was claimed that ships of 250 tons could anchor anywhere below the bridge, but by the early 19th century ships of 700 tons could dock there. Shipbuilding in the town's yards, below the docks, reflected this ocean-going and coastal trade. In the early 19th century Chepstow shipyards were building 600-ton ships, as well as rigging the barges and sloops built further upstream.

Steam boats arrived on the river in 1827 with the *Paul Pry*, owned and operated by the Wye Steam Boat Company, which was founded by local shipbuilder William Radford. The idea was to tow barges on both the Wye and Severn, but in the long term steam vessels found more employment on the Wye on pleasure cruises. Steam vessels were built in the 19th century in Hereford and Chepstow, but not necessarily to work local waters. The *Water Witch*, launched at Hereford in 1834, was sent down

The launching of the 6,500 ton *War Glory* at Chepstow in 1920. (Monmouth Museum)

to Chepstow to be fitted out and then sold in Liverpool. Mr Wegg-Prosser of Belmont took delivery in 1857 of a 42 feet 6 inch long steam boat for use on leisure excursions. Another steam pleasure boat, the *Geraldine*, was slightly longer and began work in 1866; she had been built in Norwich.[17]

Chepstow was also a place for steamship building, and finally of diesel-powered ships. The last phase of shipbuilding began in the First World War, when in 1917 the government created the National Shipyard Number 1 at Chepstow. Although the scheme was a limited success – only a single ship, the *War Forest*, had been launched by the end of the war – it gave fresh impetus to shipbuilding in the town. The Monmouthshire Shipbuilding Company launched eight ships in 1920 (one of them, *War Glory*, was wrecked off Argentina in 1924) but by 1924 the site had been sold to the Fairfield Shipbuilding and Engineering Company of Glasgow. Despite its name, the Chepstow works was mainly engaged in producing components of bridges and other structural engineering projects.

The men who worked on the river tended to do so as part of family dynasties. The Hughes family, including Luke Hughes of coracle fame, were boatmen at Wilton in the 18th and 19th centuries, and one of them, James Ross, was the landlord of the Bear Inn at Wilton. Other boatman families included the Wheatstone family of Fownhope and the Crompton or Crumpton family, members of whom were active in the river trade and as landlords of riverside inns in Hereford, Goodrich, and the Ironbridge Gorge in Shropshire.[18]

A busy scene at New Weir by James Wathen, with fishermen,
a pleasure boat and, on the right, a barge being hauled upstream.

Brockweir men included James Gethin, who left two boats to his sons in 1571. One of them was probably the John Gethin who was killed in an affray with Bristol boatmen in the Bristol Channel in 1587.[19] As late as 1851 there were two mariners and 16 watermen in the parish, and a further eight watermen in the adjoining parts of St Briavels. By this time the Brockweir river trade was dominated by the Dibden and Bowens family, the former owning the small Wye ferry until it was superseded by the bridge.

Barge crews and bow haulers were often hired on a casual basis, and pursued other occupations when there was no work on the river. They treasured their freedom, but their habits did not always endear them to the rest of society, largely, it seems, because they were gangs of young men working away from home. Barges were cut loose from their moorings at Monnington in 1772 and again in 1776, probably on behalf of land-owners who complained about bow haulers or barge crews trespassing on their land. In the same period, landlords in Hoarwithy in 1779 and Wilton in 1811 threatened tres-passing river men with legal action.[20] Watermen were usually not only adept fishermen, but also active poachers of rabbits and anything else that came their way.

Bow haulers had a reputation for hard drinking, but given that their job was the thirstiest kind of work imaginable, that is not surprising. The current was strong and 'it is with extraordinary labour and difficulty the barges are towed up. I have seen eight or ten men throwing themselves on the earth on every pull, to give force to their exer-tions.'[21] According to Archdeacon Coxe, it took 10-11 men two days to haul a coal barge from Lydbrook to Hereford. There were plenty of riverside inns where river men could obtain refreshments, although most crews on more than a single day's journey slept on board rather than on dry land.

The Wye at New Weir, where a team of horses on the left bank is pulling a barge upstream.

Bow haulers resisted the introduction of draught animals, but in the long term the Wye navigation would decline, partly because of the introduction of more efficient means of transport, but also because the river did not serve large-scale industries. In 1801 it was proposed to bypass the river by building a tramway between Hereford and Lydbrook. The coal trade thrived on the river for only two more decades until further competition came, first from horse-drawn tramways that could transport coal to Hay-on-Wye by 1822. From 1829 Hereford was linked by tramway to the Brecon and Abergavenny Canal, opening up a market for coal from the South Wales valleys. The Gloucester and Hereford Canal opened in 1845 and in 1854 came the first railway, the Newport, Abergavenny and Hereford Railway. The river navigation dwindled quickly in the wake of these developments, and the River Wye Horse Towing Path Company ceased meeting in 1855. Further downstream, the railway reached Monmouth in 1857 and when the Wye Valley Railway opened in 1876 between Chepstow and Monmouth the river was effectively superseded and barge traffic was killed off.

By the end of the 19th century the crew on a commercial river craft were most likely to be fishermen or to be hosting a party of sightseers. Chepstow declined as a port because merchant ships were getting bigger and there was competition in the Bristol Channel from Avonmouth Docks, which opened in 1877 and was expanded by the addition of the Royal Edward Dock in 1908. In 1951 Olive Phillips found that Chepstow 'still smacks of its shipping days around The Back with its tall ramshackle warehouses,

A sketch of Chepstow in the late 19th century by G. Beetlestone, showing a barge and wharf, but a scene far less busy than it was a century earlier.
(Ironbridge Gorge Museum Trust)

The Wye has become a river of small boats (this one just below Ross-on-Wye) since the decline of commercial traffic, which embody a much slower pace of life than the modes of transport that replaced the old river-going vessels.

old cottages and the derelict Boat Tavern.' She enjoyed its special atmosphere, which had a 'mixture of history, agricultural implements, hay and corn merchants, dozens of little pubs, and a few bigger hotels', but all that has since faded and the heritage of the river trade, be it in Chepstow, Brockweir, Wilton or Hereford, is now one of the most low-key aspects of the river's past.[22]

❧ 9 ❧
Fish

Writing at the time of the Great War, J. Arthur Hutton observed that 'we have a most valuable [resource] – and I am sorry to say a grossly neglected one – in our salmon fisheries'.[1] The same could be said of all British rivers and all British freshwater fish. If there is one natural resource that has been squandered without any qualms or regret it has been the abundant gift of fish offered to us by our rivers.

The consumption of fish was once a part of everyday life and a plentiful supply of them was once deemed a defining characteristic of the Wye. Hereford had its 'fish boordes' in the market place where river fish were sold, including the eels that were sold in 'sticks' of 25.[2] The eels were greatly valued and of course so were the salmon, so much tastier from the Wye than from other rivers. Few 19th-century local historians failed to mention that it was a common clause in the indentures of children apprenticed in Hereford that they should not be fed salmon more than twice a week (though more recent historians are less sure that this was so). It suggests a time when the salmon were boundless, which is part of the idyllic myth of the river, one of the things that makes the Wye special. The myth of its fish persisted well into the 20th century. For the novelist Harry Fletcher (1902-74), standing on the bridge at Rhayader during the war and watching the leaping salmon was a sight never to be forgotten: 'It was the first time I had ever seen such a thing. There was a fair bit of water coming down and it was flowing strongly. The pool below seemed to be full of fish, enormous ones, 20 pounders many of them, and the leaps they made to get over that weir were gymnastic contortions such as I had never seen in my life.'[3]

Plenty of edible species swam in the river and its tributaries. Giraldus Cambrensis, writing at the end of the 12th century, mentioned the salmon and trout, the most prized, but also umber, now better known as grayling. All kinds of other river fish have been fished from the river and eaten – including pike, gudgeon, perch, eels and elvers, shad, lampreys and lamperns. Pike has a reputation as being the most fearsome and ferocious of freshwater fish. One such pike, caught in a net near Cabalva House, by Rhydspence, in 1871, 'came floundering and lashing over the side into the boat with fierce struggles, and the noise as they were knocking it on the head was as if they were driving a pile or felling a tree'. The pike was laid on the ground, apparently dead, but when one of the fishermen put his boot into its mouth 'the pike revived enough to grip the boot viciously'.[4]

The river has many fish that swim in both salt water and freshwater, but none of them has a life cycle quite so remarkable as that of the eel. Eels mature in the fresh waters of Europe and then migrate across the Atlantic to spawn in the Sargasso Sea at depths of up to 500 fathoms. The larvae then float back across the Atlantic and, as transparent elvers, congregate in large shoals in the Bristol Channel from where they are washed by the tide into the rivers, where they make their homes in the muddy banks. Elvers were caught en masse, and needed to be if they were to provide any sort of meal, and were traditionally netted in places like Llandogo on spring evenings. 'I was told a man once caught nine hundredweight in a single night, though I was not told what he did with them.'[5]

Eels were an important part of the medieval diet, but interest in them declined because commercial fishermen preferred to go after the more valuable salmon. In the 19th century in the lower Wye elvers were scooped out of the river, washed and boiled, then pressed in a colander into greenish-white cheeses, slices of which were fried. They had to be caught before May, when the grey elvers begin to turn black, and bone starts to form in the fish, rendering them inedible until they are full grown.

Of other sea fish caught in the river, shad were particularly welcome, as a shoal of shad generally preceded a shoal of salmon. Lampreys and their smaller cousins, lamperns, are

An eel fisherman at Redbrook draws in his net.
Another fisherman is on the water in his coracle.

altogether different species. Both are suckers, sea fish that attach themselves to other, larger fish like cod, haddock or salmon, by means of their sharp and angled teeth, and literally suck their insides out. But they have to return to the rivers to spawn. Lampreys were still caught by spears in the early 19th century, mainly because their habits were predictable and their preferred hiding places in rapidly flowing waters were well known. But the fish has long fallen out of favour. One look at a lamprey on a fishmonger's slab makes it easy to see why – it is a fish without scales or gills (it has breathing holes instead), and a very ugly face.

The most prized of Wye fish has always been the salmon. A large and mysterious fish – it is one of the fish that swim in freshwater and sea water – salmon inhabit the rivers and then vanish into the ocean. In fact salmon are essentially seawater fish that seek out freshwater for spawning. The ova will not hatch in salty water. Upstream of Rhayader the Wye looks like a proper salmon river, one of boulders, rocks and rapids. So too do its tributary rivers like the Ithon, where the rapids between the pools are perfect for the hen fish to lay their eggs. Fishermen have always been close observers of salmon and know them well in all the stages of their lives.

Once the egg has hatched the young fry, or 'salmon pinks', grow into their juvenile form as parr. On the Wye the young fish were known in their first year of life as 'last-springs', a common name derived from the time of their appearance in the river as opposed to the mountain springs in which they first swam. The parr are distinguished by their striped camouflage, which they gradually lose as they grow into silvery smolt, which is a transitional phase where their bodies undergo the chemical changes (smelting) that enable them to live in salt water. In their juvenile phases salmon are prey to other fish in the river, like pike, perch, chub and trout, not to mention herons and other birds. Most young salmon stay in the river for a year and leave with the spring floods, although some last-springs swim in shoals in the river throughout the summer and for up to two years before they swim out to sea.

Salmon feed more voraciously in the sea, grow rapidly, and when they have matured sexually they return instinctively to their own river to spawn. This can take from one to four years, and the size of salmon when caught depends upon how long they have swum and fed in the sea – in other words it is sea age rather than calendar years that determines the size of the fish. The smallest of them are commonly known as grilse, but on the Wye more commonly as botchers, and have spent up to 18 months in the sea. Such fish have not always been easy to identify. Colonel Pearson, visiting Llysdinam in 1875, caught and after a quarter-hour struggle landed an 8-pound fish near Builth Wells, but only a conference with other fisherman resolved that it had a 'travelling mark' under his throat and was therefore considered to have migrated from the sea.[6] By the early 20th century anglers generally took small spring fish, salmon that had spent two years at sea and weighed on average between 10 and 12 pounds. Net fish-ermen relied on the small summer fish, that usually came into the river between May and September, and weighed on average just over 12 pounds. The larger fish – Wye salmon can weigh up to 40 pounds – are much rarer, and too unusual to be the staple of commercial fisheries.

Salmon are the best known of British river fish because they are the biggest and tastiest that native waters can offer, and no salmon was more delicious than Wye salmon. People have said so since at least the time of Giraldus Cambrensis, and no one can match the Chepstow parson, the Reverend Edward Davies, for his enthusiasm:

> Unlike the flabby fish in London sold,
> A Chepstow salmon's worth his weight in gold,
> Crimps up delightful to the taste and sight,
> In flakes alternate of fine red and white.
> Few other rivers such fine salmon feed,
> Not Taff, nor Tay, nor Tyne, nor Trent, nor Tweed.

And salmon is easy to cook. Edward Davies again:

> Adown the back the cook the fish divides,
> Take out the chine, in pieces cut the sides;
> Plung'd in the coldest water let it lie
> Till the pot boils, and foaming, bubbles high:
> Then piece by piece he souses in the fish.
> Which, boiled ten minutes, makes for kings a dish.
> A salmon whole, well dressed, I never saw;
> O'er boiled without, but in the middle raw;
> But thus divided you no hazard run,
> For every part alike is nicely done.[7]

People have always caught fish from the river, using spears or various forms of nets or traps. Some of the earliest written references to the Wye concern fishing, because in the Middle Ages fish was an important part of the diet, and an important part of the river economy. In 1308 Edward II requisitioned 3,000 dried salmon to feed his troops on campaign in Scotland, as if to say to the Scots that the English king commands just as good salmon rivers as they do.

The most common form of medieval fishing was by the construction of fish weirs, which were side channels in the river fixed with basket traps for catching mainly salmon and eels. The origin of these is obscure. Some of the documented medieval examples may be of Roman origin, like those at Kenchester and Huntsham, as well as Carey and Hadnock. The Domesday survey of 1086 records fisheries at Hadnock and Goodrich – the latter was known as Old Weare and was made by digging a leat through a riverside field to create a narrow channel and an island in the river. In 956 King Eadwig granted the manor of Tidenham to the Abbot of Bath, which included fisheries on the Severn, and on the Wye upstream as far as Lancaut. The salmon were caught in baskets known as putchers (*cytweras*) or kiddles, which were set up in ranks at fish weirs. Hackle weirs (*haecweras*) were wattle hedges placed in the river by the banks, which created an eddy in which the fish could be netted. The *Domesday Book* of 1086 records 53 fisheries in Tidenham on the two rivers.[8]

Weirs are also mentioned in the 12th-century *Book of Llandaff* as having been given to the church in perpetuity, but usually as part of a wider estate. For example a grant of over 300 acres of land at Gwent Iscoed included common pasture in fields and woods, as well as several weirs on the river. At Henllan, land given by Ithael included woodland, pasture and fish weirs.[9]

Between Ross and Monmouth there were weirs in the Middle Ages at New Weir, Bishopswere, Jetweir and Martinswere. The latter was probably named after John Martin of Goodrich Castle, who had a fishery in 1307. Tintern Abbey owned several weirs on the Wye (and a few on the Severn and Usk rivers too), in the 12th century at Plumweir, Staweir, Alfred's Weir, Walwere, Halfwere and Badingsweir. By the 14th century it had added more, at Britheksweir, Ishelsweir, Ashweir and Brocweir (Brockweir).[10]

There were fish weirs in the Welsh section of the river too, although they are less well documented. The place name Boughrood, which had acquired its name as early as 1205, may derive its name from *boch* and *rhwyd*, meaning something like jaw-shaped net, perhaps referring to traps at a weir.

Salmon were caught on their upstream journeys, although many Wye salmon were caught in the mouth of the Severn, before they had chance to swim into the Wye. Eels were caught on their downstream journeys. The traps were known as upmouths and are recorded by name as early as the 15th century. In 1454, for example, the Goodrich estate received rents on several upmouths, including '12s rent for one upmouth at Old Were' and '2s rental for 2 upmouths at Juttewere [Jetweir] formerly in the hands of Thomas Manocke and John Pye'.[11] Upmouths have also been recorded at Yakkestone or Yaxton, the old name for Rocklands near the old Hunstanton ferry (a Romano-British farmstead is in the adjacent field), at the confluence with the River Garron. Upmouths must once have been common. The fish were stored in fish houses by the river. In the early 19th century Mark Willett saw ruins of them at Coedithel weir near Llandogo, and just below Lancaut church, where the fish house was later converted to a dwelling called Marine Cottage.

Fish weirs slowly declined – Jet Weir below Symonds Yat was apparently disused by 1697 but remained as a fishery boundary. New methods of fishing gained prominence from the 17th century onwards. In 1696 the fishing rights at Dixton, by Monmouth, were let to two Monmouth fishermen, who were permitted to use 'boats cruckles hookes baites or engines' to take salmon and other fish. 'Engines' is the device that stands out in this list and probably refers to the use of wheels. Fish wheels were installed into existing fish weirs and were rotating wheels into which small nets were set. Fish that entered them would be thrown via a chute into baskets. In 1697 Monmouth weir had nine fish wheels, where bruised salmon, presumably damaged by the action of the wheels, were discarded, and there were others at New Weir.[12]

Fish weirs mainly declined at the expense of fishing with nets. Putchers were still used in the estuarine waters in the 20th century but they were found to be expensive to maintain and caught only a fraction of the fish that could be caught by nets. The Salmon Fisheries Amendment Act of 1865 allowed for a limited number of putchers to be licensed, but only in estuarine waters.

Nets take various forms, depending on the type of fish that is sought, and where in the course of the river fishing takes place. Lave nets are used in estuarine waters and have been in use since at least the 17th century when they are recorded on the Severn section of the Berkeley Estate. The lave net has a Y-shape frame, in which the arms of the Y are hung with a loose net and the end is the handle. They are used in the estuaries of South Wales rivers where the tide recedes by a distance and where there is low water. A lot of skill and patience is required to spot and trap the fish swimming in shallow water, since salmon are fast swimmers. The object of the fisherman is to intercept the fish by lowering the net as the fish approaches, then scooping it up so that the fish is caught in the fold of the net. If the fisherman stands near a bank he can ground the net and kill the salmon with a wooden knocker, sometimes known by the incongruous name of a 'priest'.

Another type of push net was the cleaching, clenching or clinch net. This was like a simple landing net, with a long pole, that was drawn through the bankside pools at feeding time. Because of its small mesh it brought up all kinds of fish, including salmon and trout. They were said to be common in the 19th century, but their last use was around Symonds Yat where they were (at least in May and June 1971) used to catch allis shad and twaite shad.[13]

Stop-net fishing was a technique used by commercial fishermen. Stop nets are loose nets attached to two poles, up to 25 feet long, that are lashed together to form a V-shape up to 30 feet wide, made stable by a cross brace known as a spreader. For this kind of fishing Wye fishermen used specially adapted stopping boats, which allowed them to lash the frame to the boat when necessary. The boat is moored in its fishing position, the whole net is lowered into the water, and bobbin strings attached to the net are held by the fishermen. These are sensitive to anything that strikes the net and indicate to the fisherman that a fish has struck it and the net should be raised. In reality there were many false alarms with this kind of fishing, since submerged logs and other flotsam could easily be trapped. Fisherman also carried forked sticks that they could use to push away any floating debris. When a salmon strikes the net the fisherman has to raise it quickly so that the net is lifted out of the water and the salmon can be killed with a knocker. Fishermen drew lots to determine which berths they could fish from, and they then changed so that all fishermen would have the opportunity to fish from the best positions. Depending on where the fishermen were stationed, the best times for fishing varied between neap and spring tides, ebb and flood tides. At the turn of the low tide the salmon run hard just below the surface, leaving a track that the fishermen could see, allowing them to warn each other of approaching fish.[14]

A report by the Inspectors of Salmon Fisheries in 1861 noted methods in use to make stop-net fishing more efficient: stone piers were erected in the river, creating an eddy that tended to drive the salmon toward the fishing stations where the stop nets were lowered. At Lydbrook boards were placed on an old fish weir, spanning most of the river, which had a similar effect of driving the fish to the stop nets, a throwback to the use of hackle weirs.[15]

Stop-net fishing was more common on the Wye than on other rivers that drain into the mouth of the Severn. In its tidal stretches the Wye is narrow, deep and muddy,

Fishermen draw in their net at dusk on the river in a painting by William Payne, c.1830. (Yale Center for British Art, Paul Mellon Collection)

John Varley's watercolour view of Chepstow in 1802 shows fishermen
unloading their boat on the bank under the bridge.

which makes other forms of net fishing difficult. It was also one of the more dangerous
methods of fishing, especially in the tidal waters, since any misjudgment of the tide
could upset the boat, which might throw the fisherman into his own net.

Stop nets were used on the Wye as far upstream as Lydbrook, but the most detailed
accounts that we have of them concern fishermen working out of Chepstow in the
estuarine waters. In 1861 there were 37 stopping boats licensed at Chepstow, of which
23 fished from below Chepstow bridge from a choice of 62 separate berths as far downstream as Black Rock in the Severn estuary, and the other 14 further into the mouth of
the Severn itself. It was also estimated that there were at least 15 nets between Chepstow
and Llandogo and a further 40 upstream as far as Monmouth.[16]

Other kinds of nets were used upstream of the tidal limit. Owen Thomas was fishing
at New Weir from the mid 17th century, using wheels, clinch nets and trammel nets.
A trammel net was set between two coracles or, if necessary, stretched from one bank
to the other. Weights would hold down the bottom while floats kept the top floating
on the surface, ensuring that fish could not pass. Francis Kilvert explained how the net
worked after having joined a group of men, including Thomas Baskerville, squire of
Clyro Court, on a trammel netting expedition in the Wye in 1871, a social occasion
with a picnic. The netting was dropped in a semi-circle in the river and then the water
was beaten with long poles in order to frighten the fish and drive them into the net.
The netting consisted of two meshes, or a double wall of netting. The fish first swam
into a fine mesh, which effectively wrapped them in a bag, and then through the larger
mesh, which they could not quite break through, leaving them hanging helpless in the
water. When the net was drawn in the fish was removed and banged on the head. In the
morning Kilvert's party caught a solitary salmon of 8½lbs, and in the afternoon a single
pike, so the river was not always a bowl of plenty, although the party was compensated

by a picnic of 'pie, rissoles, bread, cheese and butter, beer and sherry'.[17] Trammel nets were still used at Pencraig in 1889, although by this time nets were increasingly subject to regulation and stiffer licensing.

Net fishing on the Wye was regularly undertaken using coracles, which had long been part of the fishermen's kit. For example, a court Roll of Holme Lacy in 1536 ordered that no one should fish from cruckles, which are described as leather boats.[18] A traveller in 1805 noted their use around Monmouth, in a very simple technique. 'We saw two men going out in their coracles to fish. Each man lays hold of one end of a net, about 20 yards long, and paddles down the river until they feel a strike. Then they haul it up as quick as possible and draw it on shore. They paddle along at a great rate and put us much in mind of what we read concerning the Indians in their canoes'.[19] The Wye fishermen also used coracles for 'bushing', whereby a net was lowered into the water around the hiding place of a salmon, which was driven out by means of a pole and caught in the net. (This relatively quick and easy technique was favoured by poachers.) The method had its origins in the hackle weirs, and latterly the hiding places were known as cribs. They were found at natural rocks and were enhanced by the placing of further stones around them, a practice that had been illegal since the Wye Navigation Acts of the 17th century.

John Duncumb, writing in the first decade of the 19th century, offered an insight into the ways of the salmon fishermen on the Wye. Salmon were always caught on their upstream journey because once they had spawned the fish were exhausted and the flesh lost its colour. These fish were known variously as kelts, 'old fish' or spent fish, and fishermen knew that the more exhausted were the fish, the poorer the quality of fish meat. Fishermen also knew that a tidal swell would put new fish into the river, and that salmon took advantage of natural forces where they could in order to save energy. Salmon can be quite fussy about the quality of water in the river, and resist swimming up the river against a current of very cold water, so fishermen would suspend their activities at such a period. The trick of salmon fishing, then, was to know the best river conditions in which to catch the fish. And the best places too. Salmon and other sea fish did not seem to like the River Lugg, supposedly because its water was colder and harder than the Wye water.[20]

The river bank is property and so rights to fish on the Wye have always been restricted. Monastic fisheries were confiscated and sold off following the Dissolution of the monasteries between 1536 and 1539. Tintern's estates were acquired by the earl of Worcester, lord of Chepstow (later succeeded by the dukes of Beaufort), who then owned the whole river from Brockweir down. The sale of fishing rights was estimated to net the duke of Beaufort £300 per annum by the end of the 18th century, when salmon sold for about 3d per pound, serving a market extending from the locality to cover southern England. Wye salmon were sent to London, Bristol, Bath, Oxford and Gloucester. The duke of Beaufort leased fishing rights from above and below Chepstow bridge separately.

In 1767, 19 fishermen made an agreement with Edward Jorden, acting as agent to the duke of Beaufort, for fishing rights on the Wye below the old Chepstow Bridge. Fishermen were allowed to use one boat and one stop net, and to employ one person.

They agreed that their boats could be numbered and that they could not fish between Saturday night and Monday morning.[21] There were places where it was forbidden to fish, mainly for practical reasons of avoiding the bridge and the port traffic, but also because part of the fishing ground, namely Ghornwells Slake, Jorden had reserved for himself. Jorden was entitled to purchase fish at wholesale prices. Also, any old fish (i.e. salmon returning to the sea) that were caught by mistake were to be rendered to the landlord. For these rights the fishermen paid a guinea. Jorden's side of the bargain was to impound any vessel caught fishing in these waters that had not entered into the agreement, thereby providing some security for the licensed men. The fishermen drew weekly lots to determine where they should station themselves on the fishing ground, since some of the berths were more productive than others.

Fishing was big business even at that time and the duke of Beaufort decided to let his Severn and Wye fisheries by auction. For a time the industry was dominated by local men. Daniel Capel rented the fishery below Chepstow Bridge for £100 in 1799. William Waters leased the fishing from Chepstow to Coed Ithel in 1800 and had other fisheries in the estuary. He operated 11 boats, probably mostly stopping boats, and it seems that the men he fished with were members of his family.[22] In the 1840s George Waters successfully bid £165 for the fishing rights below Chepstow Bridge, which passed on his death in 1847 to his son-in-law Thomas Sargent. However, the coming of the railways made it easier to supply markets further afield, especially London, and the fishing rights attracted interest from outside the area. In 1863 the rights were taken by the Miller

Fishermen at Chepstow in the early 19th century.

family, salmon fishermen from Perth in Scotland. Alexander and David Miller already leased fisheries on the Tay and Galway rivers and their appearance in Chepstow marks the beginning of a more industrial-scale fishing. Alexander Miller (1831-92) made a lot of money and employed a lot of people on the quayside at Chepstow, where a new fish house was built in 1864, and he was a leading light and important benefactor in the Wye Preservation Society, for whom he acted as water-bailiff. He had an obvious self-interest in curtailing poaching on the river – in 1863 the 37 watchers he was allowed to employ secured 25 convictions for illegal fishing.[23] The illegal capture of parr and smolts was said to be rife, but they were also said to be sold openly in Hereford market and to be served as a delicacy in the hotels of Ross.[24] Miller was clearly an expert on salmon but in some of his arguments about the preservation of salmon in the Wye, for example that nets should only be used in salt water (which he had sole right to fish), there was clearly a conflict of interest.

Upstream of the Beaufort estate numerous other landowners owned fishing rights and had the right to claim the reward of a catch. In the 1870s Mr Bulten of Llangoed was able to have his keeper fish for salmon in the river, while he himself stood on the bank watching him. The keeper, with evident dexterity, hooked and then drew in a salmon on his rod as it resisted frantically but, ten minutes after first hooking it and when it was near the bank, the fishing rod was handed to Mr Bulten himself, while his keeper waded into the water to finally seize the catch and bring it to the bank. Mr Bulten held up the prize and personally 'knocked him on the head with great gusto and then proceeded to weigh him with a pocket steelyard'. It was a large fish, about 25lbs.[25]

Where different landowners owned opposite banks, the boundary was agreed to be the mid-line, or thread, of the river. Fisheries on stretches of the river were rented out and were known as beats. Sometimes landowners sold off their fishing rights as a separate entity – the Royal Hotel at Symonds Yat sold its fishing rights in three separate lots in 1792. Until the 19th century fishing rights were important business agreements, with clauses stipulating when and how men could catch fish, and what proportion of the catch that the owner could claim. Fishing on the Wye was carried out by independent fishermen and small and medium-sized family businesses, and it seems was largely hereditary. Fishing at Beachley was dominated by families such as Saunders and Traherne, as well as Jones, Parry, Prickett and Waters in the 18th and 19th centuries.[26]

Between Hereford and Ross there was a 7-mile stretch of river where there was a right to take fish freely. Commercial fishermen relied upon this right, established by custom, but sadly, it became one of the last battlegrounds in the decline of commercial fishing on the river. A long running case was finally settled in the House of Lords in 1911. The case had been brought by two fishermen, George Harris and Francis Bailey, who objected to the proposed privatisation of the river, not least because their livelihoods were at stake. The judgment went in their favour, but it was overturned by the Court of Appeal and was finally sent to the House of Lords. The plaintiffs were both incoming landowners, the Earl of Chesterfield and Mrs Alice Foster, who wanted to curtail the right of free fishery and reserve it as a commercial territory of their own.

Mrs Foster lived at Brockhampton Court, which had been purchased for her by her father as a wedding present, in gratitude for which she built the noted Arts-and-Crafts church, designed by W.R. Lethaby, at Brockhampton as a memorial to her parents. In reporting the free-fishery dispute the press never failed to mention that Mrs Foster was American. The ancient origin of the free fishery was not in dispute. As early as 1637 there were documents acknowledging the right of freeholders (known as brinkers) in Sellack, Kings Caple, Hentland, Ballingham and Bolstone parishes to fish in the river. It was also claimed that there was a document referring to a free fishery as early as 1292, that the right was granted by the king and may even have had its origins in Domesday. The plaintiffs sought to cast doubt on the legality of the free fishery, however, although there was no dispute that the rights of the commercial fishermen had been exercised openly. In the House of Lords the appeal verdict was upheld by four votes to three.[27]

Local people were furious. The *South Wales Daily News* described the verdict as 'contrary to common sense and popular ideas of justice'. The case was not simply a business dispute, but one that went to the heart of the local relationship to the river, and the erosion of a long-established river culture. At the end of it the people of the riverside felt that it belonged less to them than it had. The river was privatised for profit, and by siding with the landowners the Lords were accused of class prejudice and privileging a self-serving elite. The *Hereford Journal* was in a bitter mood. 'One feels with regret that another little bit of old England has disappeared with the shattering of the long cherished tradition.' It was not just the rights of professional fishermen that were curtailed, but of all freeholders who may have fished for leisure.

There is no doubt that Harris and Bailey were the main losers. It seemed like another nail in the coffin of an increasingly beleaguered trade. Both came from long-standing fishermen families, each generation of which found the fishing life harder than the previous one. The *Hereford Journal* again: 'The tendency for many years has been to make salmon netting impossible by the imposition of high duties, and by the gradual abolition of nets, so that at the present time only a draft net may be used, and that under a licence which costs £20.'

The squeeze on fishermen, at the expense of landowners who were determined that the river's natural resources should be theirs, has had a subtle effect even today in how we experience the river. Although traffic on the river is free and unrestricted, access to the bank is not – walkers on the Wye Valley path will notice how often they have to walk away from the bank itself. The ultimate reason can, perhaps, be put down to fish. If you stop access to the river bank, the poachers are thwarted. Many of the most beautiful sections of the Wye, from Glasbury downstream to Hereford, are private property. The only meaningful way in which the river is owned is the fact that fish cannot be taken from the river without purchasing permission from the owners of fishing rights. Such restrictions have never been popular and poaching is a natural, usually benign, consequence.

Today angling is a leisure pursuit – fishermen no longer go to the river because they are hungry. It is difficult to think of the Wye as anything else but an angler's paradise. As his companions fished for salmon and trout one April day in 1875, Francis Kilvert

Much of the Wye bank is private land, which has long restricted fishing rights on the river.

contemplated 'shining reaches of the river winding down between rocks and woods, gentle rushing everlasting murmur of the water, the sharp clicking of the reels, the low voices of the men as they sat a little way off on the bank'.[28]

Most historical references to fishing record its commercial side, but there have always been individuals fishing. Perhaps angling has always been a pleasure, a test of skill and patience. At one time they would have used spears, a practice that has long been illegal. Another traditional method was known as gaffing, whereby a barbed hook, or gaff, was used to grab the fish from its hiding place under a rock or bush. In the 19th century it was common for anglers, as opposed to just commercial fishermen, to fish using nets. Mr Baskerville of Clyro Court near Hay had a successful morning in April 1871 when he netted a pool near Hay with a local fisherman, Harry Pritchard. They caught three salmon, the largest 25lbs, two pike each of 12lbs, and a perch of 2½lbs.[29]

In 1913 6,408 salmon were caught in nets in the Wye (and of the 25,500 salmon netted in the Severn a fair proportion of them were heading for the Wye). By comparison only 3,538 salmon were taken by rod and line, mainly by anglers rather than commercial fishermen. In fact in that year £1,807 was paid in rod licenses but only £489 in net licences. As it became more costly to fish with nets, rod and line became a more important part of the commercial fishermen's method of work. One of them was Robert Pashley, born in 1880 at Walford, who caught 535 salmon in 1926, 461 in 1933 and a mighty 678 of them in 1936. However, it was not until the 1930s that rod-caught salmon finally outnumbered net-caught salmon.[30]

The largest recorded salmon on the Wye was caught using a rod by Doreen Davey in 1923. She used a simple split cane rod and undressed silk reel. The fish weighed

59½lbs and was 52½ inches long. It is the largest recorded salmon catch in England and is exceeded in Britain only by a salmon caught in the Tay in Scotland in 1922, also by a woman. Other women were noted anglers, including Mrs Nicholl, whom Francis Kilvert encountered fishing at Clyro in 1871. 'I was amazed to see Mrs Nicholl coolly wading more than ankle deep in the river with her ordinary lady's boots on. She walked

The Reverend J. Hollings, erstwhile curate of Mordiford, and keen River Wye angler. (By kind permission of Herefordshire Libraries)

about in the river as if she were on dry land, jumped from rock to rock, slipped off the rocks into the river, scrambled out again, splashed about like a fish. March water is cold. Mrs Nicholl must be an uncommonly plucky woman.' Other people concurred. A few days previously a young lad had struggled to land his fish 'so Mrs Nicholl plunged into the water on the edge of a deep hole, embraced the great fish round the body, and carried him out in her arms'.[31]

For as long as the river bank has been owned there have been poachers. To catch a fish and eat it may sound today like a noble pursuit, but it was not always so. Poachers may have been poor and hungry people, but they attracted little sympathy and much demonology. After the Rebecca Riots of the early 1840s gangs of men were said to have taken to poaching, in numbers large enough to intimidate the authorities trying to stop them. They caught fish by 'ball and spear', whereby a torch was carried at the end of pole to shine a light into the pools, in which the unsuspecting salmon were speared. Irish navvies working on the Elan valley project in the 1890s were also accused of joining poaching gangs and in one night were said to have taken over 200 fish, including 30-40 pounders. They must have been very skilful. Poachers were often blamed for the depletion of the Wye's fish stocks. Writing at the time of the Great War, Arthur Hutton worked up a head of steam on this issue and could see how the national crisis of food supply had been bad for Wye salmon, mainly due to poaching of fish in late autumn and winter in their spawning grounds in the Welsh mountains. But he also acknowledged that the long-term decline of Wye salmon had another cause: 'The greatest enemy of the welfare of our salmon fisheries is the capitalist and not the poor man.'[32]

The mythology of the salmon and the myth of the abundant and plentiful Wye preceded a period in which fish of all kinds declined. In the popular imagination salmon was once eaten by all classes of society, but by the 20th century it had become a luxury

An angler fishes in the river above Goodrich Castle, in an idyllic rural setting.

food, although the change did not happen suddenly. John Duncumb could remember a time when salmon sold for a penny a pound, but by the first decade of the 19th century that price had soared to anything between sixpence to half a crown, depending on the season.[33]

Human intervention was responsible for the decline in the river's fish population from the 18th century onwards. On many rivers migrating fish were impeded by industrial activities, mainly in the form of obstructions that prevented them from reaching their spawning grounds. With a result, in 1714 an Act of Parliament was passed for the better preservation of salmon, pertaining to 17 major rivers, the Wye included, although it was one of the least affected by industrialisation. It made it illegal to take young salmon, or any that were less than 18 inches long from the eye to the tail, and it expressly forbade nets or weirs that spanned the entire river and prevented any fish from swimming upstream to spawn. A Royal Commission set up in 1860 to enquire into the state of salmon fisheries in Britain had little to say about the Wye, but noted pollution of the headwaters by lead mining. The growth of towns, and the consequent increase in sewage disposal into the river had less effect on the Wye than on most other British rivers because its urban expansion was relatively modest. The most obvious cause of declining stocks in the Wye was over-fishing.

Fishermen pointed the finger of blame at each other. Commercial fishermen blamed poachers – for example by catching the fish in cribs, which were illegal by the end of the 18th century. But these were techniques that had a long history on the river. The taking of young fish in the upper river was likewise heavily criticised, although impossible to quantify. The ultimate reason for the decline of the river's fish was commercial exploitation.

In order to combat the problems of over-fishing and poaching, the Salmon Fishery Act was passed in 1861. It attempted to curb the taking of juvenile fish, especially prevalent

A fisherman at Ross, in a watercolour of 1797 by James Wathen.

with netting, and the taking of fish illegally by spearing and gaffing. It also prompted the formation of the Wye Preservation Society in 1862 by various fishery owners, followed by the Wye Board of Conservators in 1866, chaired by the duke of Beaufort himself. Their solutions did not always meet with universal approval. For example, a proposal to limit fishing to weekdays suited the net fishermen but was impractical to those who had licensed putchers. Despite or perhaps because of these measures, fishing intensified. This was to have a disastrous effect on fish stocks, as the catch of the Miller brothers of Chepstow, who fished as far upstream as Symonds Yat, testifies. In 1890 they caught over 7,000 fish, and two years later over 12,000 fish, but then the catch declined rapidly and in 1900 less than 3,000 fish were netted.

This sudden drop was caused by over-fishing not just in the Wye, but also in the Severn estuary. Anglers blamed the net fishermen, and the Miller enterprise especially, for the over-fishing. The commercial fisheries continued to blame poachers, not simply because they took fish illegally, but also because they fished irresponsibly. They were accused of destroying millions of spawn in the close season, but the reality is difficult to establish, especially as poachers were unable to answer back. And there were other factors that had contributed to salmon stock declining. The salmon disease of 1883, Saprolegnia ferox, killed thousands of Wye salmon.

The Miller enterprise was to pay for its over-fishing. The value of fishing rights rapidly plummeted and the duke of Beaufort sold the rights to the crown for £15,000 in 1901, on the condition that the nets should be leased to the Wye Fisheries Association. Immediately there was a two-year moratorium on net fishing and a bylaw that prohibited net fishing above Bigsweir. Recovery of fish stocks was slow and increasingly revenue was derived from rod fishermen rather than commercial net fishermen. Net fishing has undergone a managed decline through the 20th century – there were 19 drift net licences in 1919 but only two by 1960, 17 stop boats in 1919 reduced to eight by 1960. Labour shortages also meant that fishing operated on an increasingly part-time basis. In 1971 a mere 5,000 salmon were caught in the Wye by a combination of netsmen, trappers and rod anglers.[34]

Attempts have been made to re-stock the river with salmon. In 1869 Her Majesty's Inspector of Fisheries, Frank Buckland, introduced 700 young salmon from the Rhine, slightly larger than the native salmon; and a hatchery was established at Glasbury to introduce thousands of fry into the river in the 1960s and 1970s. In both cases, these moves preceded a rapid decline in the number of salmon in the river. In 1968 another disease struck: ulcerative dermal necrosis, which caused thousands of salmon deaths in an outbreak that lasted five years. In the first decade and a half of the 21st century, only in 2008 did the salmon catch exceed 1,000. The numbers of salmon thrown back increased until 2012, when a bylaw made it mandatory.

By 1996 the numbers of salmon spawning were insufficient to guarantee the survival of future generations. The cause of this phase of decline occurred partly in the Atlantic, where spring salmon that used to return to the Wye were more effectively hoovered up by Atlantic trawlers. The problems were also a consequence of declining habitat and pollution. Pollution from sheep dip, various blockages that formed insurmountable barriers to fish migration, excessive grazing and over-shading of water were all found to have caused the habitat to deteriorate. The Wye Foundation (now Wye and Usk Foundation), formed in 1996, has tried to tackle some of these issues. This has improved conditions in the Wye and its tributaries for the salmon, but also the brown trout, shad and lamprey, and the native white-clawed crayfish, which has encouraged other species like otters. Farming can have a negative impact on water quality through soil erosion contributing a greater sediment load, and the introduction of pesticides. Other non-agricultural pollutants include phosphate from sewage treatment works and septic tanks.

Upland forestry is thirsty and reduces the volume of water in the river. Wood in the upper valley and tributaries was coppiced on a rotational basis for logs and charcoal, but the demand collapsed after the war. With a result trees, especially the multi-stemmed alder, were left unmanaged, increasing the shade of streams. Trout and salmon prefer unshaded streams where the water is colder. At worst, trees topple and are left mid stream, deflecting the flow and causing erosion, while the loss of the root system makes banks unstable – 400 trees were removed by the Wye Foundation in its first year.[35] Upstream measures were matched by activity downstream. The Wye & Usk Foundation purchased the rights to drift netting in the Severn Estuary in 2000, which subsequently ceased, and use of putchers has also been substantially reduced.

Decline of fish in the Wye has been far more than a natural disaster. The stop-net fishermen had fixed berths from which they fished. Their names – Gut, Gloucester Hole, Slip and Cliff, Port Walls, Behind the Plane, Inside Castle, Outside Castle, etc – are testament to a river that is intimately known. Obsession with salmon has overshadowed the other species in the river, but the Wye was once rich in grayling, perch and shad, species which barely register now that anglers fish the Wye for barbel, an introduced species. The loss of fish has been a cultural loss which has changed the traditional diet of Wyeside communities, and left the vocabulary of the river much depleted.

❧ 10 ❧
At Home by the River

Once, settlers could have looked at the River Wye as an entirely natural phenomenon. Ironically the first people who we know settled, or at least sheltered, close to the river did not encounter the fertile valley of abundant resources that we might imagine. In the Upper Palaeolithic period, between about 50,000 and 10,000 years ago, hunters used the caves and rock shelters in the limestone rocks overlooking the valley on the fringe of the Forest of Dean. The best known is King Arthur's Cave in Great Doward, whose inhabitants looked over a very different countryside to the present one, a tundra-like landscape in a cold climate. From their high vantage point they could track the movement of herds of animals, for it was meat, not fish, that encouraged communities to venture here in the first place. In King Arthur's Cave excavations revealed the bones of their meals, but also the bones of extinct animals, which showed that the Wye valley was once a landscape of woolly rhinoceros, mammoth, hyena, bison, great Irish deer and cave bears.

People doubtless fished, swam and paddled on the river in boats long before they settled by it, but evidence of interaction with the river is only ever ephemeral, not least because of the tendency of the river to wash everything away. Eaton Camp west of Hereford, is sited on a promontory above the Wye at its confluence with the Cage Brook. It stands well above the river, but can nevertheless be classed as an early riverside settlement, in an Iron Age when the locations of choice for defensible settlements were the hilltops. The Romans tended to be much more confident about living by the river. Kenchester, just over 4 miles west of Hereford, was the Roman town of *Magnis*, mentioned in the 3rd-century Antonine Itinerary and the 8th-century Ravenna Cosmography. It superseded the nearby Iron Age fort of Credenhill, where the population began to decline from AD70 when the Romans became established in the area, a telling move away from the hilltop stronghold to the more inhabited lowlands.[1] Such places, however, are vulnerable to attack and at *Magnis* there is evidence of stout defensive walls. Kenchester reached its maximum extent in the 2nd century but in the 3rd and 4th centuries it had an earth and stone rampart that was strengthened by stone bastions and platforms for catapults. Interestingly, the town is not on the river and so could not have been a river port like

Roman towns such as London or Gloucester. It does not suggest that the economy of the district was founded upon river traffic, but the location of the town was indirectly determined by the river because it grew up around the crossroads of the main north-south route in the region between the fortresses of Chester and Caerleon and an east-west route to the military bases at Clifford and Clyro. The success of Kenchester can perhaps be measured by the building of villas in the countryside nearby. One possible example is the remains of a Roman building at The Weir, which overlooks a bend in the Wye and is now surrounded by informal gardens that extend to the river. (The Weir is now maintained by the National Trust and is open to visitors.)

Since Roman times the Wye has become a river of villages and small towns. Hereford enjoys the status of a city because of its cathedral and is the largest settlement on the river, and if it is now small by comparison with other metropolitan centres, it has not always been so. The sluggish economy of the border region in the centuries following the Middle Ages meant that Hereford was one of the last of the large medieval centres to break out of its original walled confines. Of the other towns, Monmouth was once more important than it seems today and Chepstow was at one time one of the largest towns in Wales and arguably its chief sea port.

Ultimately, Hereford is where it is because of the river. To the north-west of the city there was an important crossroads of Roman roads leading from Worcester westwards toward Kenchester, and north-south between Chester and Monmouth, crossing the Wye by one of the city's former fords. There have been numerous Roman finds that suggest some occupation in the Roman period, perhaps a wayside settlement by the river crossing rather than an early fort.[2] The survival of these Roman routes was probably instrumental in the development of Hereford, perhaps first the monastery of St Guthlac, followed by the cathedral church, then a Saxon *burh*, and finally the city itself.

Hereford in the late 18th century, with a quay below the cathedral.

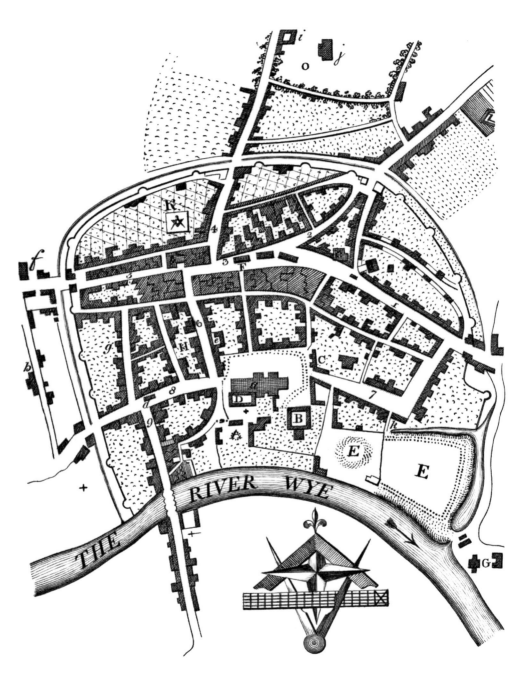

This 1796 plan of Hereford illustrates the compactness of the city, protected by the river on the south side and medieval walls on the remaining sides.

There were reputedly two fords at Hereford, the Castle Ford and the Palace Ford opposite the Bishops Palace. These were presumably the places where the river was known to be shallow in the summer months. The Palace Ford is in direct alignment with Broad Street, and the Castle Ford is aligned with Mill Street, crossing the river just below the modern Victoria Bridge, an area which is still a shallow section of river flowing over sandstone bedrock.

Hereford grew in importance as a secular centre in the kingdom of Mercia, probably in the more settled times that followed the Battle of Hereford in 760 and after the construction of Offa's Dyke in the late 8th century. Hereford was an Anglo-Saxon *burh*, a status it had acquired by 914, and is usually thought of as replacing the Roman town *Magnis* further west. Its defences pre-date the surviving medieval city wall, but in most phases of its history the city has been protected on the south side by the river, though in Saxon times there also appears to have been a defended area south of the river. In the 8th century it was a town of 40 acres, about the size of the Roman settlement it replaced, *Magnis*. Bishop Aethelstan rebuilt the cathedral in the 1030s and, after recovering from being sacked by Gruffydd ap Llywelyn in 1055, the city was allowed to prosper unhindered. The town's medieval extent, still defined partly by the medieval wall, and also by the road system around the city centre, was reached in the 12th century, and it did not expand much beyond that until the 19th century; the only overspill was on the south bank of the river leading to the bridge. Wye Bridge was first constructed about 1100, to the west and just upstream of the earlier crossings.

Ross is a town on two levels, a higher level on sandstone cliffs, which is the centre of the town, and a lower riverside level near Wilton Bridge, which developed into a port. In this it is much like Bridgnorth on the Severn. It could regard itself a town as early as the 12th century when King Stephen, in 1138, granted a charter for a market there. In the 16th century it was renowned for iron working and the manufacture of leather goods, and in 1637 it acquired an unenviable reputation for plague. The town was effectively quarantined. Supplies were brought in and left on Wilton Bridge, and the money for payment was left in bowls of vinegar. The 315 dead were buried in a plague pit, and there is a commemorative cross in the churchyard. But that earlier aspect of the town's history has been overshadowed by the influence of a man born in that very plague year, Sir John Kyrle (1637-1724), the man Alexander Pope later called the Man of Ross. Kyrle, a wealthy man of simple habits, was of an unusually philanthropic cast of mind and his legacy to the town was a number of public-spirited initiatives about which we shall hear in due course.

The town of Monmouth owes its existence to the Norman Conquest and its strategic position at the confluence of the Monnow and Wye. There was a settlement here in Roman times, known as *Blestium*, but whether it was still inhabited in an organised way in 1066 had little to do with the construction of the castle and priory. The town was walled from 1297 to about 1320, when the gate on Monnow Bridge was erected. The Wye Bridge also had a gateway but by the early 19th century its exact position and appearance had slipped beyond memory.[3] Chepstow was founded beneath the castle as a port and trading centre and was a major Welsh town from the

John Speed's map of Monmouth in the early 17th century shows how it was built between the Monnow at the top of the picture, and the Wye at the bottom.

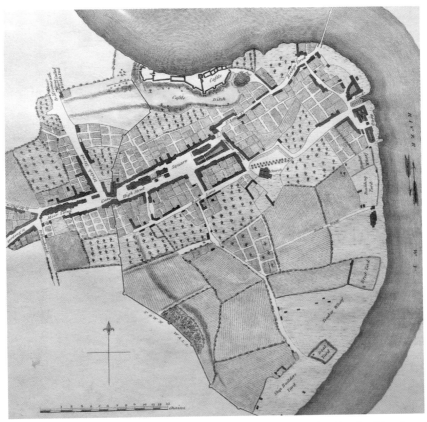

Chepstow is defined by the river and the road leading from the bridge. In this plan of 1801 the town is enclosed by the river on the east side and wall on the west side. Settlement is linear along the road leading uphill from the bridge. Within the walled town, by the river, are brick, timber and shipbuilding yards.

Middle Ages until the industrial revolution. It was dominated by its castle and priory and enclosed within town walls constructed in the 1270s and protected on the east side by the river. As late as 1800, however, the settlement within the town walls was little more than a ribbon development of the route up from the bridge to the Town Gate at the upper end of the High street, leading into Wales. The ground also rose sharply above the river, which prompted the Reverend Edward Davies, vicar of nearby Mathern, to quip that

> But strange to tell, there cannot be found
> One single inch of horizontal ground.

The origin of the Wye's Welsh towns was largely defensive. Builth, Rhayader and Hay were all built where castles had been established in the 11th and 12th centuries. Builth was granted borough status in 1277, immediately after Edward I's conquest of north Wales, although only the church survives from the Middle Ages in a town that was largely destroyed by fire in 1691. Hay was a walled town in the Middle Ages when its economy was based on the woollen industry, although most of the wall was taken down in the 18th and 19th centuries. Rhayader was a borough by 1360 and the layout of the streets suggests that it was a planned settlement, although nothing much survives in the town earlier than the 19th century. By the end of the 18th century, when the turnpike road was built between Kington and Aberystwyth, Rhayader became a coaching town, then found a new lease of life a century later when the Elan Valley reservoirs were built.

T.H. Fielding's view of Builth, published in 1841,
portrays the town as little more than a village among the hills.

Other Welsh settlements originated with castles, like Aberedw and Boughrood, or grew up close to important river crossings, like Glasbury and Newbridge. In Llangurig it all began with the church.

The larger Wye towns owed their prosperity in large part due to the river. Although it was often seen as a problem it remained essential, and the success of the navigation was a measure of the prosperity of its towns. Daniel Defoe provides a valuable insight into the relative fortunes of the Wye towns in the 1720s. Hereford was at this time 'an old, mean built, and very dirty city', but further downstream the outlook was much brighter. Ross was 'a good old town, famous for good cider, a great manufacture of iron ware and a good trade on the River Wye'. Monmouth was a town of recession at this time, and yet 'drives a considerable trade with the city of Bristol, by the navigation of the Wye', but it was Chepstow that was the regional centre of commerce, 'a place of very good trade'.[4] The river, then, was a major factor in the prosperity of its towns and would remain so until the improvement of roads later in the 18th century and especially with the coming of railways in the mid 19th. After that Chepstow and Ross reinvented themselves as tourist towns, relying on the river in a new way.

The countryside is close to the heart of every settlement on the Wye and it remains essentially a rural river. Parts of it were once remote enough for hermits to live by. At the time of the Wye Tour in the late 18th century there were vagrants and beggars living in or near places like Tintern Abbey. Wordsworth also makes an indirect mention of poor and marginal people, although they remained nameless and romanticised:

> ... wreaths of smoke
> Sent up, in silence, from among the trees,
> With some uncertain notice, as might seem,
> Of vagrant dwellers in the houseless woods,
> Or of some hermit's cave, where by his fire
> The hermit sits alone.[5]

But the river never had to worry that the poor would spoil its reputation. The Wye provided an invaluable setting for many country residences, especially fortuitous when rural beauty became a fashionable setting for a house, and at the same time raised the social status of the river itself. The famed beauty of the Wye derives at least something from the quality of the people who lived by it, and wrote about it. Poets like Anna Seward, in her 1796 'Pastoral Ballad', written in a Wyseide cottage, made the Wye's reputation as a desirable place to live in rural bliss:

> Oh, share my cottage, dearest maid! –
> Beneath a mountain, wild and high,
> It nestles, in a silent glade;
> And Wye's clear currents wander by
>
> ...

Far from the city's vain parade,
No scornful brow shall there be seen;
No dull impertinence invade,
Nor envy base, nor sullen spleen.
The shadowy rocks, which circle round,
From storms shall guard our sylvan cell;
And there shall every joy be found,
That loves in peaceful vales do dwell.

River terraces were a perfect site for a house, keeping them free of floodwater but also offering views over the river. There are many of them: The Weir and Belmont above Hereford; and Rotherwas, Holme Lacy and Sufton Court below Hereford. 'The views from [Belmont], in each direction of the river, are highly attractive, and art and nature under the guidance of taste, are happily combined to produce a rich and beautiful effect.'[6] Many of the houses, like Holme Lacy and Monnington-on-Wye, have ancient roots and were for many generations inhabited by the same families; this simply adds to the Arcadian feel of the place.

The great age of Wyeside country houses was the late 18th century. During that period Herefordshire was the centre of the Picturesque movement, and home to two of its most influential landscape connoisseurs, Uvedale Price and Richard Payne Knight. Humphry Repton and Capability Brown were at work in the county and their work was enhanced by, and enhanced, the Wye. Moccas Court, rebuilt in the 1770s for the Cornewall family by Anthony Keck, stands close to a former motte and bailey castle, and its long transition from defended site to idyllic country house is part of the story

James Wathen's view of Moccas in 1788.

Belmont House overlooking the Wye, by James Wathen, 1821.

of the Wye. The grounds were landscaped by Capability Brown, with input later from Humphrey Repton, and made the most of its Wye setting by extending to both banks of the river, incorporating part of a medieval deer park and including riverside walks. Belmont near Hereford was built in 1788 to a design by Thomas Wyatt, and has a landscape park designed by Repton, with views over a ha-ha to the river.

Piercefield Park, just north of Chepstow, was laid out on a greater scale and had the advantage of dramatic natural scenery as a starting point. The popularity of the Wye Tour, and the fact that the park was accessible to the public, meant that Piercefield was by far the best known of Wyeside residences. A landing stage was even provided for pleasure boats. Picturesque walks were laid out on the west bank of the Wye above Chepstow, first by Valentine Morris after he inherited Piercefield in 1752. Although they had become disused by the 1780s when Morris had to sell it to George Smith, they were re-opened in 1794 with alterations designed to accommodate increasing numbers of visitors, most of whom started at Chepstow. The walks remained open, albeit with reduced public access (alas for Richard Warner, when he visited on his walking tour in 1797 the grounds were closed), until the 1850s and subsequently became ruinous and overgrown, so much so that the discovery and interpretation of most of its features has been achieved by the trained eye of archaeologists.

Piercefield offered hilltop viewpoints over the Wye downstream to its confluence with the Severn. From the Iron Age fort there was an extensive view northwards up the Wye valley. The walks included several viewpoints where the river could be appreciated and a riverside walk. A lot of people loved the place. Dr Richard Pococke described being conducted in 1756 to a seat at the highest of the viewpoints, from where the view was 'the most beautiful I ever beheld; the river winds so as to make a peninsula on the other side, which is a piece of ground gently rising to a point, on which there are two or three houses, and all this ground is diversified with an agreeable mixture of corn fields,

Piercefield was the most extensive landscape park by the Wye, although the house is set well back. The landscape is dominated by the high Wyndcliff, which offered extensive views over the river and was a favourite vantage point for artists.

meadow, wood.'[7] Like everything fashionable, however, a later generation was getting bored with it. Thomas Roscoe, after having experienced the grandeur and simplicity of nature on the journey down the Wye was unimpressed by something so artificial as a landscape garden: 'A ramble through the three-mile walk of Piercefield Terrace is far less gratifying than the same distance would prove through the wild greenwood.'[8]

The Wye did not always add anything picturesque to the scene. Even though the river carves a dramatic S-curve through the rocks, here it is tidal; or, as Samuel Ireland put it in 1797, it is polluted by the mud of the Severn. 'I was disappointed in the famous view from the Wynd Cliff', wrote Francis Kilvert in July 1875. 'The view may be fine on a clear day but any view would be spoilt by the filthy ditch which they call the Wye in the foreground, a ditch full of muddy water at the best of times, namely high water, but now a scene of ugly foreshore and wastes of hideous mud banks with a sluggish brown stream winding low in the bottom between.'[9] Some 19th-century tourists also visited Goodrich Court, which was built in 1828 in a commanding position above the river. It stood opposite the genuine medieval castle like an impertinent upstart, which did not meet universal approval. Built for the antiquarian Samuel Meyrick, this Gothic turreted fantasy was, according to Thomas Roscoe in the 1830s, a 'romance of stone and lime' and a place to dream 'of arms and chivalry'. It was demolished in 1949, except for the gatehouse.

A later generation of country residences was built beside the Wye further upstream in Wales in the 19th century. The Birmingham-based engineer James Watt bought a large

Women take their washing to the river at Rhayader, in a drawing
made soon after the bridge was built in 1780.

estate at Doldowlod below Rhayader in 1803. In Watt's time Doldowlod was a farm-house and it was his son and business partner, also James, who in the 1840s built the first phase of the country house that stands today, modelling it on his splendid 17th-century house, Aston Hall in Birmingham. The Reverend Richard Venables, Archdeacon of Carmarthen, built Llysdinam in 1829, a restrained country house opposite Newbridge. In this comparatively isolated upriver section the emphasis was on peace and quiet. Glyn Gwy, on the river bank above Rhayader, was built in the 19th century by Mr Foxton, apparently a recluse, who moved there from a house close by because he feared that the new railway would disturb him.[10] Clochfaen was built in 1914 for the courtier Harry Lloyd Verney (1872-1950) in a vernacular timber-framed style overlooking the river near Llangurig. The house was grand enough to accommodate some earlier fireplaces brought from houses in London. The new house was a fresh start for the Clochfaen estate as it replaced a derelict earlier house that had been built in 1810.

Contemporary depictions of the river in the 18th and 19th centuries often show women doing their laundry in the river, or carrying pitchers of water on their heads. It is a reminder that the river has long had a role in domestic water supply. Washing in the river was common, but so in many places was taking water for other domestic uses, although in general people preferred to use well water if they could. There were several wells in Hereford that, in theory at least, offered a much cleaner supply than the river with its sediments, but they seem to have been insufficient to cover all of the city's needs.

Plans to supply Hereford with pumped river water were prepared in 1695, similar to schemes operated in other urban areas like London and Shrewsbury. Ambrose

Crowley, an ironmaster from Stourbridge, in partnership with Daniel Desmile and Edward Dyson, made an agreement with the city to supply water for 21 years from a waterwheel at the Castle Mills, which was to pipe water to cisterns in the town, one of them by St Peter's Cross. It is thought unlikely that the scheme ever came to fruition.[11]

The first town on the Wye that we know to have enjoyed a piped water supply was Ross, which had the benefit of a system instigated by John Kyrle in the first decade of the 18th century. River water was channelled into a pond, and then a waterwheel was used to pump the water to a tank (which has survived) beneath The Prospect, the public garden that Kyrle established near the church. From here it was piped around the town and a public fountain was set up. This system remained in use into the 19th century, although it was said to be in disrepair by 1827. The system was eventually replaced when the Alton Court Waterworks was built in 1887; this draws water from an artesian well, not from the river.

Like most towns Hereford suffered from sanitary inadequacies when it expanded in the 19th century. The Public Health Acts of 1848 and 1849 recognised the need for urban centres to establish a public water supply but it was left to the towns and cities themselves to organise it. Under the auspices of the General Board of Health, Thomas Rammell produced a report on the sanitary condition of Hereford in 1853. The subsequent Hereford Improvement Act that was passed in 1854 was a landmark in the provision of civilised living conditions and also in the development of local government.

By the mid 19th century Hereford was supplied with water from wells around the city, supplemented by river water, which was sold in the city at a halfpenny a bucket, and was the preferred source of water for the brewing industry. Unusually, well water was considered inferior for drinking to river and stream water. In particular there were problems with lead poisoning and with well water that was contaminated by nearby sewers and cesspools. In 1853 samples of local water were sent to London for testing, with some unexpected conclusions. The river water, taken upstream of the city, was described as clear, 'but had a slight tinge, and decided taste of peat'. But it was classed as soft water and was therefore considered to be much superior to the hard water from wells. The soft river water was deemed 'best for cooking, and especially for tea making. For instance, equal quantities of the leaf will make four cups of tea with the Wye water, but only three cups equally strong' from the well in High Town Square opposite the Sun Inn. Water from the streams around the city was also better than well water, albeit with a problem of particle suspension, but the best source was considered to be the city's Moor spring. One of the recommendations of the Board of Health report was that the city should if possible be supplied from the Moor spring, the quality of whose water would be improved if it could be treated with quick lime.[12]

Thomas Rammell's report also considered the sanitary condition of Hereford and gives a valuable, if unpalatable, insight into the daily lives of people in the city. Drains carried sewage away either directly to the river, or via the Town brook and Stonebow brook. However, the numerous mill ponds, of which the pond at the Castle Mill, next to Castle Green, was the chief offender, were places where sewage stagnated, with a consequence that parts of Hereford stank in summer, as well as being a health hazard. The

The waterworks at Broomy Hill in Hereford.

insanitary state of Hereford was said to account annually for 40 deaths from disease, in a town with a population just over 11,000. Hereford was by no means as bad as many British towns and cities, where population growth in the 19th century was putting a much greater strain on long-established infrastructures. Even so, Rammell's conclusion was that the Public Health Acts of 1848 and 1849 should be applied to Hereford, paving the way for a properly organised public water supply and for an efficient system of sewers.

The solution to the problem of water supply was the River Wye. A site was chosen just west of the city on Broomy Hill, to which water was pumped and where the water was filtered in tanks before delivery to the city. Timothy Curley, an engineer who had come to Hereford with the construction of the railway, was responsible for the new water system, including the pumping station and a staged process of filtration. Water was lifted to tanks where there were large mechanical filters and was then screened by spraying water over granite pebbles, before being passed through a sand bed. The water was not yet chlorinated but the result was an improvement on the wells and there was less sediment in the water tanks of domestic users. When Hereford expanded in the 19th century and houses were built on Aylestone Hill, an additional water tower was added, completed in 1893, with a capacity of 45,000 gallons.

Demand placed on the river increased as Hereford's population grew further. In the 19th century the waterworks had used steam engines, but electric engines were installed in 1911. From the 1960s the area served by the waterworks has also increased, since piped water was now to be supplied to rural Herefordshire as well. The Herefordshire Wye has been included within the Welsh water authority since 1974, largely because the river catchment is mainly in Wales. From that time a new treatment works has operated at Broomy Hill that can take up to 12 million gallons from the river every day for treatment. By the beginning of the 21st century the Broomy Hill plant supplied 110,000 customers covering 80 per cent of Herefordshire.

The other Wye towns did not take their main water supply from the river, but from wells and tributaries instead. The greatest demand for domestic water on the River Wye system is in the Elan Valley, where reservoirs collect water and pipe it to Birmingham. Work by the Birmingham Corporation on what was to be one of the foremost civil engineering projects of late-Victorian Britain began in 1892 with the construction of the reservoirs and the laying of a pipe – the 'Birmingham Aqueduct' – from Mid Wales to the English Midlands. It crosses the Wye by means of a subterranean siphon just south of Rhayader, and the only signs of it on the surface are the inlet and outlet houses where the valves are controlled. They are set well back from the bank and you would have to know they are there to be able to spot them.

Equally heroic, if less well publicised, has been the improvement made to the treatment of sewage from the end of the 19th century. This has significantly improved a river environment that was invariably more polluted downstream of a town that it was upstream. Sewage treatment works are among the most inconspicuous of riverside structures, and their locations have been carefully planned so that they go mostly unnoticed. The purpose of sewage treatment works is to remove enough impurities to enable water to be delivered back to rivers and therefore rejoin the natural water cycle. By screening, settling and then spreading waste water over beds of rough stones where colonies of bacteria can consume organic material, the water is progressively purified. It then receives a last filter, known by the unlikely term of polishing, before it is pumped back into the river. Wherever possible, foul water and rainwater run-off are kept separate, so that storm water can more easily drain into the river, although this has not always been possible. In 2015, for example, storm water overwhelmed the sewage works at Hay-on-Wye, causing untreated sewage to be released into the river. That such an occurrence should be regarded as wholly unacceptable by the public today is a measure of how far we have come from the days when all the Wyeside towns availed themselves of the river as a natural outlet.[13]

The Wye has long been a river of leisure and pleasure and seems ideal for the purpose. It is predominantly a rural river and, because it has no large industrial towns, has always been comparatively free of pollution. There used to be commercial traffic, but from the mid 19th century the railway took over an already declining river trade and the more placid stretches of river became ideal for recreational boating. The scenery of the Wye has been appreciated since at least the early 18th century and before the Wye Tour became popular. John Kyrle laid out The Prospect in Ross, overlooking the Wye toward Wilton Bridge and castle, and created 'The Man of Ross Walk' on a rocky eminence parallel with the river, which ended in a summer house, although by the 1830s, when Thomas Roscoe visited it, he found it in 'a deserted and somewhat desolate condition'.[14] Castle Green became a place to promenade by the river in Hereford after the castle was dismantled at the end of the Civil War and was a well-established place with mature trees by the late

Paddling on the Wye below Victoria Bridge in the late 19th century. The river was a natural focus of outdoor recreation. (By kind permission of Herefordshire Libraries)

The river has a natural gravitational pull in fine weather.
Here people gather on a summer evening at Bredwardine.

The Kyrle Gate leading to the Prospect at Ross, overlooking the Wye,
built when the river was first being conceived as one of the town's amenities.

18th century. Bartonsham Meadows were also much frequented in summer by this time, and its Civil War entrenchments had by then become an object of curiosity.[15]

When the commercial navigation declined there was a new, if smaller, economy of pleasure boats. Steam pleasure boats were operating from Ross as early as 1834 and could be hired with crews from inns including the Swan, the King's Head and the George. Steam-powered pleasure cruises were also offered from Hereford by, among others, Francis Wegg-Prosser (1824-1911), the wealthy Roman-Catholic convert of Belmont who founded there the Abbey of St Michael the Archangel in the 1850s.

Organised boat racing has a long history on the Wye. There were boat races at Hereford sporadically in the first half of the 19th century, beginning in 1801 and 1802, and a series in the 1830s. Races between Hunderton Bridge and Wye Bridge took place in 1852 and this section of the river henceforth became the venue for the city's regattas.[16] In 1859 there were crowds of people lining the river and standing on Wye Bridge, the band of the Newport Abergavenny and Hereford Railway provided the musical accompaniment for the dances, and Richard Jordan supplied most of the boats. By the end of the decade there were cups for the fours and punts and it was hoped to add a ladies cup too. For the 1860 regatta Hunderton Bridge was decorated and the band of the Hunderton Rifles was in attendance. The regatta had taken on the character of a festival for the city.[17]

The Hereford Rowing Club was formed in 1861 and the following year they supplied boats for races and a procession, in an event organised in honour of Richard Jordan. A show boat preceded the main flotilla, with the band of the West Midland Railway Works on board. Races for fours and pairs, and also for 'whiffs' (narrow sculling boats) were

The Pavilion on Castle Green, Hereford, is much altered.
It once housed public baths and is now home to a canoe club.

Pleasure cruising near Symonds Yat.

Hereford Regatta in 1892. (By kind permission of Herefordshire Libraries)

between Hunderton Villa and the boatyard at Wye Bridge. By the late 19th century the regatta was well established at Hereford, following a nice straight course from Belmont to Wye Bridge and reckoned just as good as Henley, if about a hundred yards shorter.[18] Rival clubs could now compete in a period when the railways could carry boats to away events. Monmouth Rowing Club was formed in 1928, although Monmouth Grammar School had already taken up the sport by this time and rowing remains one of the school's chief sports in its current incarnation as Monmouth School.

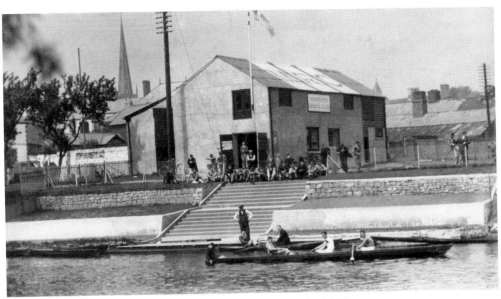

Monmouth Rowing Club in the 1930s.

Raft racing at Monmouth c.1960.

By 1860 an evening boat race at Chepstow could attract a large crowd on Castle Green and by the bridge. Races were held over varying courses between the road and railway bridges, a highlight of what was really a big town fête. 'After the boat racing was over, hundreds of persons adjourned to the castle to witness the fireworks and balloon ascents', while a band provided an accompaniment and tents offered refreshments and children's entertainment. In 1867 there were races in Ross, organised for single sculls (i.e. a pair of oars), pairs and coracles.[19] And there is a modern tradition

Canoeing on the river has become an important part of the Wye valley economy.

of raft racing. A formal raft race has been run every year between Monmouth and Whitebrook since 1967, with exceptions in the Foot and Mouth year of 2001 and the floods of 2007.

Canoeing has been popular since at least the 1950s when the Hereford County Canoe Club was formed, first in Ross and then in Hereford. However, not every activity on the river can be classed as sport. In the early 20th century rowing and sailing on the river was treated as a healthy outdoor pursuit like rambling or cycling, a way to see and enjoy the countryside.

Boats for pleasure could be hired at various places along the river, for example from Richard Jordan of Hereford, Hobbs of Ross and Fuller of Monmouth, of various sizes, and capable of taking up to 20 people.[20] The general presumption was that boats were navigated downstream, where there were few dangerous natural obstacles, with the exception of Monnington Rocks above Hereford where the river is bisected by an island, with a deep channel on one side and rapids on the other. Carey Island, near Fownhope, posed a similar problem, because it was essential to take the narrow channel and avoid the weirs on what looked like the wider channel. Bigsweir was the highest point on the river at which the effect of the tide was felt, so only lower down would the navigation get difficult. By the end of the 19th century all this could be enjoyed safe in the knowledge that a hired boat could simply be placed on a train and taken back to whence it came.

There are many places where canoes can now be hired, or brought to a launching site on top of a car. Taking to the river is one way to know it intimately, to experience the alternation of deep pools with shallows, which can shift their positions in times of flood. The Wye may be famous for the ruins of Tintern and Goodrich, but many people just want to experience the river as a work of nature.

❧ 11 ☙
Ice Floes and Inundations

When we think of natural disasters and rivers, the mind invariably turns to floods. In its natural state a river is a volatile thing, prone to quick changes of mood, and this is usually more marked closer to the source because that tends to be the area with the highest precipitation. The Wye, draining as it does the rain-drenched hills of central Wales, can rise quickly. Daniel Defoe, visiting in the 1720s, remarked how the citizens of Hereford could be at the mercy 'of the violent freshes that come down from the mountains of Wales'. It is a reminder that the sudden swelling of the river that enabled it to be navigable was only a degree short of a destructive flood.

We say that rivers have 'channels' and 'floodplains', but in reality those distinctions exist only in our own minds, and this is also true of the ways we talk about rivers in flood. We say they 'burst their banks' as if they are flowing in places they are not supposed to as a result of freakish conditions, but in fact they merely respond to natural events, taking up as much space as is necessary. The river is always just the river. What we call the floodplain on which we build houses might just as easily be labelled the occasional river bed; in times of high water the river merely asserts its sovereignty over low-lying ground.

Floods are the most notable events on the river and are often described in dramatic language. In 1795, the bridge at Hay was destroyed. 'The river having already swept away the bridge of Glasbury, brought down every material that the ruin of its banks supplied, and quickly formed a dam across its arches; till the structure, no longer able to support such an accumulation of wreck and waters, fell with a horrible crash before the raging element, and the whole poured down on the country below, carrying ruin and dismay among the habitations near its course.'[1]

It is not simply the ferociousness of the river in flood that impresses us, but also the mood swings that give it its personality. 'In dry weather this interesting river shrinks to a comparative rivulet' and walking along its banks the gravels and stones of its beds are 'dried out in the sun', commented John Thelwall while he lived at Llyswen in the winter of 1797-8. 'At other times it will suddenly swell to a boisterous and overwhelming sea, rising many feet, nay, many yards, in a single night, sweeping everything before it, overwhelming the valleys wherever it finds an opening between the hills, and exhibiting one continuous scene of terrible and tumultuous grandeur.'[2]

It is self-evident that floods are purveyors of human misery, but when a river is demonstrating its devastating power it is also a magnificent spectacle. For John Thelwall, a flood was something to be seen: 'wrapped up in a large rough coat, I enjoyed the interesting scenes from an elevated alcove'. From here 'the torrent came pouring in a rapid and majestic course … foaming and dashing and raging against the banks, tumbling from rock to rock with a deafening roar, and whirling in its impetuous eddies, fragments and limbs and trunks of trees, which it had torn away in its course.'[3]

The *Hereford Times* was equally expressive when reporting the floods of February 1852. In fact many people had climbed the cathedral tower to admire the scene:

> For miles, the meadows presented the appearance of a chain of lakes, in the midst of which houses, churches, and trees seemed to be half submerged. From the bridge, the foaming and headlong torrent was seen in all its tumultuous grandeur. So powerful was the current that it dashed against the piers with a surf that mounted from two to three feet in height … The evening was singularly bright and beautiful, and the unclouded moon gave to the wide expanse of waters, and the distant twinkling lights, as seen from the Castle-green, and to the restless, turbid, eddying stream, a singular beauty of effect, which attracted hundreds of spectators, who had not all departed homeward until nearly midnight.[4]

Floods are also subtle things. The Wye catchment drains a large area of mountainous mid Wales, but also the lower hills of the borderland whose waters join the main river further along its course. Floods therefore affect different parts of the river at different times, and the severity of flooding is never equal along its course. After the torrential rain in the summer of 2007 it was the river in Herefordshire that flooded severely, whereas the upper Welsh section was largely free of inundation. In the Herefordshire stretch of the Wye the worst flood occurred in 1795. Chepstow, being at the tidal end of the river, was especially vulnerable to a combination of a high river level and a powerful tidal bore in the Severn. The great storm of 1703, reckoned by some to have been a tsunami, was the worst recorded flood, just a few inches above that of 1737 when the water was said to have risen 70 feet at high tide. There were further high tides in 1768 and 1799, and again in 1899 when the riverside inhabitants tried to protect their homes by boarding and 'mudding'.[5]

For as long as there has been literature describing the river, its floods have been chronicled to some extent, but in greater detail since the establishment of local newspapers such as the *Hereford Journal* in 1770 and *Hereford Times* in 1832. The occurrence of a serious flood is often apparent from the need to repair or rebuild bridges or riverside buildings. For example, the New Weir was severely damaged by a flood in 1609 and had to be rebuilt. In 1660 Glasbury church was badly damaged by floods and in 1730

The stone bridge at Glasbury depicted in 1794, just months before it was destroyed by flood. Samuel Ireland offered this engraving as a memorial to the lost bridge.

the same thing happened to Whitney. In both cases new churches were built on higher ground. November 1770 saw a severe flood that badly damaged Bredwardine Bridge, following which the toll house was erected to fund bridge repairs into the future. Dixton church was seriously flooded in 1795, 'the water having forced its way through the windows and doors, and torn up the pulpit, pews and pavement'.[6]

But flooding was not always so destructive and in the rural sections of the river seems to have been commonplace. Edward Williams of Clyro, speaking during the floods of 1871, remembered a time when 'all the valley was frequently flooded in the winter and under water from Hay up to Llyswen', but he said that in recent years (i.e. after 1852) it had not flooded so heavily or so often.[7]

The nature of serious flooding on the Wye has changed over time. Inundations have affected Wyeside settlements in the 21st century but freezes are much less frequent now than they were in the 18th and 19th centuries, when it was common to see large blocks of ice careering downstream. The popular image of a winter freeze is to see children out sliding on the ice, as they certainly have done on the Wye, but they were not the only creatures to venture on to the slippery and dangerous surface. In a field a river forms a natural boundary but when the water freezes the sudden removal of the barrier tempts unwary livestock to wander.

Francis Kilvert noted several freezes during his stints as curate at Clyro and vicar of Bredwardine in the 1870s. In February 1870 there were 'large masses of ice 3 and 4 inches thick' under Hay Bridge and in December the following year the Wye was completely frozen across above Glasbury Bridge. The winter of 1878-79 was particularly

Skating on the frozen river at Hereford, just upstream of Wye Bridge, in 1892.
(By kind permission of Herefordshire Libraries)

severe at Bredwardine. In December ice was floating down the river and the thermometers dropped as low as 16 Fahrenheit (-9 Celsius) by day. By the 12th the Wye was already frozen about half way across below Bredwardine Bridge, and was entirely frozen over at Moccas four days later, by which time children were out sliding on the river surface. A week later the ice had spanned the entire river at Bredwardine. A thaw started suddenly, on 29 December: 'Huge masses and floes of ice have been coming down the river all day rearing, crushing, grinding against each other, and thundering against the bridge. A crowd of people were on the bridge looking over the parapet and watching the ice pass through the arches.' But it was to be a brief respite only, as it snowed again on New Year's Day 1879, and two weeks later Kilvert reported a second thaw: 'Last night the river rose rapidly and at midnight the ice was rushing down in vast masses, roaring, cracking and thundering against the bridge like the rolling of a hundred waggons.'[8]

Kilvert's graphic descriptions remind us that the first casualties of a flood were the bridges. Bridges with several arch spans were always a slight impediment to the flow of the river, with the result that the water level was lower on the downstream side than it was on the upstream side. That disparity increased when the river was in spate. Flood water brought down all sorts of large objects – tree trunks, barges broken free of their moorings and large blocks of ice – which were liable to become wedged under arches, effectively turning a bridge into a dam and causing a flood on the upstream side. For that reason settlements were usually focussed on the downstream side of bridges. Alternatively, large objects floating out of control on a fast flowing current would strike bridges with considerable force. Five barges were dashed and wrecked against Wye Bridge in Hereford on one afternoon in February 1852, to the terror of spectators on the bridge itself:

The Wye at Hereford in the winter of 1917, turned into an ice rink.
(By kind permission of Herefordshire Libraries)

A rare summer flood in Hereford in August 1912.
(By kind permission of Herefordshire Libraries)

On reaching the bridge, the height of the water of course prevented [the barges] from passing under, and they were dashed with tremendous violence against the southernmost pier, in which was afterwards found a wide yawning crack, of considerable length. Persons who were on the bridge at the time, describe the shock as having made the whole fabric shake. A general rush of the spectators took place, women screaming with alarm, and expecting the instant fall of the ancient structure. It, however, stood its ground.[9]

The emergence on the Wye in the 19th century of single-span bridges like Bigsweir was not simply technical, aesthetic or economic. Single-span bridges were less vulnerable to flood damage and reduced the risk of upstream flooding. The absence of bridges in medieval Herefordshire, outside of the city itself, was long put down to the high cost of building and maintaining structures at the mercy of the river's destructive power. It remained true of Herefordshire and Radnorshire well into the 18th century. Three Glasbury bridges were destroyed in the 18th century – in 1738, 1777 and 1795. At Whitney the first bridge was built in 1774 and by 1802 the bridge was in its fourth incarnation.

Railway bridges too were brought down by floods, with potentially dramatic consequences if the railway was not alerted. In March 1947, the last year in which the Great Western Railway was operating, Strangford Viaduct near Ross came down at about 11 o'clock at night, about 10 minutes after a goods train had passed over it. The rapid flow of the river washed out the stonework protecting the central pier, causing the girders to collapse and leaving the rails hanging about 40 feet in the air. Fortunately two men nearly half a mile away at the British Lion pub at Fawley station, heard the crash of the girders and were able to raise the alarm.[10]

The Stank at Hampton Bishop. In 1852 the bank partially collapsed, allowing water to flood the cottages by the adjoining road.

The site of Hereford was well chosen with regard to keeping it safe from rising water. As John Price mentioned in 1796, it was 'those houses which stand on the south-side of Wye-bridge' that were susceptible to flooding. On the south side of the river is Bishop's Meadow, which is ideal for the overflow of the river when needed. This was a characteristic early example of flood defence, diverting water away to a temporarily expendable part of the landscape. Other towns and villages built more formal defences, as Dr Richard Pococke noticed as he passed through Builth in 1753. 'From the end of the bridge a wall is built about 177 yards long and six feet broad, with a wooden frame on the top to keep out the river.'[11] The Stank is an earthen bank that protects Hampton Bishop from the river where it bends sharply. It is shown on maps as early as the 1720s and continues to provide the main barrier against floodwater for the river at this point, and the Bunch of Carrots Inn, sited precariously beneath the bank.

The worst flood years on the Wye were 1770, 1795 and 1852, all caused by a sudden thaw following a long winter freeze. In July 1794 the *Hereford Journal* had been reporting on the unusually low water level, saying that 'barges have been laying at Hereford for upwards [of] four months', but that year brought the coldest winter in living memory, until a warm front brought rain in the first week of February and everything melted. In Herefordshire the river level rose 15 feet in the space of 24 hours, 'and did enormous damage through the whole county, destroying bridges, drowning cattle and sheep, sweeping off timber'.[12] The river level peaked in Bredwardine on 10 February and in Hereford the following day, when the water was already several feet deep in riverside houses. There was damage to commercial property in the city. The cellars and vaults of cider warehouses were inundated and, because the barrels were not properly stopped before they were set afloat, an enormous quantity of cider and perry was wasted.[13]

The flood was severe enough to damage or destroy several Wye bridges. Newbridge was destroyed and remained ruinous for two decades – proposals were invited for a new bridge of timber in 1814. Glasbury Bridge was lost, and in the aftermath no one had the confidence to design a new stone bridge so it was replaced in 1800 in timber instead. Samuel Ireland had made a drawing of the bridge only six months earlier but, by the time he came to write about it, it was 'little more than a wreck; every arch of it having been blown up by the torrent of ice, which poured down on the very sudden thaw'.[14] At Hay only two of the arches were left standing. Whitney Bridge was also largely destroyed and the nearby ford remained the only, and as it happened dangerous, alternative: in December 1795 a post-chaise overturned fording the river when it was in spate, and the driver, three passengers and the horses all drowned. One brighter note for many people was that the New Weir near Monmouth was almost destroyed and there were voices that spoke out against repairing it.

The golden rule in times of flood is to keep away from it, which is usually possible because the river takes a while to swell to its full capacity, and its peak can be predicted. Drownings are rare in times of flood but not everybody can easily retreat above the flood line. The London coach had already been abandoned by its passengers when it was thrown off the causeway leading to Wilton Bridge in the 1770 flood. The mail coach was caught in a flood on Bredwardine bridge in the 1820s, when three of the horses were drowned. In 1852 at Tintern a horse, still attached to its (now wheel-less) carriage, was found drowned. In such times of crisis, heroic efforts were made to keep mail services operable. 'The turnpike road was completely submerged in water' at Whitchurch in 1852, so much so 'that it required six horses to take the mail through, the water reaching up to the horses' bellies'. In Hereford, meanwhile, although coach services were suspended mail bags and coachman from Ross were brought in on the top of a wagon.[15]

There were several fatalities in the 1795 flood. A man from Eign drowned on 10 February, and upstream Mr Lloyd, a farmer from Clyro, drowned when part of the Hay Bridge gave way as he crossed it with his horse and cart. Mr Crowder, a Monmouth grocer, drowned in the riverside meadows having taken a boat in an attempt to rescue some property. Three men were on the river at Chepstow when the powerful current drove them against a pier of Chepstow Bridge. They all drowned.[16]

Livestock fared much worse than humans. Where pigs or horses were penned up they had no chance of escape if their owners had been unable to free them before they were inundated. A Hereford butcher lost the 13 sheep he had penned up near the Tanbrook in 1795. Beasts of the field were also vulnerable, especially if the water rose quickly at night. 'A number of cattle and colts were seen to pass under [Bredwardine] bridge in the moonlight and it was feared they would be drowned', wrote Kilvert in 1878. 'Some women saw a bullock swept down under the bridge at noon today.'[17]

The river sometimes rose much more quickly than riverside inhabitants expected. In 1878, for example, the Jenkins family had to run for their lives. Soon after Francis Kilvert had passed their house by Bredwardine Bridge at night, 'the river came down with a sudden rush and wave and filled the road with water and they had to escape to the trap, carrying their children on their backs, wading through water knee deep, and leaving 3 feet of water in the house'. As the water rose, other people had to flee their homes. 'Many people were flooded out of their homes at Letton and Staunton and spent the night on Bredwardine Bridge watching the flood.'[18]

Forewarning was much easier during the day than it was at night, as the experiences of 1852 showed. In Builth the water rose during the day and so there were few losses of possessions or livestock to report. Further downstream events were more dramatic. Unfortunately, many homes were inundated after dark, leaving their occupants little time to rescue their possessions. Many people in Monmouth spent a night 'anxiously removing their pigs, horses, and other animals from the reach of the flood, which was fast closing upon them. Others were engaged in removing the contents of their cellars, and their furniture and provisions from the ground floors to the higher apartments of their houses.' In Monmouth, as in Hay-on-Wye, the water entered the gas works and disrupted the provision of street lighting. At Ross water entered houses in Brookend at 8 o'clock in the evening and the water continued rising until past midnight. In Hampton Bishop The Stank was unexpectedly breached for a length of only about 6 yards, but enough to send a tidal wave of water on to the turnpike road below. 'The cottagers living by the road side, opposite to the Field Farm, saw the approach of the enemy, and, in some measure, endeavoured to prepare for it; but before they could remove their chattels, the tops of the hedges on each side of the turnpike-road were covered, and the stream rushed into their houses, despoiling their humble furniture, and causing the inmates of the houses to fly upstairs to safety.'[19]

Apart from the unlucky cottagers, everybody in Hampton Bishop moved their stuff upstairs, including their pigs and poultry. A Mr Wheatstone moved his furniture on to the first floor, in addition to which 'one of the bedrooms was converted into a sty for seven pigs, and, in another were stationed geese, ducks, fowls, and rabbits.'[20]

At times of flood small boats, especially coracles, were a lifeline to stranded householders. Wading around in waist-deep water was not recommended as all manner of lethal obstacles lay unseen beneath the surface, and it is often difficult to judge the exact depth of water. At Whitchurch in 1852, the Rector's pigs were rescued by boats which were rowed with ease across the meadows. In Hay-on-Wye stranded householders were rescued by ladder from their bedrooms and taken to safety in boats, while coracles delivered food to those who could not escape. In Monnington-on-Wye several neighbours commandeered a boat to rescue a family from a cottage, where the water level had risen so high that thatch was removed from the roof to allow them to escape. In Stretton Sugwas the river was so high that it submerged the joists supporting the first floor of a cottage.

After the water had subsided came the full realisation of what had been destroyed. The destruction wrought in 1795 was well documented, and was well remembered when John Thelwall came to describe it three years later. 'Rails, land-marks, trees innumerable, and even sheep and cattle, were borne down by the rapid torrents from the mountains, or whirled away from the meadows and low lands by the infuriated course of the river; whole plantations were shattered, and several bridges were entirely swept away.'[21] The brewing industry invariably suffered as it tended to be located by the river. In 1852 the malting house at the Grapes Tavern (adjoining Drybridge House) in Hereford was inundated and the barley laid out on the floor was lost. Other neighbouring properties, including the Dog Inn, were flooded, and everything the river washed away – garden walls, hurdles, pieces of broken boats, railings – was found strewn across the

The flooded May Hill Station, on the east bank of the River Wye at Monmouth, in 1910.
(Monmouth Museum)

neighbouring meadows where it all lay in 'promiscuous heaps'. Farmers too suffered serious losses, as at Hampton Bishop in 1852. 'Considerable mischief was done to the property of farmers in the neighbourhood. Their fences were swept away – trees torn up by the roots – and their corn and hay ricks were several feet deep in water, necessarily inflicting a serious loss.' At Monnington Court the farm lost 'five large wheat ricks, two barley ricks, one bean rick, one pea rick and two hay ricks' estimated to have been worth £100. In Monmouth a riverside timber yard lost much of its stock. 'Many of these oak timbers being new, have, it is feared, after floating away for a great distance in the heaviest water, sunk in the middle of the river, and have been covered with sand and gravel, so they will probably never be recovered.'[22]

It has to be admitted that amid the carnage there were unexpected benefits. The flood was not to be regarded as purely destructive, although it was the observant outsider John Thelwall, rather than the local press, who drew attention to it: 'The ravages ... are more than compensated by the good which they distribute. The wood that is thus born down furnishes a supply of fuel to the surrounding cottagers; who, on these occasions, plant themselves on the banks of the river, with hooks in their hands, mounted upon long poles, and fish for the logs as they are swept along. I am credibly informed that, by means of these heavy floods ... this species of log-fishing has been so profitable to the poorer people of the town of Hay, that there are few of them who are not by this resource supplied with a sufficient quantity of fuel for the consumption of the whole winter.'[23]

There were other advantages to flood water. 'Wherever the inundation has room to spread, a more permanent advantage is dispensed to the country at large: a cheap and invaluable manure is spread over the meadows.' The downside was when inundations occurred at the wrong time of year, or deposited the wrong kind of material if the deluge had been too powerful. 'Instead of a coat of manure, a thick stratum of pebbles

Floods inundating Monnow Street in Monmouth in 1929. (Monmouth Museum)

and coarse gravel is sometimes thrown up by the torrent; and I am informed, that some meadows belonging to a farmer in Herefordshire, have been very materially injured in this manner during the present winter.'[24] These instances were rare, however, and because low-lying land was almost always given over to pasture, the long-term effect of flooding was usually beneficial.

The nature of flooding depends on the changing climate. The serious floods of 1770, 1795, 1852 and even 1947 were all caused by a long freeze curtailed by a warm front that brought the substantial accumulations of snow and ice in the headwaters and tributaries down in such volume that the normal river channels were unable to cope. The flood was the culmination of a pattern of weather extending over two or three months. In future, floods seem more likely to result from extreme short-term weather events. As the climate warms scientists predict that there will be more severe storms, a perfect example of which occurred in 2007, when the river rose rapidly in summer – almost unheard of in the 18th, 19th and 20th centuries – caused simply by a few days' torrential rain.

Severe floods at the turn of the present century stimulated new investment in flood defences. Over five million pounds was spent protecting Hereford from river floods in a scheme that was completed in 2008 and comprised grass mounds and brick walls on Hinton Road and the former St Martins Quay. The walls along the quay have slots for infill panels that can be inserted in extreme circumstances. These defences are designed to protect the south side of the city, as well as the main road passing through the city from south-north across the river. Money has also been spent on strengthening the flood embankments at Hampton Bishop and Mordiford, but much attention on flood prevention has been concerned with groundwater and tributary streams. For example, in Ross severe flooding in 2000 was caused not by the Wye but by the Rudhall and

Modern flood defences erected in 2008 on the former St Martin's Quay in Hereford.

Monmouth in 1947, when supplies were distributed to the stranded by boat.
(Monmouth Museum)

Chatterley brooks that flow into it, a problem alleviated by building culverts to carry off excess water. In Hereford the Yazor Brook scheme was similar, diverting water through a 1.3 kilometre long culvert into the Wye at Credenhill, protecting the north-west side of the city from flooding. Flood marks are often placed on walls to commemorate severe episodes of flooding, as if a permanent marker is necessary to provide evidence of what, in normal times, seems unimaginable. The existence of these is referred to by authors from the 18th century onwards, and yet it is remarkable how ephemeral they turn out to be. There was once a 1947 flood marker in Dixton church. A tablet on Mr Morgan's coal wharf in Hereford marked the height of the 1795 flood, from which it could be determined that the 1852 flood rose 7 inches higher than 1826 but 18 inches below 1795.[25] These markers have long since disappeared. Society has a habit of forgetting about flooding just as the human body forgets about pain. We will continue to see floods as the river acting out of character, whereas in reality it is simply going about its natural business. The river is unpredictable. In times of flood we don't worry about drought and in times of drought we seldom put money into flood defences. As the climate changes, the long-term nature of the river flow is perhaps its greatest unknowable.

A flood high-water mark by Chepstow Bridge. Such marks were once seen in several places along the river but have been ephemeral.

12

The Deceitful Stream

One of the things that Ian Clayton always remembered about his fateful journey down the Wye in April 2006 was what a beautiful fine day it was. It is remarkable how often the river is at its most fatal when it looks most inviting. It can change as quickly as an idyllic weekend break can turn to tragedy. That was the case when the Clayton family hired their canoe at Hay-on-Wye and set off down river, enjoying what they came from Yorkshire to see: the spring sunshine, lambs in the fields, birds overhead, swans on the water. But when they turned a bend the hitherto sluggish water suddenly became fast and furious. Out of control, the boat was dashed against a fallen tree trunk and overturned, throwing the father out into the icy water, but leaving the children stranded inside the upturned wreckage. Recovering himself, and fuelled by adrenalin, Ian Clayton sought frantically to save the two children. Feeling around under the water he thought he had hold of his children's arms, but when he pulled he found it was only the arm and leg of his son, and not the boy's twin sister. His daughter was nowhere to be seen. The emergency services recovered her later and she was pronounced dead at Hereford hospital. She was only nine.[1]

This is the face of the river that we prefer not to see. But the ripples on the surface conceal powerful and unpredictable undercurrents, and the glinting water is many degrees colder than it looks. The river is both beautiful and dangerous, and the two cannot be uncoupled. The tragedy of Billie Clayton is all too familiar in the history of the river. The danger was not visible, tragedy struck in an instant and without warning, and the disorientating shock of the water hampered the rescue effort. At the inquest it emerged that the company that hired out the canoe was in its first (and last) day of trading. The briefing offered to the Clayton family about navigating the river was rudimentary and they were given no idea that the place where the tragedy happened was known to be hazardous. They also had no training in how to respond to an emergency. So Billie Clayton died on a beautiful day, as did 19-year-old Gareth Jones in the summer of the same year, a north Wales farm worker cooling off in the river by the Royal Welsh Showground at Builth Wells.

Looking at this from a historical perspective, people drowned in the 19th century for much the same reasons as those who have fallen victim to the river in the 21st century. The danger is repeatedly underestimated and the call for regulation of canoe hire that followed Billie Clayton's death is part of a long echo going back at least 200 years.

The memorial to Scott Trout by the Wye in Hereford.

As people always cry, 'Something must be done to stop these things from happening again.' On the riverside at Hereford is a memorial to Scott Trout, dedicated to him and everyone who lost their lives in the Wye. 'Don't let it be you' exclaims the memorial, set up by the Wye Drown Campaign in 1995. On Bredwardine Bridge there is a small plaque commemorating Stuart Thomson, who drowned there in 2009. As much a warning as a commemoration, it emphasises that he died 'in shallow water on a beautiful summer's day'.

The setting up of riverside memorials is nothing new. Robert Bloomfield and Charles Heath noted the memorial that remains standing near Coldwell Rocks. Sixteen-year-old John Whitefield Warre drowned on a family boating trip in 1804 after they had moored at Coldwell for a picnic. Later, John decided on a swim, never a good idea after lunch, while the crew were apparently off in the woods gathering nuts. The memorial was erected by his parents, who had watched helpless as the horror unfolded. Not just a simple memorial, it also attempted to do a public service. After extolling the virtues of the deceased, it continued: 'This monument is here erected to warn parents and others how they trust the deceitful stream; and particularly to exhort them to learn and observe the directions of the Humane Society, for the recovery of persons apparently drowned.' Details were lodged in the neighbouring Coldwell church.[2]

In 1898 the death of a young swimmer at Chepstow occasioned the coroner to advocate erecting signs to warn potential bathers of the dangers of the river, especially powerful here as the river could sweep a person out to sea or, on the flood tide, upriver. When William Thomas, 56-year-old resident of the Chepstow Union Workhouse, jumped off Chepstow Bridge in 1916 his body was recovered at Brockweir.[3]

In the 19th century inquests were held almost as soon as a body was recovered, usually at the public building nearest to the place where the body was found – which often meant a public house. This sombre duty fell to many riverside drinking places, including the Boat Inn in Stretton Sugwas, the Saracen's Head in Hereford, the Whalebone Inn at Eign, the Bunch of Carrots at Hampton Bishop, the Green Man in Fownhope, the Plough Inn at Ross, the King's Head Inn in Wilton and the Boat Inn at Chepstow. Fatalities were a part of riverside life and the local community was usually responsible for recovering the bodies. Harry Pritchard, a fisherman from Clyro, remembered a time netting for salmon near Hay-on-Wye, but fished out a dead man instead – apparently a missing local pauper who probably drowned while bathing in the river.[4] As part of his evidence at an inquest in Ross in 1862, George Davies of Monmouth added, almost as a throwaway remark, that 'I have saved many people's lives and have picked up many dead bodies in the water'. This could be deeply unpleasant. Occasionally bodies were in the water for weeks, as in the case of Thomas Dale, a private in the Shropshire Infantry, whose body was washed 31 miles downstream in two weeks in 1894 before it was recovered in Ross.[5]

The Wye was a commercial waterway and a proportion of the fatal accidents on the river were associated with barge traffic. In 1828 a barge collided with Wilton Bridge in the fog, and Joseph Thackway of New Weir was cast overboard and drowned. Captain W. Watters was wielding a pole used to lever barges off the shallows in 1809, but drowned when the pole snapped and he fell into the water. Wiliam Jenkins of Ross tried to leap from the bank to his barge at Foy in 1796 but fatally misjudged it and plunged into the river. Tragedy struck the Goodrich ferry after it became detached from the guide rope one December night in 1814 and drifted downstream, although its passengers managed to secure the boat to the bank further downstream. The ferryman had clung to the rope and eventually, having at first reached the bank, slipped and fell into the dark river.[6]

Local newspapers regularly reported drownings in the Wye in the 19th and 20th centuries; apart from revealing its dangers, these remind us of a time when there were more people by and on the river, whether in boats or in swimming costumes. The dangers of swimming in the river were – or should have been – widely known. The Herefordshire Wye might look an inviting place for a swim, but a correspondent to the *Gentleman's Magazine* in 1819 urged that its dangers were underestimated by many, especially the increasing numbers of tourists who turned up in summer. Out of the summer tourist season the Wye could be 'a tremendous torrent, eddying like the Thames at London Bridge; and the bottom is full of immense rocks upon the sides, and deep holes, some of which, called salmon-holes, are from thirty to forty feet in depth. Immersion at such a period is, even to excellent swimmers, almost certain death. The rapidity of the current prevents their making a short cut across to the bank; and the cold of the water in the winter season, mostly produces the cramp.'[7] Cramp was regularly cited until the middle of the 20th century as a cause of drowning. Today it is known as cold-water shock.

Wild swimmers on the Wye near Chepstow in the early 19th century, in a print made from a drawing by Turner. Swimming in the Wye is often more dangerous than it looks.
(Yale Center for British Art, Paul Mellon Collection)

Cold-water shock seems to have afflicted the young and fit, not just the elderly and children. Richard Edkins of Lancaut was only 20 when, on a summer evening after a hard day's labour, he and his brother decided to cool off in the river. Richard, the older brother, jumped in first but immediately sank and was never seen alive again. The inquest concluded that 'sudden immersion either caused the heart to stop or cramp ensued'. Like William Watkins, the young Glasbury station-master who drowned while swimming in 1891, it was probably not the first time Richard Edkins had swum in the Wye. But cold-water shock was not always fatal. Richard Roberts from Coventry, only 14 at the time, entered the river at Symonds Yat 'and was overcome by a cramp seizure', although he was still able to call for help and be rescued.[8]

In a period when there were no public swimming baths, the Wye was a natural place of recreation, and certainly *the* place to cool off on a hot day. Arthur Payne, visiting Ross from London in 1862, certainly thought so. While he was swimming in the river he noticed a group of four boys, none of whom, it later transpired, could swim. Having given some advice and encouragement he offered to swim across the river with one of the boys on his back. He had done this before at the seaside, so it seemed an innocuous thing to do. On the return leg, however, he suddenly tired in mid stream and turned over, at which point 11-year-old Thomas Tranter slid off and into the water. Payne tried to save him, as did men in boats who were at hand, but the boy slipped under and never surfaced again until his body was recovered. Payne reached the shore but was exhausted. Ironically, Thomas Tranter's father was downstream fishing at the time. A verdict of accidental death was returned.[9]

On a summer evening in 1863 Edward Reed discovered that, if the cold was not fatal, the current could be. With a friend he had gone from Hereford up to Belmont and swam across the river without difficulty. On his return, however, the river seemed to change and he was swept downstream by the current. Cries for help were heard on the bank and by boatmen on the water, but no one was able to save him and he was found in nine feet of water. The unpredictability of the river also accounted for a Mr Battiscombe, who was fishing at Boughrood ford in the spring of 1890. According to the reports, 'there was a freshet and the river rose rapidly', sweeping the angler away with it.[10]

Other fatalities arose from people trying to ford the river in dangerous times or swim across in the absence of a ferry or a bridge. This gives us one of the most romanticised stories of the Civil War, at the siege of Goodrich Castle in 1645, and of the River Wye. The Parliamentarian forces laying siege to the castle were led by Colonel Birch. Charles Clifford, a Royalist, and his lover Alice Birch, niece of the said Parliamentary leader, had taken refuge in the castle but were allowed to leave before hostilities commenced. Unfortunately they made their getaway at night in bad weather, and had enemy lines to avoid. In the event, they either failed to locate the ford precisely or miscalculated the depth of water at the ford. It has given Goodrich Castle a good ghost story, although it should be the river that is haunted by two figures looking for the way across.

Charles Clifford and Alice Birch have passed into local folklore and their ordeal no longer horrifies us, but there have been similar though less romantic misadventures. Lloyd Jones was employed as a driver at the Crown Livery Stables in Builth Wells and on an October evening in 1895 he took a horse and trap to escort two people back to Aberedw. On the outward journey he crossed the Wye at Builth and took the road on the east side of the river, but on the return journey he tried a short cut and decided to cross the river about a mile above Aberedw at Sciog Ford (the place is no longer marked on the Ordnance Survey maps). However, heavy rainfall had swelled the river and the depth of water at the ford, unbeknown to Jones, had risen to between five and six feet. The horse and trap were swept away. The horse was discovered on the opposite bank the next day, miraculously alive, and the trap was found by a whirlpool. Others recklessly tried to swim across the river. John Greenow had been drinking with a friend in Hereford, who admitted that they were both very drunk, when a police constable tried to arrest Greenow in the early hours of the morning for causing a public disturbance. The two scuffled and Greenow escaped, only to be pursued by the policeman. To shake of his pursuer Greenow decided to swim across the Wye.[11] There is no more deadly combination than alcohol, darkness and river.

But the most bizarre case of reckless misadventure following a drinking session is that of Ernest Bowen, a Pontypool sailor on leave who spent the day and evening drinking with friends in Brockweir. Looking for a place to spend the night he decided to head for Tintern and, as the ferry ceased operating at 10pm, decided to swim across the river instead. They found his body in six feet of water. It later transpired that, by an incredible coincidence, 21 years earlier, in 1874, his father Richard Bowen, then 32, had also drowned at Brockweir while trying to swim across the river.[12]

Most river fatalities were a consequence of boating accidents. In the 19th and early 20th centuries it was very common to see all manner of craft on the river – rowing boats, skiffs, canoes, all sorts of fishing boats and ferries. The Monmouth Grammar School's promotion of river sports for its boarding pupils was not without cost. A four-oared vessel capsized in rough water at Dixton in 1886, killing two of its crew, and during a race with Hereford Cathedral School in 1921 a boy was drowned when their boat was swamped. Many accidents occurred in bad weather when the river was more tempestuous, but the number of accidents seems also to have increased in the 19th century as more bridges were built, especially in the stretch of the river downstream of Hereford. Examples include the misadventures of experienced boatmen and of novices. William Hudson was certainly an experienced boatman. He regularly took to his small flat-bottomed boat and took up position in the river besides the football ground at Redbrook (where there is still a recreation area), which was so close to the river that the corner flag was only five yards from the bank. On one December Saturday in 1909 he was coming to the railway bridge by the Boat Inn, where his craft struck one of the piers and broke up in the fast flowing water. Both he and his young son were drowned.[13]

A similar fate befell the Crawley family in 1899, after hiring a vessel from Fullers landing stage in Monmouth for an excursion down the Wye. The boatman was James Smith, 70 years old and experienced on the river – in 1890 he had rescued two people from drowning at Chepstow. The boat struck one of the bridge piers at Tintern and rapidly filled up with water. Mr and Mrs Crawley and their daughter Elizabeth were swept downstream to their deaths. Two other daughters, and another passenger named

The piers of Redbrook bridge, which the boat carrying William and Harold Hudson struck in 1909, with fatal consequences.

Arthur Studd of London, managed to get to the river bank. Smith clung to the wreckage for over an hour before he was rescued. Nearly two years later something similar happened to a boat hired by two ladies from Ross. After passing through the bridge at Tintern the boat capsized and, although the ladies managed to get ashore, the boatman, Richard Thomas, clung to the wreckage until his strength left him, and he drowned.[14]

Given that experienced boatmen could come to grief passing under the bridges, it is perhaps surprising that someone with no experience was allowed to hire a vessel and take it on to the river, but there seem to have been no health and safety regulations to save people from themselves. In 1861 a works outing to Monmouth was arranged for employees of the West Midland Railway in Hereford. Six of them decided to make the journey by water, and hired a 40-foot out-rigger named the *Fawn* from Hereford. At Monmouth it all went wrong. 'They got to within thirty or forty yards of Wye-bridge when by the force of the current, or some unskilfulness possibly in the steering of the boat, the out-rigger became entangled in a crevice at the pier of the bridge and they were unable to free themselves from this position. The current ran very strong at the time, and forcing the boat against the bridge broke it in two pieces, and they were all immersed in the water. Boats were immediately launched, and every assistance rendered but unfortunately John Wall (29), Henry Prowley (17), and Henry Harris (45) sank to rise no more alive.'[15]

A common cause of accidents among inexperienced river people was upsetting the boat when changing places. At Ross in 1902 that seems to have been enough to tip

The River Wye at Tintern. Many accidents have happened in small boats crossing the river after dark.

Catherine Smith-Wood overboard while her sister looked on in horror. Catherine told her sister that it would be easier for her to swim to the bank than to try to climb back in the boat while it was in mid stream, but she was fatally mistaken. Something similar may have caused Alfred Davies to fall overboard when he was on a boat one Sunday afternoon at Chepstow in the spring of 1879.[16]

These kinds of accidents were always more fatal at night. Moreover, in the darkness it was not always possible to establish why a vessel had sunk, especially if the experienced crew perished. Four fishermen were on board a small boat that capsized before dawn one January morning near Builth, one of them drowning. At Hampton Bishop in 1902 William Lydiatt, a local farmer, was one of two men who drowned in a boating accident on the way home on the river on a Sunday night; two other men were rescued by people at the Bunch of Carrots Inn. In the previous year Albert Mansell and John Harris, two Birmingham holiday-makers, wanted to cross the river late at night at Symonds Yat, long after the ferryman had gone home. They hired Edward Jarrett, a 20-year-old local man, to row them across the river, but of the three of them only Harris made it to the opposite bank. Whether alcohol was involved in any of these incidents is anyone's guess.[17]

A similar nocturnal tragedy befell one of the river's most experienced boatmen in 1855. Edmund Crompton took a skiff upriver one October evening to the home at Belmont of Mr Wegg-Prosser, owner of a pleasure steamer that Crompton managed. On the return, after 11 o'clock, the journey was uneventful until they reached Hunderton. Apparently, Crompton stood up in the boat and it unexpectedly capsized (or perhaps the boat struck the new railway bridge). Crompton and his young nephew, both good swimmers, reached safety, albeit on opposite banks of the river, but Crompton's wife perished. The tragedy must have played on Crompton's mind, but less than a year later he won a race in punts at the Hereford Regatta, which took place on the same stretch of river between Hunderton and Wye Bridge.[18]

Not everybody who drowned in the river did so by accident. People seek out the river for pleasure, but they are also drawn to it in times of despair. Perhaps they hoped that the water would wash them away as if cleansing them from the world; perhaps it was a subliminal way of surrendering themselves to nature; or perhaps there were just few other practical ways that they could end their own lives. But without a suicide note, there is always a mystery about apparently self-inflicted drownings. At the inquest in the Plough Inn at Ross in 1877, witnesses claimed that Mr Organ was in low spirits before his disappearance and eventual discovery in the river. His widow, who was at first too intoxicated to give evidence, later testified that he had given her all of his money before leaving the house. A policeman traced his route upstream and found his final footprints in the muddy river bank, but the coroner was still not wholly convinced that he had taken his own life, which was a felony in Victorian Britain. A verdict of 'found drowned' was reached, which was the river equivalent of an open verdict. There were many similar cases – William Preece was found floating in the river in 1881 at Stretton Sugwas, and Jacob Huggins, known to be 'ill' and observed to have been behaving 'oddly', drowned at Wilton in 1893, to name but two.[19]

If the river offered oblivion for those who needed the ultimate way out, only occasionally do we get an inkling of the reason. An inquest was held at the Blue Boar in Hay-on-Wye in 1870 into the death of one of its barmaids, who went out one night as far as Glasbury where she threw herself in the river. Only afterwards was it discovered that she was pregnant. James Phillips, a Boer War veteran, hired a boat at Hereford in the summer of 1902 and rowed himself upstream. The river became a metaphor for ending his life, as if by stepping off dry land he had left his life behind and once on the water had entered a separate realm. He was found a day later, still in his boat on the water, with a self-inflicted gunshot wound.[20]

✎ 13 ✎
The Wye Tour

'A succession of nameless wonders', and 'the most beautiful I ever beheld' were the responses of Thomas Gray and Bishop Richard Pococke, just two voices among many who celebrated the scenery of the Wye valley in the 18th century. The Wye was a phenomenon, praised in guide books and poems, paintings and engravings, making it one of the first recognised tourist destinations in Britain. There was a well established Wye Tour by boat from Ross to Chepstow, founded by John Egerton (1722-1787), the Rector of Ross who moved to the town in 1745 (and later became the bishop of Bangor, Lichfield and then Durham). Egerton and his wife were a wealthy, well-connected and sociable couple who had plenty of free time to welcome numerous guests. Egerton had a pleasure boat built in order to host excursions down the Wye, an idea that quickly caught on. Soon there were boats for hire and inns offering accommodation for the newly fashionable Wye Tour. But by no means did every visitor to the Wye take the established river cruise. Many others travelled by road, or made a journey upstream from Chepstow. Even without a 'Wye Tour', people would have come here.

Several elements coincided to make Wye tourism a phenomenon. Britain had long been a place of travellers – in the Middle Ages they were pilgrims – but a strain of writing emerged after the 16th-century Reformation of the church and the union of England and Wales in 1536, that set out to discover, describe and praise the hinterland of Britain. By the 17th century the 'bare ruined choirs' of the old monasteries that had been shut down in the 1530s were beginning to stimulate curiosity about the past. William Dugdale published the first volume of his *Monasticon Anglicanum* in 1655, intended to be a record of the nation's monastic ruins before they were entirely lost. Old abbeys shared with crumbling castles the notion of lost greatness, and a strain of writing emerged that emphasised the historical dimension of Britain through the medium of its ruins. Artists followed this trend with the publication of topographical prints. Samuel and Nathaniel Buck toured the country in the 1730s and early 1740s, issuing engravings of England and Wales. Castles and old abbeys were their stock-in-trade, categories in which the Wye valley excelled.

Landscape painting, particularly the work of continental painters such as Claude Lorrain and Salvator Rosa, together with the fashion for picturesque landscape parks inspired a taste for rural scenery, and especially dramatic scenery. In Britain, artists such as John Boydell (1720-1804) and Paul Sandby (1731-1809) published prints that opened the public's eyes to the scenic attractions of Wales for the first time. But the pre-eminent reputation of the Wye for seekers of picturesque scenery owed most to the writer and aesthete William Gilpin (1724-1804), whom we will meet later.

The 18th century saw the first generation of travellers who called themselves tourists. Economic prosperity gave the rich plenty of leisure time, while books and prints made

Tintern Abbey was admired not just as scenery but as an important antiquity, a relic of the Catholic past of England and Wales. This view was published by William Coxe in 1801.

them curious, but it was not simply aristocrats and the middle class who took the Wye Tour. Plenty of them were under-employed clergymen, like Richard Warner (1763-1857) of Bath and Stebbing Shaw (1762-1802) of Hartshorne in Derbyshire. The Wye Tour grew in popularity just when tourism began in the wilder margins of Britain, most of which are now National Parks. The advantage of the River Wye as a tourist destination was its relative accessibility. Other competing regions like the Peak District, the Lake District, North Wales and the Scottish Highlands, were all much more remote.

The taste for antiquities and rural scenery also coincided with the Celtic Revival, the period when people started taking an interest in Britain's ancient past. For the English especially, the ancient Britons, or Celts, were Britain's version of classical antiquity. Thomas Gray's poem 'The Bard' appeared in 1757 during the Seven Years War and, despite the fact that the bard in question was standing defiant against the invasion of Edward I, Gray appropriated the figure as an emblem of British independence and an important figure in the origin of British national identity. Plenty of tourists visited Wales then, and even more of them did during the years of war with France between 1793 and 1815. A Celtic Grand Tour replaced its European counterpart, and thrived until the continent was safe again for English travellers.

The Wye Tour emerged in the 1750s, at around the time that Castle Green became a recreation area in Hereford and after the Prospect had been created in Ross-on-Wye – so local people clearly already enjoyed the river, although from comments in the journals of visitors we gather that Wye tourists liked to think that the locals were oblivious to the beauties around them. But through the Wye Tour, the Wye came to be appreciated as part of our national culture – and of course the local economy benefited from the influx of visitors. Inns began to cater for tourists as the tour gained in popularity, and watermen learned the places on the river that visitors appreciated most. Richard Warner stayed at the Beaufort Arms in Tintern (though he got little sleep in the sweltering heat), described as a very comfortable inn kept by the village antiquary, Mr Gething. Charles Heath recommended the Swan, the King's Head and the George in Ross, and the Beaufort Arms, the King's Head and the Crown and Thistle in Monmouth. The Royal Hotel in Ross was built in 1837 specifically to cater for river tourists.

One could start one's Wye Tour from Ross-on-Wye, which was the best known of the Tour centres, and embark on a two-day excursions to Chepstow. Alternatively, for those who just wanted to see Tintern Abbey, the journey upstream from Chepstow was quicker and could be timed to take advantage of the incoming tide. Most visitors took the tour by boat. The land route between Ross and Chepstow was hardly conducive to sightseeing since the road did not follow the riverside and the road network was notoriously poor, and sometimes dangerous – the heir to the first duke of Beaufort died in a coach accident near Troy House by Monmouth in 1698 and there were no improvements to the road in the decades that followed. Tintern was not served by a decent road until the 1820s, and the road from Ross to Monmouth did not enjoy the comparative luxury of Kerne Bridge, replacing the Walford ferry, until 1828. Even at this time, however, there were determined walkers, like the Reverend Richard Warner of Bath, whose journey down the Wye in 1797 was part of a longer walk around Wales. In places the road was actually a quicker route, much more direct than the meandering Wye. The distance between Goodrich and the ferry near Whitchurch called Hunson's Rope was a mile over land but seven miles by water.[1]

But the main reason why the tour was conducted by river was that the best way to enjoy the scenery was from a boat. Archdeacon William Coxe described his journey on the road from Chepstow to Monmouth, in which he was frustrated by 'extensive forests, among which the Wye winds, unseen, in a profound abyss'.[2] But there were other, unexpected pleasures in viewing the world from a boat. Passing Wilton Castle William Gilpin admired the ruins 'and also the vivid images reflected from the water; which were continually disturbed, as we sailed past them; and thrown into tremulous confusion, by the dashing of our oars'.[3]

New boats were constructed especially to serve the tourist market. According to Charles Heath's guide book, by 1808 there were eight vessels offering excursions down-river from Ross. In 1787 the Honourable John Byng was rowed downstream in a boat spacious enough to accommodate 14 passengers in addition to its crew of three, on a deck that was carpeted and featured a dining table. The steersman often doubled as a guide. George Evans, who spent decades on the river, was one of the crew of John Egerton's original boat that launched the Wye Tour, and was later accorded the honorary title Commodore. The level of comfort on board was improved over the decades. The earliest boats were open to the elements, but by 1807 A.M. Cuyler could describe

Two pleasure boats make their way toward Goodrich Castle in this view by Thomas Hearne (1744-1817) of 1785. (Yale Center for British Art, Paul Mellon Collection)

his tour vessel as a 'house-boat', covered over and with windows in the sides. In the 1830s Thomas Roscoe likened his 'light bark' to a gondola, 'when its tarpauling cover was spread over the framework; but, being favoured by a radiantly bright morning, I preferred sitting under the skeleton ... a table in the centre of the part allotted to passengers, and cushioned seats around, made this small floating parlour a most commodious conveyance'.[4] When Richard Colt Hoare travelled down the river in 1797 the journey from Ross to Monmouth and from Monmouth to Chepstow was £1/11/6 for each stretch, with 10 shillings 'for waterman's victuals'. Colt Hoare was more generous to the watermen than he had been to the poor occupants of Tintern Abbey, whom he wanted removed. 'The men were well satisfied with the 10/6 I gave them extra' to his fare from Monmouth to Chepstow.[5]

A voyage by river was not always smooth. Tour boats had a shallow draught, but even so occasionally they grounded on shoals in dry weather and had to be pushed off manually or levered into deeper water with punts. When the river level was low in summer the boat sat on the water at a much lower level, impeding the view of the interesting features on the banks. At other times a strong current could make sections of the excursion overly hasty, as Samuel Ireland found when leaving Tintern, when his lingering view of the ruins was curtailed by the breeze and tide. More often than not, however, the journey was slow. The full Tour from Ross to Chepstow could be done in nine hours in theory, but that was without stopping to admire and embark at places of interest. The Wye Tour was therefore more satisfying if it was made into a two-day excursion. As soon

'On the River Wye with Wilton Castle ruins' by John Glover, after 1794.
(Yale Center for British Art, Paul Mellon Collection)

as the road from Monmouth to Chepstow was completed many visitors took the coach instead. And if the downstream journey was slow it was at least aided by the current, until about 10 miles from Chepstow where the effect of the tide began to be felt. Away from the influence of the tide the upstream journey was a slog, the two oarsmen having to row against the current, and where the current was especially strong, more strength was needed. Below New Weir, for example, the strength of the current often meant that eight to ten men were needed to haul a boat upstream.[6]

The scenic highlights of the Wye tour were well established. It began with Wilton Castle, then Goodrich Castle, Coldwell Rocks, Symonds Yat and New Weir on the first day to Monmouth; Tintern and Piercefield Park were the highlights of the second day to Chepstow. After Ross, which had little of special interest for the traveller, Wilton Castle was an early foretaste of things to come. For Richard Warner it 'lends its ruins to add to the variety, and heighten the beauty of the magic scenery of this place'. Not everyone was impressed, however. 'A modern house built in the middle of the old ruins – dreadful!', sneered Richard Colt Hoare – he was quite an accomplished sneerer.[7] By contrast, Goodrich Castle had reverted to nature by the 18th century. Trees had colonised the interior, and its overgrown appearance made it an ideal place to contemplate the ravages of time and the vanities of human endeavour. For Warner, the ivy-clad ruins, 'the crumbling turrets of the massive walls, and the waving heads of the surrounding

Inside Goodrich Castle in 1788, by John Webber (1751-1793), an artist best known for accompanying Captain Cook on his third Pacific expedition.
(Yale Center for British Art, Paul Mellon Collection)

wood, reflecting a reciprocal charm on each other, form a combination extremely agreeable to the imagination, and impressive to the mind'.[8] The castle occupies a hilltop position above the river, which for visitors meant landing and making the trek up the slope. Some preferred to view it from a distance – after all, it was its commanding presence on a rock that people came to see, not the mouldings of its weathered doorways and chimneypieces. In any case, the ferry house offered refreshments, and this enjoyed just as much trade as the crumbling old ruins on the hill.

Further downstream the river meandered to Coldwell Rocks, an ideal picnic spot where there were large rocks that the boatmen, presumably in the hope of earning tips, christened after their distinguished passengers. Robert Bloomfield, then a famous poet, was particularly chuffed to hear that one of the rocks was to be named after him, if only for one day. He and his party stayed afloat at Coldwell to enjoy their lunch in the summer of 1807.

> Here, in one gay according mind,
> Upon the sparkling stream we din'd;
> As shepherds free on mountain heath,
> Free as the fish that watch'd beneath
> For falling crumbs, where cooling lay
> The wine that cheer'd us on our way.[9]

From Coldwell there was a four mile journey by boat to New Weir. Alternatively, the more energetic could go on foot up to the top of Symonds Yat to admire the view, and then descend to the boat again at New Weir. The weir itself was not high, but enough to be labelled a cascade by William Gilpin and others. Robert Bloomfield enjoyed shooting the rapids of the cascade after his lunch at Coldwell Rocks:

> Here rush'd the keel like lightning by;
> The helmsman watch'd with anxious eye;
> And oars alternate touch'd the brim,
> To keep the flying boat in trim.[10]

The other item of interest at New Weir was the forge. Perceptive visitors would already have noticed the charcoal burners in the woods and the carts delivering charcoal. This was a period when industry was by no means regarded as an eyesore, but fascinated the leisured classes for whom heat, smoke and noise were quite exotic. Several industrial scenes were interspersed with the more conventional scenic highlights of the river. Samuel Ireland's description of Lydbrook wharf, which tourists passed after leaving Goodrich, expressed the same satisfaction that Daniel Defoe would have felt in the 1720s. 'With all the dark and dingy attributes of this place, involved as it is smoke, and begirt with coal barges, it yet affords a very pleasing and interesting landscape. The high road that ascends the woody hill, screening the background of this wharf, is perpetually enlivened by horses and carriages in this sooty and sable commerce, while on the bank of the river beneath, the lading and unlading the vessels, afford additional business and variety to the scene.'[11] New Weir forge stood on the opposite bank to the towpath and the lock, so the more curious visitors would have to wait until they reached Tintern on the second day of their excursion if they wanted to see the operation of a forge close at hand. Tintern forge had many visitors, at a time when curious tourists could gain access to industrial buildings and see the arcane metallurgical trades at work. Few of them seem to have understood what they saw, instead coming away with their preconceptions confirmed. Richard Warner, visiting Tintern in 1797, fell back on his classical education. 'We saw Virgil's description realized, and the interior of Etna, the forges of the Cyclops, and their fearful employment, immediately occurred to us.'[12] References to mythological smiths like Cyclops and Vulcan were among the clichés of contemporary guide books.

The labouring classes were often seen as an enhancement to the general scenery, especially if they were in coracles. As Charles Heath noted, whether they were iron workmen or fishermen, 'all the employments of the people seem to require either exertion or caution; and the ideas of force or of danger which attend them, give to the scene an animation unknown to a solitary, though perfectly compatible with the wildest romantic situations'.[13] The workmen at New Weir Forge lived in scattered dwellings

Tintern Abbey viewed from the east, showing the ferry and old slipway by the Anchor Inn where tourists disembarked, from Frederick Calbert's 'Four views of Tintern Abbey', 1815. (British Library)

by the winding road that brought charcoal to the forge. 'The little cottages ... the neat residences of industrious labour, form a pleasing accompaniment; exhibiting simplicity contrasted with majesty.'[14] Apart from Tintern, there were more industrial scenes below Monmouth, including the forge and tinplate works at Redbrook and a paper mill at Whitebrook. Occasionally however, industrial plant marred the scene, as when lime kilns were erected close to the river near Coldwell. Charles Heath claimed that 'the effluvia from it is not only disagreeable in itself, but obscures by its smoke the appearance, in some places, of those beautiful greens, with which the rocks are cloathed'.[15]

Further downstream the scenery became more dramatic, especially near journey's end at Chepstow, and here the best way to appreciate the scenery was from a boat: 'The views from the Wye are exceedingly magnificent; the rocks on each seem to be from 300 to 600 feet high; they are sometimes perpendicular and wholly naked, and sometimes the very precipices are covered with wood.'[16]

However, Tintern Abbey was *the* highlight of the Wye Tour, and Samuel Ireland felt no need to temper his enthusiasm for it: 'Approaching this sublime and sequestered spot, the enthusiastic lover of simplicity in art and nature, the admirer of the picturesque and beautiful, the antiquary and the moralist will feel the effect, as it were, of enchantment, and become lost almost in a pleasing melancholy.'[17] Even so, the abbey ruins were hardly ready to receive visitors when the Tour gained in popularity in the mid 18th century. The site, overgrown with scrub and trees, was apparently the repository of all kinds of rubbish, and what open space remained was used as a fives court. What was worse, the abbey ruins were home to an indigent community, a mini shanty town that in turns moved and irritated the passing trade. Tintern Abbey was owned by the duke of Beaufort, who in 1756 employed a contractor from Chepstow to clean up the ruins a little and grass over the interior. It made the ruins accessible, and there was already a convenient landing stage by the original Watergate, where the ferry operated.

As the abbey stands close to the river bank many more people visited its lofty interior than walked up to Goodrich Castle. By 1793 Tintern was so popular that it warranted a guide book of its own, published by Charles Heath. It was also one of the first heritage attractions to be under lock and key. Its custodian was Mr Gething of the Beaufort Arms although, despite stopping there overnight in 1797, Richard Warner still had trouble tracking down the key.

The management of Tintern Abbey introduced a conundrum. What was important about a Gothic ruin, the Gothic or the ruin? Today that has been answered emphatically, because we value historical remains first and foremost as evidence. In the 18th century, however, travellers were more ambivalent about the clean up, with varying opinions on whether ruins should be valued as history or romance. Henry Penruddocke Wyndham liked what the duke of Beaufort had done. 'The present remains are carefully preserved from further destruction, while the fallen ornaments of its once vaulted roof, and the broken monuments of ancient abbots and benefactors, are so disposed in moderate piles, that all their sculpture ... may be inspected with the utmost facility.'[18] Later the duke erected high-level iron railings so that visitors could climb the mural stairs and walk the gallery above the arcades.

Visitors took an antiquarian interest in the place and wanted to appreciate its architecture, but they also delighted in a ruin 'roofed only by the vault of heaven'. After all, there were lots of ruined abbeys to be seen, but none (bar perhaps Fountains Abbey in Yorkshire) in such a romantic situation. And different people saw different things. Where Wyndham had seen order Samuel Ireland delighted in disorder: 'the various ruinated fragments of capitals and pillars below, which lie scattered indiscriminately and in part overgrown and buried in beds of wild flowers, [that] create an interesting disorder'.[19] Unsurprisingly, therefore, he thought that 'the smooth and trim manner' in which the ground was kept was incongruous with the picturesque chaos. The ivy that clothed the walls was often singled out for comment. 'Nature … as if to render the ruin compleat, has taken abundant pains in decorating its columns and walls with a profuse coating of ivy.'[20] Sir Richard Colt Hoare took a different view when visiting in 1797: 'In some parts I think the ivy conceals too much of the building, as none of the architecture or stonework can be distinguished.' But there was worse: 'many shabby cottages which surround the abbey diminish much from the grand appearance which it would assume' if the duke of Beaufort had removed them and the orchards when he cleaned up the site. A year later and he had not changed his mind. The abbey was 'so surrounded with ragged cottages and orchards that half of its height is completely hidden by them'.[21]

Philippe Jacques de Loutherbourg's view of Tintern Abbey, published in 1805, makes a virtue of the poor community living by the ruins, turning the place into an idyll of simple rusticity.

A view of the ivy-clad interior of Tintern Abbey by Thomas Sunderland (1744-1823).
(Yale Center for British Art, Paul Mellon Collection)

Thomas Sunderland's view of the west window Tintern Abbey.
(Yale Center for British Art, Paul Mellon Collection)

The approach to Tintern Abbey by river was marred for some visitors by the cottages built
in front of it, seen here in an 1850 print in one of the early Bradshaw's Guides.
(Yale Center for British Art, Paul Mellon Collection)

In Robert Taylor's engraving of Tintern, published in 1854,
the ruins stand in well-maintained parkland.

Nearly 40 years later Thomas Roscoe was still complaining about 'the low miserable cottages that surround' the abbey.[22]

As time went on the vegetation was controlled to a greater extent and the shanty town disappeared, so by the time Francis Kilvert went there in the 1870s it was quite a different place from what it had been a hundred years previously. 'One wants a little more ruin and ivy', according to Francis Kilvert, and 'the long line of the building should be broken by trees', but he was luckier than he perhaps realised in having the place to himself for most of his visit.[23] Tintern Abbey was one of the first sites to be taken into the guardianship of the state following the passing in 1913 of the Ancient Monuments Consolidation and Amendment Act.

Below Tintern the main attractions were Piercefield Park, which was open only on certain days after 1794, and then Chepstow, where there were several points of interest, chiefly the castle, but also the unusual timber bridge, the former priory, which had been converted to the parish church, and the bustling wharf. Here the tour ended for most, although Samuel Ireland carried on and sailed to the mouth of the Wye, where the whole character of the river changed: this was a place 'where we found the tide uncommonly rapid, and where if the wind is brisk, the waters are troublesomely rough'.[24]

Piercefield was a popular place for artists like Edward Dayes (1763-1804), giving extensive views over the river, here toward the confluence with the Severn. (Yale Center for British Art, Paul Mellon Collection)

The appeal of Chepstow for the Wye tourists was that it was a place of castle, bridge and boats, depicted here by Samuel Ireland in 1794.

Chepstow Castle by Edward Francis Burney (1760-1848).
(Yale Center for British Art, Paul Mellon Collection)

The ruins of Chepstow Castle, as portrayed by Philippe Jacques de Loutherbourg
(1740-1812) in his *Romantic and Picturesque Scenery of England and Wales* (1805).
The castle is portrayed as a part of a rural scene, completely ignoring
the bustling small town that would greet the viewer by looking left.

A pencil sketch of Chepstow by the Irish artist Francis Danby (1793-1861).
(Yale Center for British Art, Paul Mellon Collection)

The entrance to Chepstow Castle by Paul Sandby (1730-1809),
one version of a well-known print that was first published in 1777.
(Yale Center for British Art, Paul Mellon Collection)

Visitors travelled for a variety of reasons, claimed William Gilpin in 1782, including the desire to view antiquities, the beauties of nature and the manners and customs of other people. But he added a new dimension that elevated the Wye Tour to a leading cultural phenomenon, by proposing a new object of pursuit: 'that of examining the face of a country by the rules of picturesque beauty'. Gilpin published his *Observations on the River Wye* 12 years after he made a journey there in 1770, by which time he had left his post as headmaster of Cheam School and was vicar of Boldre in Hampshire. Gilpin's aesthetic manifesto was greatly respected by some but was soon also mocked in his own day and has been criticised ever since. He attempted to view the countryside in terms of a painting, to put a three-dimensional experience into a two-dimensional one, and place himself always as the onlooker, leaving the places he visited as separate objects. In other words, he looked at, but never inhabited the places he visited and the elements that made up his picturesque landscapes were essentially ornamental.

In general, the Wye offered plenty of picturesque views, but they had to conform to quite rigid guide lines. 'Every view on a river ... is composed of four grand parts; the area, which is the river itself; the two side-screens, which are the opposite banks, and mark the perspective; and the front-screen, which points out the winding of the river.'[25] In practice Gilpin argued that by framing the landscape with such simple elements, it was possible to appreciate a variety of picturesque scenery on the Wye below Ross.

The four elements, or 'ornaments', of the landscape were ground, wood, rocks and buildings, each of which contributed to the scenery. The Wye is noted for its wood, but it was a pity for Gilpin that the trees never overhung the river banks, which would have obstructed the navigation. Although the eye can range around the natural scenery, for picturesque purposes a scene needs a focal point, and this is why Gilpin thought that artists needed a building in their picture, to 'give consequence to the scene'.[26]

The imposition of strict rules on landscape was a recipe for noticing imperfections. At Ross the view from the churchyard 'consists of an easy sweep of the Wye; and of an extensive country beyond it. But it is not picturesque.' The view of Goodrich Castle might have been 'one of the grandest on the river', but alas 'I should not scruple to call [it] correctly picturesque'. The views from the Wyndcliff were not properly picturesque because the vantage point was too high. At Tintern, 'though the parts are beautiful, the whole is ill-shaped' and 'a number of gabel-ends hurt the eye with their regularity', which could easily be rectified if anyone had the courage to do it: 'A mallet judiciously used … might be of service in fracturing some of them.' Some of the scenes that he did endorse as properly picturesque probably surprised (or baffled) his readers. The coal wharf at Lydbrook, for example, was all bustle with horses and carts following the road down to the waterfront where small vessels were loaded. All this was set against a woody background, producing 'all together a picturesque assemblage'.[27]

Gilpin was criticised for his overly prescriptive approach and it was widely noticed that the pictures that adorned his book were some of the most uninteresting views of

Samuel Palmer's (1805-1881) 1835 watercolour of Tintern Abbey.
(Yale Center for British Art, Paul Mellon Collection)

Wye scenery in print. In 1809 a satirical title, *The Tour of Dr Syntax in Search of the Picturesque*, was published by Thomas Rowlandson and William Combe, mocking the pomposity and absurdity of Gilpin's manifesto. In the long term Gilpin has come to look like a man of his own times. His book is written for people like him, classically educated men who did not need their Latin quotes translated. He implicitly assumed that only a person of education would have the wherewithal to appreciate the Wye scenery, and he was not alone in this. When he met a disabled old woman at Tintern, 'shuffling along her palsied limbs, and meagre, contracted body, by the help of two sticks', he was horrified by the makeshift home she had made for herself in the old cloisters. She showed him the remains of the old library, and he was surprised that he found her engaging. He sympathised with her plight, but it never occurred to him that the poor woman might also have derived pleasure from the beauty of the place.[28]

People may have disagreed with him but Gilpin did make contemporary artists and travellers think about what they were looking at and why they liked it. He was an aesthetic disciplinarian, and there was value in that. And he was also revered for many years as the author of the most authoritative guide to the Wye Tour. Charles Heath acknowledged Gilpin's contribution to the popularity of the Wye Tour, since people wanted to experience for themselves the places he described in his *Observations*.

Gilpin also influenced the numerous artists, both amateur and professional, who travelled down the Wye filling their sketchbooks with the standard scenes. There was a market for topographical prints of the Wye and some professional artists even travelled with writers, like Samuel Hieronymus Grimm, who travelled through Wales via the Wye valley with Henry Penruddocke Wyndham in 1774. In this period prints were published individually or in series, making the highlights of the Wye Tour yet more widely known. It was a period in which the topographical drawing was superseded by landscape painting in watercolours, and a gallery of Wye views could chart a transition

In Samuel Palmer's 'Tintern Abbey at Sunset' of 1861 the place has become a landscape of the imagination, very different from what the place really looked like.
(Yale Center for British Art, Paul Mellon Collection)

from the Buck brothers' engravings of the 1730s, through the rise of print makers like Paul Sandby to romantic painters like Samuel Palmer.

The subject matter was surprisingly limited, however. Pictures of Goodrich, New Weir, Chepstow, the view from Wyndcliff and especially Tintern dominate. It is difficult to find a purely natural scene among the catalogue of works created in this period. Even those views that show stretches of river without buildings are invariably given a human context by a boat, a fisherman or a party enjoying a picnic. Only later, with artists like Turner and Samuel Palmer, did artists become less interested in depicting the real places they were visiting than in transforming what they saw before them into landscapes of the imagination.

Drawing was fashionable and the boat was an ideal place for sitting and sketching. One such amateur artist, Margaret Martineau, was surprised to discover that one of the crew was an accomplished artist himself – indeed, better than she was, despite the gulf between his social class and her own. She was gracious in acknowledging his talent: 'It seemed odd to hear our boatman recommending me to attempt something more than pencil and to see him standing over me when I was sketching and telling me that I was beginning it too large. He was a very intelligent young man.'[29] Sketchers were the amateur photographers of their day, but they could interpret the landscape in a very critical way. Sir Richard Colt Hoare was especially choosy. At Goodrich he encountered the castle 'on an eminence surrounded by trees, rather too much so for drawing'. A better view could be had by crossing the river, although he did concede that the interior 'presents some picturesque studies'.[30] At Chepstow he thought the bridge was a better subject for the pencil than the castle ruins.

The Wye Tour produced a large body of literature, from guide books and verses to major literary works such as William Gilpin's *Observations* and Wordsworth's 'Lines Written above Tintern Abbey'. Much of the literature is derivative, and even William Gilpin based some of his descriptions on previous work by Thomas Whately. With the exception of Wordsworth, whose poem we shall meet later, the Wye poetry of the period has never been highly regarded. Robert Bloomfield, who had made a name for himself as a 'peasant poet', took the Wye Tour with friends in 1807, visiting scenery that he had never before witnessed, but *The Banks of the Wye* is little more than a guide book in verse form. Earlier, in 1786 Edward Davies, vicar of Mathern, had published his *Chepstow: a poem in six cantos*, which was lighter than it sounds and was less a work of high culture than a useful guide for visitors to Tintern from Chepstow. Later in the 19th century the personal impressions of Wye tourists, many of whom visited the area as part of longer tours of Wales, gave way to more practical guide books, such as Nicholson's *Cambrian Traveller's Guide* and John Murray's *Handbook for Travellers*.

Practical guide books to the Wye had been pioneered by local men: Charles Heath set himself up in Monmouth as a printer and publisher and issued the first edition of his *Excursion down the Wye from Ross to Monmouth* in 1791. He followed it with other guides to Monmouth and Tintern. Mark Willett, a Chepstow publisher brought up in Tintern, published *An Excursion from the source of the Wye* in 1810, and T.D. Fosbroke, vicar of Walford, published the first edition of *The Wye Tour* in 1818. Heath filled his pages with

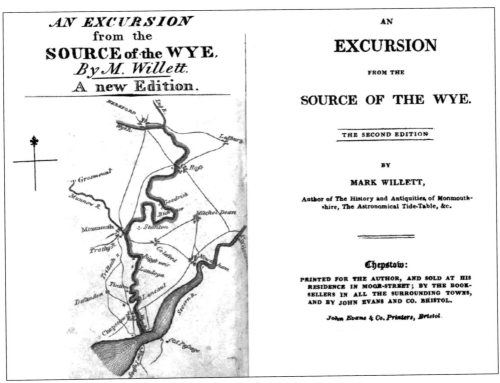

Title page and frontispiece of Mark Willett's *An Excursion from the source of the Wye*, published in Chepstow in 1810.

sober and practical advice, descriptions of Wye scenery that deferred to Gilpin, quotations from the poets, and a smattering of history drawn from leading antiquaries. Plenty of the places he described, however, were distant from the river itself, so it could be used as a guide to the region rather than the riverside. Detours to places like Raglan Castle were not unknown. Likewise, Fosbroke quoted Gilpin at length and gave background information on the antiquities on the Tour. The first edition of his guide was published in 1818 and by 1834 he had followed Mark Willett's lead and expanded it to take in the upper river, thereby moving on from the confines of the river tour.

Guide books continued to be published throughout the 19th century, but the character of the Wye Tour changed over that period. The heyday of the Celtic Grand Tour had come to an end in the peace that followed Waterloo. Road improvements in the 1820s made travelling by river less essential and the increase in traffic made the Wye valley busier than it had previously been. Kerne Bridge replaced the old Walford ferry and a new iron bridge was built downstream at Bigsweir. Then came the railway. Trains not only made it easier to reach the Wye valley, which lost some of its mystique in the process, but they also required the construction of many more bridges over the river. Just below Monmouth were the Duke of Beaufort Bridge and Monmouth Viaduct, a little further down was Redbrook Bridge, and there were girder bridges at Tintern, all

Chepstow railway bridge in the late 19th century,
as a pleasure steamer makes its way upstream.

of which eroded the illusion of timelessness on the river. In 1822 steam-boats began a regular service from Bristol to Chepstow and so Ross began to decline as the starting point of the tour. The railways improved access to the Wye from central England and Gloucester became an alternative starting point of many tours. The Wye Tour was conceived as a journey by river, but today it is only a novel way of seeing what can easily be seen in other ways. And there were other parts of the river that were hitherto largely undiscovered. As early 1797 Samuel Ireland recognised that the stretch between Ross and Chepstow covered less than a third of the course of the Wye. The upper river was also worth exploring, and had the advantage that descriptions of its scenery were less familiar, it was a less crowded place, and offered more satisfaction for the independent-minded traveller.

❧ 14 ❧
For King and Country Men

On Castle Green in Hereford is the Nelson Column, erected after the victory at Trafalgar in 1805, a smaller version of the more famous memorial in London, crowned by an urn rather than a statue. A riverside site in Herefordshire might at first seem an odd place to celebrate a national triumph, but there are many examples of commemorative structures on or overlooking rivers. At the end of Castle Green is the Victoria Bridge, erected to celebrate Victoria's 1897 Diamond Jubilee, and millennium bridges are found in many places across Britain. The Nelson Column was erected during the heyday of the Wye Tour, which coincided with the period of the Revolutionary and Napoleonic Wars with France, between 1793 and 1815. In this period the landscape of the Wye, more than any other place, was a canvas for reactionary and radical politics, and also a symbol of national unity that was to be eclipsed by the modern prevailing notion of landscape as personal memory and reflection.

The Nelson Column erected on Castle Green in Hereford in 1809.

Victoria Bridge, erected in Hereford to commemorate the Diamond Jubilee of
Queen Victoria, and linking Castle Green with Bishops Meadow.

The Union Jack on the cliff opposite Chepstow, originally painted for the
Silver Jubilee of King George V in 1935, next to the Gloucester Hole,
the small opening to a much larger underground chamber.

Rivers are natural expressions of nationhood, flowing as they do over such large areas of land, and they were once celebrated as repositories of collective memory. Many English writers have invoked rivers as the spirit of the nation; perhaps the best known example is Alexander Pope's poem 'Windsor Forest', in which the poet saw the Thames as the journey from the primeval forest of Windsor to London, the celestial city of a golden future, and then flowing out to sea in the conquest of the world. The Wye and the Severn have each also been invoked in nationalist terms and, while the Thames is an English river, the Wye and the Severn flow through both Wales and England and enjoy the special status of being British rivers.

The creation of a national identity was one of the achievements of Elizabethan and Jacobean literary culture, following and expanding on the pioneering work of John Leland, who described England and Wales at the behest of Henry VIII. It reached its peak in the publication in 1586 of William Camden's *Britannia*, the avowed aim of which was 'to restore Britain to its Antiquities, and its Antiquities to Britain', and in which the individual special character of the nation was defined by its island status and internal geography. In 1612 Michael Drayton published the first part of *Poly-Olbion*, the poetical equivalent of Leland, Camden, William Harrison and other prose topographers of the period. It was also the poetical equivalent of Christopher Saxton's county maps, which were first published as an atlas in 1579. The subtitle of Drayton's poem is more informative than the title: *A Chorographical Description of Tracts, Rivers, Mountains, Forests, and other Parts of this renowned Isle of Great Britaine, With intermixture of the most Remarquable Stories, Antiquities, Wonders, Rarityes, Pleasures, and Commodities of the same.*

Drayton's Albion is held together by rivers that dominate the landscape in the same way that they dominate Saxton's maps, and the unity of the nation is symbolised by fluvial marriage, a device Drayton had learned from Edmund Spenser's *Faerie Queene*. And so the River Lugg is bridegroom to the Wye, a naturalised counterpart to the marriage of great families, one of the means by which national unity was achieved in Elizabethan England, eschewing the baronial feuding of earlier times.

In describing the course of the Wye Drayton imagined the section 'Twixt the Brecknockian earth, and the Radnorian ground', as the heart of Wales, and by extension of ancient Britain.

> … The ancient *Britons* here
> The River calls to mind, and what those British were
> Whilst *Britain* was herself, the Queen of all the West.[1]

The river sang the song of the Britons, 'expressing wondrous grief' as a succession of invaders,

> The Roman, next the Pict, the Saxon, then the Dane,
> All landing in this Isle, each like a horrid rain
> Deforming her … [2]

Through all efforts past and present to 'exile all brave and ancient things, for ever from this Isle' the river has and will endure. The River Wye represents something inviolable and embodies an unbreakable national spirit.

During the war with France, aristocrats who would normally have embarked on a Grand Tour of Europe had to make do with a Celtic alternative. Against a background of war, republicanism and revolution, patriotism underlies much of the writing and art of the Wye Tour. The nearest the Wye has to Pope and Windsor Forest is *The Springs of Plynlimmon*, written by Luke Booker, vicar of St Edmunds in Dudley, and published in 1834. Although Booker was writing a century after Pope and his is manifestly an inferior poem, he was equally keen to portray rivers as symbols of British greatness and to assert that this sceptred isle is also a heavenly-blessed one. In *The Springs of Plynlimmon* the legend of the sister rivers, now increased to five from the original three, is the vehicle by which he praises England and Wales in patriotic terms. Plynlimmon's chief rivers, Wye and Severn, are also its Anglo-Welsh rivers and Booker wanted to stress that these rivers unify the nation, and that somehow the old division into separate nations was unnatural:

> Twin rivers – none more beauteous seen
> In rocky dell, or meadow green,
> Effusing, as with joy, to crown
> The Union (mark'd for high renown)
> Of Cambria grand, and Anglia fair, –
> On Earth's vast chart the loveliest pair
> Of nations, blended now in one, –
> More fine, – more brave – Earth boasted none.[3]

Booker describes the upper Wye as an Eden-like place and as 'Plynlimmon' sends his five rivers on their way he bids them to

> … bless the vales thro' which ye stray:
> The grateful vales their flow'rs shall bring,
> And waving fields shall laugh and sing.[4]

The essence of the British nation is found in this bountiful valley, and to follow its course is to follow the British story from a land of natural abundance to the building of a great civilisation. The 'verdant vallies' of the upper Wye above Rhayader are places of 'wild and hilly plains / where unperverted Nature reigns'. On past 'Builth's gay meads', the river flows to Hereford, where 'mid four harvests, plenty reigns'. Like Michael Drayton, Booker sees the Wye as a symbol that Britain will endure, whatever empires are built there. At *Magnis* (Kenchester), the pride of the Roman Empire once stood:

> … where that pride erst rear'd its head,
> The pomp and grandeur all are fled!

...
Such monuments of man depart,
To check the swellings of the heart,
And shew how frail is human pow'r
While Time the Works of Art devour;
Yet Nature still unchang'd is seen,
And Vaga, blithe, thro' meadows green
Displays her bright and silvery line.[5]

The wreckage of English power and pride near the Welsh border was a different matter. Luke Booker was as thrilled by Goodrich Castle as countless other tourists, but the castle owed its magnificence to the river, in other words to the narrative of Britain's steady rise to greatness.

Yet, Vaga! there it had not been,
Hadst thou nor travers'd first the scene,
To mark a site for future fame,
And blend its honours with thy name.[6]

The river's glorious associations continue at Monmouth, which gave its name to 'Harry of Monmouth', King Henry V, who triumphed at Agincourt in 1415. But it is at The Kymin that the great traditions of Britain past and present combine. Here, amid a druidic grove of oaks stood a natural rocking stone, or 'buck stone' (according to Samuel Ireland and several other contemporary writers) which had withstood numerous attempts to cast it down, making it a symbol of indestructibility.

... oft the prodigy has brav'd
Rude violence, and yet been sav'd
From all attempts of Goth and clown
To hurl the ponderous Wonder down;
And still, for ages, may it prove
The solemn Guardian of the grove![7]

In 1794 members of the Kymin Club, a group of Monmouth gentlemen led by Philip Hardwick, erected a summer house, or pavilion, on the hilltop above the Wye not far from the rocking stone, chosen for its panoramic views. The pavilion, as Booker calls it, is a two-storey round tower which had a kitchen on the lower floor and banqueting room on the upper storey. Five windows offer commanding views, weather permitting, of Monmouthshire, Herefordshire and Gloucestershire, and only on an extremely clear day would even an optimist hope to glimpse Worcestershire, Shropshire, Radnorshire, Brecknock, Glamorgan and Somerset, as was claimed. It also, needless to say, looked down on the silvery Wye at its confluence with the Monnow. William Coxe had 'the pleasure of dining in this delightful apartment, with a company of Monmouth corps

Britannia crowns the Naval Temple at The Kymin.

Public celebrations at the Naval Temple in 1905
to celebrate the centenary of the Battle of Trafalgar. (Monmouth Museum)

of volunteers, who assembled in celebration of the king's birthday'. In 1800 members erected a Naval Temple 200 yards away to celebrate the victories of British admirals since the beginning of the Revolutionary War with France, culminating with the Battle of the Nile (Trafalgar was still five years away). Britannia is the crowning glory of the Doric temple, which has marble inscription panels and an entablature proclaiming 'Britain's glory'. Richard Colt Hoare, who visited it in 1803, thought it in bad taste, but it is an insight into its own jingoistic times.

The Naval Temple and Luke Booker's poem coincide with the age of the Romantics, among whom there were writers who came to the Wye and admired the natural scene against the backdrop of their political ideals. Conventional poets like Robert Bloomfield might have found in 'rock-founded Chepstow's mouldering pride' a romantic and satisfying spectacle, but Chepstow Castle had a much bleaker message for radical poets. At Chepstow Robert Southey recognised the failure of the last period of hope for republican ideals. It was here that Henry Marten was imprisoned for life for his part in the judgement and execution of Charles I:

> For thirty years secluded from mankind,
> Here Marten linger'd. Often have these walls
> Echoed his footsteps, as with even tread
> He paced around his prison: not to him
> Did Nature's fair varieties exist;
> He never saw the Sun's delightful beams,
> Save when thro' yon high bars it pour'd a sad
> And broken splendor. Dost thou ask his crime?
> He had rebell'd against the King, and sat
> In judgment on him.[8]

Southey contrasted the barren and joyless cell in which Marten lived, with 'Nature's fair varieties' beyond the high bars of his prison window, placed where he never saw a shaft of sunlight fall on the river below. Southey considered Marten's imprisonment not merely unjust, but unnatural.

For a Republican as much as Royalists, access to nature was vital, and landscapes like that around the River Wye were a repository for their ideals, hopes and despairs. These writers had no time for sitting passively in a boat, like the majority of Wye tourists. Walking was a way by which young radicals like Robert Southey, Wordsworth and Coleridge identified themselves with the poor travellers who lived life on the road. Wordsworth first visited the Wye valley on a solitary walking tour in 1793. It was the year that Britain declared war on France when, homeless and dispirited, he walked from Salisbury Plain, up the Wye valley to north Wales. For a poet like him it was not an act of pleasure, but an expression of his restlessness, uprootedness and general feeling of disconnection from conventional society.

The political activist John Thelwall (1764-1834) was also disconnected from conventional society. In the winter of 1797-8 he stayed in a cottage at Llyswen, where he found refuge from London following his acquittal on a charge of treason for being a member of the banned London Corresponding Society. Regarding himself as a victim of state persecution, Thelwall identified with Henry Marten in his cell in Chepstow Castle. Thelwall wrote about his experiences in an essay 'The phenomena of the Wye' for *The Monthly Magazine* in 1798. Thelwall's voice is not that of the traveller who describes a fleeting glimpse of what he happens to see on a particular day, but of the patient observer who notices the things that are not immediately apparent. To begin with, his essay is concerned with winter on the Wye, whereas most travellers and especially artists visited the river in summer. He walked by night when the rules of picturesque appreciation of landscape could not possibly apply. And he stayed a long way upriver in Llyswen, where the danger of meeting other tourists was small.

For Thelwall the landscape was a political metaphor and winter perfectly summed up the state of the nation. In his sights he had the Wye tourists and the artists and conventional writers who indirectly endorsed the status quo. Thelwall characterises them as a butterfly race, spreading their wings only in the genial rays of the sun. Summer visitors inevitably saw a harmonious landscape where everything was in its right order. This, as academics have been pointing out since the 1970s, was a political point of view as well, asserting that rural society as it then existed was the natural state of things, as opposed to those trends that threatened it, namely industrialisation and the republicanism fired by the ideals of the French Revolution. The result was that, in contemporary art and literature, inhabitants of rural landscapes were portrayed as little more than ciphers, uncomplaining people who needed no voice and little attention, blissfully unaware as they were of the paradise in which they lived. There was little social focus in picturesque travel writing, and Thelwall thought the balance needed to be redressed. He therefore made a point of describing the floods he saw and what he was told of the floods of 1795. In many ways a grim tale, there were also grounds for faith in the future, which reflected his own political optimism. Floods spread silt and fertilise the ground, providing hope for what might blossom afresh in the spring. He also noted how the poor people hooked floating branches from the rivers and stocked them for use as firewood. Since access to firewood was restricted by landowners, the prospect of gathering it for free was not to be passed up. It was said that some of the poorer people of Hay gathered enough wood to see them through a whole winter.

Another counterpoint to traditional patriotic views of the river was expressed by Wordsworth in the most famous poem to have been written about the Wye. Wordsworth was acquainted with the literature of the Wye valley, but he was not to be a conventional Wye tourist. He was also familiar with allusive landscape poetry, deriving from Milton's *Paradise Lost*. Both have a bearing on 'Lines written a few miles above Tintern Abbey, on revisiting the banks of the Wye during a tour, July 13, 1798', published as part of *Lyrical Ballads* in 1798. Wordsworth was already an experienced walker, but his visits to Wales in 1793 and 1798 remind us that war prevented him from walking on the Continent as he had done in 1790. On his second visit to the Wye he was accompanied by his sister Dorothy. They walked from Chepstow to Tintern on the first day, then crossed the river and walked as far up as Goodrich on the second day. On the third day they walked back to Chepstow, and in the 'four or five days' between leaving Tintern and arriving in Bristol the poem was written.

The five years that separated his two Wye tours had been tumultuous personally and politically. Wordsworth's Republican ideals had been sorely challenged by the Terror that followed the French Revolution and by Britain's declaration of war against France. The seemingly unchanging landscape of the Wye was therefore partly an escape route out of political realities for the poet. An alternative argument asserts that Wordsworth wrote the poem as an act not of political escapism but of political retrenchment, allowing him to recuperate from the failures of the French Revolution. The Wye valley certainly gave him a place to think. From his lofty cliff top he surveyed a scene where

> ... on a wild secluded scene impress
> Thoughts of more deep seclusion; and connect
> The landscape with the quiet of the sky.[9]

Despite its title, the poem makes no reference to Tintern Abbey, nor to any of the other antiquities that visitors customarily sought out for praise. Writers had long invoked the river as national symbol by reference to the buildings on its banks, be it the ruined monastery, the medieval castles, industry or the Roman ruins at Kenchester. Luke Booker shows that the taste for this kind of writing was far from over when Wordsworth was writing in 1798, but Wordsworth gives himself no room for national sentiment.

The marked absence of human beings in the poem has been credited to Wordsworth's political disappointments: to omit beggars, pleasure boats and industry might be an attempt to purify his mind of political thoughts. He certainly left out many of the details he would have seen. The cottagers around Tintern are only hinted at, in phrases that echoed the words of William Gilpin – he refers to 'vagrant dwellers in the houseless woods', the only sign that they are there being 'wreaths of smoke / sent up, in silence, from among the trees'. Their homes were close to nature, 'green to the very door', suggesting the idealised world imagined earlier by his radical poet friends Southey and Coleridge. But the cottagers are never more than a notional presence and as the poem progresses it is not the political that concerns him but the personal.

For Republicans like Wordsworth and Robert Southey the Wye had been coded with political meaning because of Henry Marten's incarceration at Chepstow, but Wordsworth now lacked the optimism of Southey, Thelwall and his own early years. The Wye allowed Wordsworth to reconnect with an earlier self, which will ultimately allow him to abandon his former Republican fervour and the events that unfolded from it – 'the fever of the world' – and move on:

> ... when the fretful stir
> Unprofitable, and the fever of the world,
> Have hung upon the beatings of my heart,
> How oft, in spirit, have I turned to thee

O sylvan Wye! Thou wanderer through the wood
How often has my spirit turned to thee![10]

It might have been a poetic trope to find consolation in nature, but it was Wordsworth's way of transcending recent history. The poem allows him to unburden himself from the last five years of his personal life and the times he had lived through. His visit to the Wye was a process of self-renewal, allowing him to cast off his republicanism and class struggle, in favour of the healing influence of nature: 'Nature never did betray / the heart that loved her'.[11]

Wordsworth takes us in an unexpected direction. Starting out from the turmoil of his life and times, he ended with the river not as the repository of the collective memory of a nation, but as the carrier of personal memory. Written in contemplation of the Wye, his poem was one of the defining moments that transformed the place of Nature in our culture.

❧ 15 ❧
Picturesque, Various and Interesting in the Extreme – the Tour of the Upper Wye

The Wye Tour was a self-contained spectacle that never extended further upstream than Ross. From here the river had to be followed by water, as the road diverted away from the river bank, and the scenery was not seen as picturesque. (Today, walkers can stay close to sections of the river on the Wye Valley footpath.) Hereford was much visited by tourists by the late 18th century but, although writers had much to say about the city itself, few of their observations were associated with the river. The same applied further upstream at places like Bredwardine. The Wye that visitors responded to was further up, beyond Builth and especially upstream of Rhayader. This was a very different river to the lower Wye. The lower river was a busy commercial waterway and had many towns and villages on its banks. Above Rhayader there were no vessels on the water, and very few settlements of any consequence. It was the river as a work of nature that people enjoyed, in a world inhabited by natives who eked out a Spartan existence in isolated communities.

The upper Wye, and upland scenery in general, was not always seen as a place of aesthetic beauty. Edmund Gibson, editing an expanded edition of Camden's *Britannia* in 1695, described the Wye above Rhayader as 'a vast wilderness, dismal to behold by reason of many crooked ways and high mountains'.[1] By the mid 18th century, of course, that was exactly what tourists were looking for.

In later editions of his Wye tour, William Gilpin provided a brief description of the entire river, even if only at second-hand, based on the journal written by an unnamed friend or colleague. Gilpin imagined travelling upstream from Ross, but later writers tended to follow the river downstream from the source. Not until the 1790s was there a full account of the whole river, written and illustrated by Samuel Ireland (1744-1800). Ireland specialised in producing books of picturesque tours (of Holland and France) and of picturesque views of some of Britain's chief rivers, the Thames (1792), Medway

(1793), Warwickshire Avon (1795) and the Wye (1797). Ireland was no great artist but there was a healthy market for topographical views of British scenery. For the historian, however, Ireland proved in his words and pictures to be a valuable eyewitness to life by the riverside, often giving us the only views of some of the ferries on the river. But Ireland's account of the Wye was not really a practical guide for tourists. Not until 1841 did Leitch Ritchie publish his description of the Wye, subtitled 'a picturesque ramble', pointing out that previous books had covered only part of the Wye and that 'something more was due to the most celebrated river in England [sic]'.[2] In practice, the independent travellers who journeyed to the upper Wye usually followed only part of its course, or made a special visit to the source. Many were interested in visiting tributary rivers like the Lugg, and especially the Elan valley and its bleak mountain road from Rhayader to Aberystwyth.

The Elan valley was also the way to the waterfall at Devil's Bridge, one of the prime destinations for travellers in mid Wales. (It had the happy consequence that on the Wye above Rhayader the English traveller was unlikely to bump into one of his compatriots.) As for the appeal of upland scenery, in Wales there was plenty of competition. Apart from the Wye Tour there were other well-trodden routes in Wales, notably around Snowdonia. Between 1770 and 1815 at least 80 books describing tours in Wales were published. The reading public was alerted to the undiscovered delights of Wales by the publication of Thomas Pennant's tours, first published in 1778, and by the success of topographical prints; the work of Paul Sandby was widely distributed and made many

Samuel Ireland's view of the Wye valley above Rhayader,
with two travellers on horseback in the distance.

places in north Wales well known to a wider public. The improvement of many of the roads in Wales and the availability of suitable accommodation also drew more people in. None of these tours was based around a single topographical feature like a river – the Wye Tour from Ross to Chepstow was an exception in that respect, but also because it was undertaken by water, and was serviced by so many facilities along the route. Many travellers sought out natural wonders like waterfalls, while others like Thomas Pennant and Richard Fenton were mainly interested in antiquities. Travellers tended to follow well-worn itineraries that took in Snowdonia via a route along the Dee valley, Devil's Bridge in mid Wales and industrial and scenic south Wales, as well as the lower Wye. The popularity of Devil's Bridge and the added profile it enjoyed through the development of the nearby Hafod Estate by Thomas Johnes, from 1785, undoubtedly helped swell the numbers visiting mid Wales and the upper River Wye between Rhayader and Builth.

The upper Wye was very different from the lower Wye for travellers in the 18th and 19th centuries. One of the obvious differences was that there was no public transport in the upper part of the river valley. There was a coach from Hereford to Aberystwyth, by way of Hay, Builth and Rhayader, but beyond that the tourist had to rely on his own resources. Radnorshire had only a single post-chaise according to Benjamin Malkin in 1803. Even as late as the 1830s the visitor to Rhayader in October would 'find no means of communication with the rest of the world, except for those who journey with post horses, and those who make use of the locomotive powers of their own limbs'.[3] Upstream of Glasbury, the Radnorshire roads left much to be desired. 'The road on this side of the river is not turnpike, and very bad. It is no where fit for a carriage, and believe will not admit of one between Aberedwy to Buallt [Aberedw to Builth].'[4]

Some travellers followed part of the Wye on a longer itinerary through Wales. In his 1797 tour, for example, Richard Warner travelled from Brecon to join the river at Builth; he followed it up to Rhayader, whence he set out on the mountain road toward Devil's Bridge and Aberystwyth. Often the road deviated from the river bank. The pedestrian traveller did not have to follow the roads, however, and Leitch Ritchie described being able to follow the river bank at will, at a time before wandering about in fields was deemed to be trespass.[5] Travellers on foot or horseback could also take advantage of numerous ferries. Benjamin Malkin crossed the river seven times in the 20-mile stretch between Hay and Builth, to view the scenery from different angles. Malkin encouraged pedestrian travellers near Rhayader to take advantage of a 'new and unfinished turnpike road, cut with a labour apparently not to be compensated by any traffic here'.[6] The roads slowly improved, and in any case were better the further downstream the traveller had reached. By the 1830s Ritchie could advise travellers to stop and admire the views at the fourth and seventh milestones downstream of Builth.[7]

For more independent-minded travellers who found ticking off the major sights of the Wye Tour unsatisfying, the upper river offered much more in the way of adventure. John Thelwall criticised the limited ambitions of Wye Tour artists, and by implication its tourists too, who sought the established viewpoints and followed rigid rules on what made a good landscape painting. When every picturesque view needed the correct foreground, middle distance and background, and the correct proportion of light and shade, the landscape was rendered bland and predictable. Thelwall argued that mountainous country did not need to follow these rules, and proved it by striding out on to the hills at night when the effects of light and shade were nullified. 'I was particularly impressed at the latter end of last autumn, during a nocturnal walk in the neighbourhood of Builth. The night was dark and comfortless – no moon, no star in the firmament; and the atmosphere was so thick with vapours and descending showers, that even the course of the river was scarcely discernible. In short nothing was visible but a sky of sullen grey, and one vast sable mass of surrounding mountain. ... Never before was I so deeply impressed with the power of mere outline', a scene unrelieved by the play of light and a varied palette, 'and yet the eye was feasted, and the imagination was filled with mingled impressions of sublimity and beauty'. As we have seen, in the winter of 1797-8 Thelwall was living in a cottage at Llyswen, which provided a refuge from the many enemies he had made in positions of authority in London. Llyswen was too far upstream to be part of the Wye Tour. Thelwall liked it because it was relatively remote and unappreciated, and because the delights of its scenery had nothing to do with polite notions of taste. He had in mind especially fashionable landscape parks and pleasure grounds that were designed to be at their best in spring and summer, which made no contribution this far up the river valley. 'Its rocks, its mountains, its dingles, its precipices, constitute a more permanent and superior charm.'[8]

There were clichés in the literature of the upper river, just as there were on the lower river. To start at Plynlimon was to start at the beginning of the world, according to one mid 19th-century guide book: 'We appear to have commenced our tour at the beginning of civilization, improving as we advance. The whole is thoroughly Welsh, and the people – original in manners and appearance – seem to have learnt contentment in the lap of poverty, to have but few wants.'[9] Nothing eases the consciences of the privileged more than to know that the poor are happy in their poverty.

Travellers were not guaranteed to see the splendours of the Wye valley in their prime. The upper river was much more changeable than the lower river, at the mercy of the weather and the seasons. So at the source Samuel Ireland was lucky. 'We were peculiarly fortunate in having a bright and clear day to view in all its grandeur this sublime and picturesque scenery', which their 'experienced guide informed us had scarce ever occurred during a course of many years in those airy regions'. At Rhayader, however, he had cause to be disappointed by the dry weather at this 'miserable place'. Drought meant that 'we had the misfortune to lose the display and thunder of its cataract', and they were treated instead to the 'ponderous rocky substances' that made up the river bed.[10]

Although the upper Wye was deemed to have plenty of scenery worth seeing, not all of it was worth making a special effort to see, at least according to some contemporary observers. Upstream of Llangurig the rewards did not always repay the effort of travelling there, which applied especially to Plynlimon, the chief attraction of which is that it is the source of three rivers. The problem for the upland area around Plynlimon is that the whole countryside is high and the peaks are not especially prominent. The high altitude contributes to the cold and windy climate, with few sheltered valleys or opportunity to find sanctuary in the lee of a hill. The uplands were quite treeless, in marked contrast to the river valley around and below Rhayader. In the literature of the period, the upper Wye seemed even more primitive and bleak because it was not a place that actively catered for tourists, but also because travellers wanted to find a wilderness and emphasised that in their writing.

Plynlimon, where the sources of the Wye and Severn were both places of pilgrimage, was very often approached from the south west, from Ponterwyd and Dyffryn Castell, which are both in Ceredigion on the Llangurig-Aberystwyth road. Nearby Eisteddfa Gurig was a small hamlet with one inn and a rival ale house set up by a mountain guide, which advertised guided tours of the mountain.[11] The hospitality was simple but ample. The traveller stepping from the Aberystwyth mail coach would find in the Plynlimon Inn comfortable if rustic hospitality, a turf-fuelled fire, home-brewed ale, and a clean and comfortable bed.

Plynlimon was wild enough to warrant hiring a guide to the sources of the Wye, as well as the sources of the Rheidol and Severn. Leitch Ritchie stayed at the Plynlimon Inn in 1841, home to the only English speakers in the place, and was taken to the source of the Wye by the landlord. George Borrow hired the services of a man at Dyffryn Castell who worked partly as a shepherd, to show him the sources of the rivers. The man was described as 'a tall, athletic fellow, dressed in brown coat, round buff hat, corduroy trousers, linen leggings and highlows, and though a Cumro had much more the appearance of a native of Tipperary'.[12] The guide clearly knew the hills, but what paths they may have trod have now disappeared. The top of Plynlimon is largely free of paths, except for sheep tracks, but it must once have been easier to walk on as Borrow's guide claimed that it took a quarter of an hour to walk from the source of the Severn to the source of the Wye. It would take much longer now.

One of the principal attractions of the source was that it seemed to be a self-contained world completely detached from contemporary society. Leitch Ritchie commented on the independence of the people who lived at Eisteddfa Gurig, and noted that the head of every household was a shepherd. 'The husband, assisted by the sons, when young, tends the sheep on the mountain; the wife makes flannel, and knits stockings; and the daughters go out to service at an early age. Their little ménage is comfortable. Their bread is barley cakes; they sometimes salt a pig; they provide themselves with a quarter of beef at one time and, like their betters, live at home and kill their own mutton.'[13]

Authors did not always praise the beauty of Plynlimon scenery. Gilpin thought it too wild, dreary and unadorned to qualify as a scene of grandeur or beauty. Travellers wanted incident and detail, unlike a modern walker who might like the light, the air and the solitude. Thomas Roscoe had the impression that few people bothered to go to the source by the 1830s, largely because the journey was 'rendered dangerous by swamps and turbaries', and that the view from the top failed to offer 'a sufficient reward for the toil and difficulty of the pilgrimage'.[14]

Heading downstream, the first settlement of any consequence was Llangurig. Visitors rarely wrote flatteringly of it – wretched, squalid, mean are some of the adjectives it inspired. Llangurig was described by Samuel Ireland as a place of 'clay cottages without chimneys, churlish boors, sour milk and black bread', its only saving grace its dramatic scenery. It was certainly very different from the experiences to be had on the Wye Tour proper. Thomas Roscoe left Llangurig replete with anecdotes, and seems to have enjoyed himself as he was 'indulged with Welsh singing, much rapid, Welsh converse, and peals of light-hearted laughter from the merry crowd of both sexes there congregated', drinking the stout Welsh ale and eating bread tinged with peat smoke.[15] These sparsely inhabited parts of Wales were as good as venturing abroad for many English travellers. What Leitch Ritchie like about the river as far down as Rhayader was its Welshness – 'it possesses that foreign aspect which is so exciting to the curiosity'.[16]

Travellers to the upper Wye could experience landscapes that were in turn dramatic and grand to those that seemed to them monotonous and insipid. The landscape opens out around Llangurig, where the river meanders in a wide valley floor, but this expanse was not to everyone's taste. T.H. Fielding was unimpressed, as 'immense beds of gravel extending on all sides, and denuded of the turf, present a picture of desolation, in character very different to the country from whence the river descends'.[17] William Gilpin summed up the problem, that the river was insufficient for the scale of the valley.

Where the river enters Radnorshire, however, the valley floor narrows and the hills seem closer at hand. Here visitors found the scenery offered them the aesthetic pleasures they were looking for, a river of character in a natural landscape. The river, especially close to Nannerth Rocks near Rhayader, becomes quite moody: 'The Wye rolls onward

T.H. Fielding's 19th-century view of the landscape above Rhayader,
a place of dramatic mountain scenery, little settlement, and poor roads.

over a rocky channel, sometimes in calm and deep silence, at others, foaming over banks of rock, and bounding from ledge to ledge; now pent in a narrow channel, it runs with amazing rapidity.'[18] Richard Warner took the trouble to climb the hill above Rhayader to survey the river valley. It was 'a pleasing, varied landscape. The sinuous course of the river; the vivid verdure of the meadows which it waters; the little town of Rhaiddar, with its neat white-washed cottages; and the dark mountains which surround it on every side, combined to produce a picture new and striking.'[19]

When Richard Warner reached Rhayader in his 1797 walk, the Lion Inn had room only for one guest, and Warner had to walk a quarter of a mile in torrential rain to the cottage where it was arranged for him to spend the night. Richard Colt Hoare was also unimpressed by the Red Lion – 'bad' – and was equally terse about the river – 'an insignificant stream'.[20] Colt Hoare was travelling across country from Devil's Bridge towards New Radnor. But Rhayader was a busy, self-contained place, as was apparent when Warner and his fellow traveller entered the kitchen of the inn. 'A large table covered with rounds of beef, loins of pork, fragments of geese &c &c appeared at one end, round which was seated a motley group of noisy Welsh rustics, who voraciously devoured the good things before them. Opposite to these were two Scotch pedlars' while 'the middle of the kitchen was occupied by a number of sportsmen just returned from growse-shooting on the mountains'.[21]

Rhayader was only a small town by the 19th century, but it was interesting by virtue of its position on the upper part of the river, and because from there the traveller could

The 'calm and deep silence' near Nannerth Rocks,
one of the few places on the Wye where trees overhang the river.

239

set out up the Elan valley toward Devil's Bridge and then Aberystwyth. It also had the air of a formerly important place. And beyond the town the scenery changed again, with rich meadows and oak woodlands, less bleak and more abundant as the river drew in the waters of the Elan, Claerwen and later the Ithon. This section of the river provided plenty of picturesque encounters with its steep hillsides, plentiful woods, the river cut through rocks, at times gentle and others turbulent. This 'continuous series of picturesque views' was deemed 'sufficient of themselves to make the reputation of the river'.[22]

There was epic history in these hills. Vortigern was well known in England throughout the Middle Ages thanks to Geoffrey of Monmouth's *History of the Kings of Britain* (1136). He was the British king who invited the Saxons Hengist and Horsa to become allies against the Picts. William Camden had noted that after the Saxons had ousted Vortigern, this traitor to the British found refuge in the mountain fastness above Rhayader, where by 'God's vengeance pursuing him, he was consumed by lightning'.[23] There were legends of Vortigern in several places in Britain, including on the Wye at Little Doward, and his Rhayader association was in decline by the time tourists started visiting. Instead, near Builth travellers could visit Cefn-y-bedd where Llywelyn ap Gruffudd, last native Prince of Wales, was killed in a skirmish in 1282. Richard Warner liked to think of Llywelyn as a 'Cambrian chieftain' living in a Celtic Heroic Age, brought down when 'the spear of Adam de Francton pierced his heart whilst he was performing prodigies of valour'. Warner, like all of his contemporaries, recounted, and not without some relish, the brutality of the times, describing how Llywelyn's corpse was taken to Edward I at Conwy where the English king gloated over his Celtic foe. It was Britain's answer to the *Iliad*, the nation's equivalent of a classical past. After ruminating on these great events, Warner entered Builth, which 'contains nothing that deserves particular attention'.[24]

By 1800 Builth was only a small town. Here was the arched bridge 'whose appearance gives at once importance to the town, and beauty to the river'. But for T.H. Fielding in 1841 the town itself was nothing special: 'the interior of the town does not answer to its outward appearance, being old and mean in the lower parts, though the higher street is less objectionable, and contains some good houses'.[25] To others it had the air of an ancient settlement. The mounds by the bridge were the remains of a medieval castle; the town was thought to be the Roman Bullaeum Siluram.[26] By the 1830s the town had entered the second phase in its history, when it became known as a spa resort and acquired its more upmarket name of Builth Wells. It had saline, sulphurous and chalybeate springs, and a pump room, to complement its growing reputation as a land of plenty – the game in its woods, the salmon, trout and grayling in its river and tributary streams.

Aberedw again offers the delights of precipitous rocks closing in on the river, with a castle at the confluence of Wye and Edw that was never as grand as its setting. The river hence was ideal picturesque travelling country, neither too rugged and bleak, nor too level and monotonous. Glasbury was where the 'orchards, groves and careful cultivation about this smiling spot, remind us that we are leaving the mountain country'.[27] Surrounding land that was agreeable, fertile, richly wooded and far from the madding

The appeal of the upper Wye was its grand isolation;
this is how Samuel Ireland portrayed Builth in 1794.

T.H. Fielding, who sold himself as a teacher of painting and watercolours at the East India
Company's military college, was one of a minority of artists to portray the upper Wye,
here looking towards Aberedw church.

crowd is what the final Welsh stretch of the river offered and it was widely appreciated. The river runs partly through smooth eroded rocks, occasionally turbulent, but often placid. Benjamin Malkin was loaned a servant of Mr Macnamara of Llangoed Castle, who acted as a guide to ascending the steep valley sides to appreciate the scenery of the river valley. The castle at Aberedw, built to command the Wye and Edw valleys, found a renewed attraction as a place to appreciate the scenery. The stretch of river between Hay and Whitney, William Gilpin concluded, was a special section of river. 'The Wye may in this place be more beautiful than in any other part of its course. Between Ross and Chepstow the grandeur and beauty of its banks are its chief praise. The river itself has no other merit than that of a winding surface of smooth water. But here, added to the same decoration from its banks, the Wye itself assumes a more beautiful character; pouring over shelving rocks; and forming itself into eddies, and cascades, which a solemn parading stream through a flat channel cannot exhibit.'[28]

T.H. Fielding expressed the attraction of the Wye in Herefordshire, a county seemingly untouched by the industrial revolution even as late as the mid 19th century. 'The Wye long retains the rural simplicity of its secluded course, undisturbed, and undefiled by the presence of manufactories.'[29] And it was also much more inhabited than the landscape around the upper river, Moccas Court, Clifford Castle, Monnington, Rotherwas and Holme Lacy all being attractions that enhanced the scene for travellers.

Perceptions of the Wye changed in the second half of the 19th century. Tastes and the nature of travel had changed. Men took up angling and other country sports, as Leitch Ritchie had noted at Builth. Murray's *Handbook for travellers in South Wales* (1860) could not travel up the Wye without remarking on the church architecture en route, a reflection of the growing interest in historic architecture and the revival in taste for things medieval. Bridge Sollers was noted mainly for its Decorated church, and Bredwardine

Hay-on-Wye, 'an irregular, ill-paved town with narrow streets built on uneven ground' according to Richard Colt Hoare in 1802, a few years after this engraving was published.

was cited as the oldest church in the county, whatever that means.[30] The railway made a difference, making it possible for travellers to follow the course of the Wye from Hay upwards to just north of Rhayader. This was the Mid Wales Railway, which opened in 1864 and ran along the Wye from Three Cocks Junction near Glasbury to Marteg above Rhayader, from where it left the Wye valley in the direction of Llanidloes. In the same year the Hereford, Hay & Brecon Railway opened from Three Cocks Junction, passing along the Wye from Glasbury to Whitney.

The upper River Wye was largely forgotten as a place of scenic beauty in the century that followed the arrival of the railways. The major events of that period, including the construction of reservoirs in the Elan Valley, and the designation elsewhere of Areas of Outstanding Natural Beauty and National Parks, bypassed the Wye valley and had the effect of downgrading its status. It is ironic that one of the finest descriptions of the Wye above Glasbury was written in this period. Francis Kilvert was a resident, not a tourist, and a regular train passenger too. From the train carriage he 'saw all the old familiar sights, the broad river reach at Boughrood flashing round the great curve in the sunlight over its hundred steps and rock ledges, the luxuriant woods which fringe the gleaming river lit up here and there by the golden flame of a solitary ash, the castled rock towers and battlements and bastions of the Rocks of Aberedw'.[31]

❧ References ❧

Chapter 1 A noble and glorious river

1 W. Plomer (ed), *Kilvert's Diary*, i (1938), p.351.

Chapter 2 The natural river

1 R. Warner, *A walk through Wales* (1798), p.55.
2 S. Owen et al, *Rivers and the British Landscape* (2005), p.232.
3 C. Park, 'Introduction to British Rivers', in Owen, *Rivers and the British Landscape*, p.24.
4 A. Richards, 'Herefordshire', in C. Lewis and A. Richards, *The glaciations of Wales and adjacent areas* (2005), pp.129-30, 141-4.
5 W. Plomer (ed), *Kilvert's Diary*, ii (1939), p.128; i (1938), pp.320, 333, 351.
6 V. Stockinger, *The Rivers Wye and Lugg navigation* (1996), p.124.
7 *Kilvert's Diary*, iii (1940), p.455.
8 J. Duncumb, *Collections towards the history and antiquities of the county of Hereford*, i (1804), p.13.
9 *Kilvert's Diary*, ii, p.126
10 L. Toulmin Smith (ed), *Leland's Itinerary in England and Wales*, iii (1964), p.109.
11 R. Silvester & R. Hankinson, 'Clas, church and village at Glasbury', *Radnorshire Society Transactions*, 73 (2003), pp.116-7.
12 Natural Resources Wales, *Wye Abstraction Licensing Strategy* (2015).

Chapter 3 Plynlimon

1 J. Harvey (ed), *William Worcestre: Itineraries* (1969), pp.67, 199.
2 Giraldus Cambrensis, *The Description of Wales*, i, 5.
3 G. Borrow, *Wild Wales* (3rd edition 1872), pp.274-5.
4 G. Jones and K. Rowntree, *A Prospect of Wales* (1948), p.6.
5 E.R. Henken, *National Redeemer: Owain Glyndwr in Welsh Tradition* (1996), pp.77, 152.
6 Borrow, *Wild Wales*, p.274.
7. *The Mabinogion*, translated by Sioned Davies (2007), p.206.

8 M. Drayton, *Poly-Olbion*, song vi, lines 103-7, 115-23.
9 W. Harrison, *Description of Britain* (1587), xiii, lines 65-6
10 B. Malkin, *The Scenery, Antiquities and Biography of South Wales* (1804), p.332
11 L. Ritchie, *The Wye and its associations* (1841), p.14.
12 L. A. Twamley, *An Autumn ramble by the Wye* (1839).
13 T. Roscoe, *Wanderings and Excursions in South Wales* (1837), p.59.
14 D. Bick, *The Old Metal Mines of Mid Wales, part 4: West Montgomeryshire* (1990), pp.54-8.

Chapter 4 A river of churches

1 T.H. Fielding, *A picturesque description of the River Wye* (1841), p.18.
2 *Book of Llandaff*, ii, 11, I-III.
3 Ibid., iv.1.V-VII.
4 Ibid., iv.1.VIII.
5 Ibid., iv.3.
6 R. Silvester & R. Hankinson, *Early medieval ecclesiastical and burial sites in mid and north-east Wales*, Clwyd Powys Archaeological Trust report 612 (2004), plan e.
7 *VCH Gloucestershire*, x, pp.50-62.
8 D. Brook, 'The early medieval church in Gwent', *Monmouthshire Antiquary*, 5 (1988), p.78.
9. T. Rowley, *The Welsh Border* (1997), p.117.
10. *Book of Llandaf*, v.2.
11 A.H. Smith (ed), *The place-names of Gloucestershire*, iii (1964), p.265.
12 R. Silvester, *Radnorshire historic settlements*, part 1, Clwyd Powys Archaeological Trust report 92 (1994), p.147.
13 R. Silvester & R. Hankinson, 'Clas, church and village at Glasbury', *Radnorshire Society Transactions*, 73 (2003), pp.116-7.
14 W. Plomer (ed), *Kilvert's Diary*, ii (1939), p.98; R. Scourfield & R. Haslam, *The Buildings of Wales: Powys* (2013), p.321.

15 S. Ireland, *Picturesque views on the River Wye* (1797), p.103.

16 *VCH Gloucestershire*, v, pp.150-9.

Chapter 5 River crossings

1 B. Malkin, *The Scenery, Antiquities and Biography of South Wales* (1804), p.298.

2 F. Ellison, 'Whitney Bridge and Whitney Ferry', *Transactions of the Woolhope Naturalists Field Club*, (1935), p.119.

3 H. Hurley, *Landscape origins of the Wye valley* (2008), p.158.

4 *VCH Gloucestershire* v, pp.247-71.

5 *Book of Llandaf*, iv.3.

6 L. Toulmin Smith (ed), *Leland's Itinerary in England and Wales*, iii (1964), p.110.

7. *Gentleman's Magazine* (1819), p.381; his memorial is in Kings Caple church.

8 J Webb, *Memorials of the Civil War*, i (1879), p.9.

9. A. Lamont, 'Fords and ferries of the Wye', *Transactions of the Woolhope Naturalists Field Club* (1922), p.81.

10 H. Hurley, 'The river crossing at Hoarwithy', *Transactions of the Woolhope Naturalists Field Club*, 44.1 (1982), p.215.

11 Ellison, 'Whitney Bridge and Whitney Ferry', p.119.

12 G. Fairs, *A history of the Hay* (1972), pp.42-3, 46, 51.

13 J. Tucker, *The ferries of Gloucestershire* (2010), pp.140-1.

14 *VCH Gloucestershire* v, pp.150-9.

15 R. Lowe, 'Upmouths, cruckles and gillyns: notes on Wye fisheries between Ross and Monmouth', *Transactions of the Woolhope Naturalists Field Club*, 56 (2008), p.102.

16 Hurley, 'The river crossing at Hoarwithy', p.216.

17. R. Warner, *A walk through Wales* (1798), p.219.

18 A. Crow, *Bridges on the River Wye* (1995), pp.152, 94; D. Chapman, *Hereford, Herefordshire and the Wye* (1880), p.83.

19. L. Toulmin Smith (ed), *Leland's Itinerary in England and Wales*, ii (1906), p.69.

20, A. Cooper, *Bridges, Law and Power in Medieval England* (2006), pp.159, 165, 167.

21 R. Johnson, *The ancient customs of the city of Hereford* (1868), pp.49-50.

22 Ibid., p.49.

23 S. Rigold, 'Structural aspects of medieval timber bridges', *Medieval Archaeology*, 19 (1975), p.54.

24 Toulmin Smith (ed), *Leland's Itinerary*, iii, p.43; ii, p.69.

25 C. Hart, *Royal Forest: a history of Dean's woods as producers of timber* (1966), p.138.

26 S. Ireland, *Picturesque views on the River Wye* (1797), p.26.

27. M. Rowlands, *Monnow Bridge and Gate* (1995).

28 H. Fletcher, *Portrait of the Wye valley* (1968), p.128.

29 M. Cook, *Medieval bridges* (1998), pp.21-2.

30 *Gentleman's Magazine* (1819), p.401.

31 Ibid., pp.400, 401.

32 Malkin, *Scenery, Antiquities and Biography of South Wales*, p.89.

33 Ireland, *Picturesque views on the River Wye*, p.29.

34 Crow, *Bridges on the River Wye*, p.80.

35 Fairs, *History of the Hay*, pp.254-5; *Hereford Times* 29/4/1865.

36 Fairs, *History of the Hay*, p.255.

37. Ibid., pp.256-57.

38 Crow, *Bridges on the River Wye*, pp.76, 26; Ireland, *Picturesque views on the River Wye*, p.7.

39. Hurley, 'The river crossing at Hoarwithy', p.221.

40 Nicholson, *Cambrian Traveller's Guide* (1840), p.645.

41 I. Waters, *Brunel's Tubular suspension bridge over the River Wye* (1976).

Chapter 6 Frontier and battleground

1 J. Harvey (ed), *William Worcestre: Itineraries* (1969), pp.199-201.

2 *Book of Llandaf*, vi. 24; iv. 3.

3 Geoffrey of Monmouth, *History of the Kings of Britain*, translated by Lewis Thorpe (1966), viii.2 (p 187).

4 W. Camden, *Britannia* (1695), p.586.

5 *Anglo-Saxon Chronicles*, translated by G.N. Garmonsway (1972), pp.98-9.

6 A. Brooks & N. Pevsner, *The Buildings of England: Herefordshire* (2012), p.247.

7 W. Plomer (ed), *Kilvert's Diary*, iii (1940), p.160.

8 J. Corbet, *An Historical Relation of the Military Government of Gloucester* (1645), reprinted in J. Washbourn, *Bibliotheca Gloucestrensis* (1823), p.71.

9. Ibid., p.117.

10 Ibid., p.123-4.

11 Ibid., pp.119, 128.

12 Ibid., p.137.

13 J. Washbourn, *Bibliotheca Gloucestrensis* (1823), pp.341-2.

14 Corbet, *Military Government of Gloucester*, p.97.

15 Quoted in J. Duncumb, *Collections towards the history and antiquities of the county of Hereford*, i (1804), p.276.

16 R. Shoesmith, 'A curious feature on the old Wye Bridge', *Transactions of the Woolhope Naturalists Field Club*, 57 (2009), p.90.

17. D. Parsons, *The diary of Sir Henry Slingsby* (1836), pp.163-4.

18 quoted in Duncumb, *History and antiquities of the county of Hereford*, p.284; T.W. Webb (ed), *Military memoir of Colonel John Birch* (1873), p.30.

19. T. Roscoe, *Wanderings and Excursions in South Wales* (1854), p.113.

20 A.L. Rowse, *The Regicides* (1994), pp.104-6.

Chapter 7 Industry

1 H.L.V. Fletcher, *Portrait of the Wye valley* (1968), p.154.

2 E. Taylor, 'The 17th-century iron forge at Carey Mill', *Transactions of the Woolhope Naturalists Field Club*, 45.2 (1986), p.450.

3 Hereford Mills Act 1555, in V. Stockinger, *The Rivers Wye and Lugg navigation* (1996), pp.57-9.

4 R. Johnson, *The ancient customs of the city of Hereford* (1868), p.89; Stockinger, *Rivers Wye and Lugg navigation*, pp.124-5.

5 J. Thelwall, 'The Phenomena of the Wye, during the winter of 1797-8', *Monthly Magazine*, 5 (May 1798), p.345.

6 R. Lowe, 'New Weir, Whitchurch or Symonds Yat: from ironworks to tourist destination', *Transactions of the Woolhope Naturalists Field Club*, 58 (2010), pp.28, 32.

7. Stockinger, *Rivers Wye and Lugg navigation*, p.102.

8 P. Barton, 'Montgomeryshire water corn mills', *Montgomeryshire Collections*, 87 (1999), p.88.

9. Ibid.

10 G.W. Ridyard, 'Supplementary notes on the watermills of Radnorshire - part vi', *Melin: the Journal of the Welsh Mills Society*, 15 (1999), pp.35-40.

11 H. Hurley, *Landscape origins of the Wye valley* (2008), pp.121-2.

12 Ibid., p.124.

13 J. Meredith, *The iron industry of the Forest of Dean* (2006), pp.124-6.

14 P. Dorling & T. Young, *New Weir Forge* (2010), Herefordshire Archaeology unpublished report.

15 S. Ireland, *Picturesque views on the River Wye* (1797), p.139.

16, Ibid., pp.138-9.

17. Hurley, *Landscape origins of the Wye valley*, pp.123-4.

18 T. Whately, *Observations on modern gardening* (1771), pp.109-10.

19. J. Newman, *The Buildings of Wales: Gwent/ Monmouthshire* (2000), pp.274-5.

20 Hurley, *Landscape origins of the Wye valley*, p.133.

21 D. Chapman, *Hereford, Herefordshire and the Wye* (1880), p.90.

Chapter 8 The working river

1 S. Dimmock, 'Urban and commercial networks in the later Middle Ages: Chepstow, Severnside and the ports of southern Wales', *Archaeologia Cambrensis*, 152 (2003), pp.53-68.

2 Ibid., p.57.

3 J. Chandler (ed), *Travels through Stuart Britain: the adventures of John Taylor, the water poet* (1999), p.197.

4 quoted in J. Eisel, 'Aspects of the Wye navigation', *Transactions of the Woolhope Naturalists Field Club*, 60 (2012), p.35.

5 Ibid., p.44.

6 W. Coxe, *An historical tour through Monmouthshire* (1801), p.292.

7. C.W. Oulton, *The Travellers Guide, or English Itinerary*, i (1805), p.235.

8 H. Hurley, *Herefordshire's river trade* (2013), p.56.

9. R. Bloomfield, *The Banks of Wye*, i, lines 471-6.

10 S. Ireland, *Picturesque views on the River Wye* (1797), pp.97-8.

11 T. Roscoe, *Wanderings and Excursions in South Wales* (1854), p.132.

12 M. Willett, *An excursion from the source of the Wye*, 2nd edition (1820), p.37.

13 Eisel, 'Aspects of the Wye navigation', pp.41, 37-39.

14 J. Duncumb, *Collections towards the history and antiquities of the county of Hereford*, i (1804), p.159.

15 Hurley, *Herefordshire's river trade*, pp.59-61.

16 *VCH Gloucestershire*, v, pp.150-9.

17 Hurley, *Herefordshire's river trade*, pp.62-4; Eisel, 'Aspects of the Wye navigation', p.49.

18 Hurley, *Herefordshire's river trade*, pp.33-5.

19 *VCH Gloucestershire*, v, pp.150-9.

20 Hurley, *Herefordshire's river trade*, pp.36-7.

21 Ireland, *Picturesque views on the River Wye*, p.97.

22 quoted in H.L.V. Fletcher, *Portrait of the Wye valley* (1968), p.191.

Chapter 9 Fish

1 J.A. Hutton, 'The life history of Wye salmon', *Transactions of the Woolhope Naturalists Field Club* (1918), p.5.

2 R. Johnson, *The ancient customs of the city of Hereford* (1868), p.91.

3 H. Fletcher, *Portrait of the Wye valley* (1968), p.58.

4 W. Plomer (ed), *Kilvert's Diary*, i (1938), pp.333-4.

5 Fletcher, *Portrait of the Wye valley*, p.183.

6 *Kilvert's Diary*, iii (1940), p.167.

7 E. Davies, Chepstow: a poem in six cantos (1786).

8 I. Waters, 'The salmon fisheries at Chepstow in the nineteenth century', *Gwent Local History*, 42 (1977), pp.21-22.

9 *Book of Llandaf*, iv.20; vi.11.

10 G. Jenkins, *Nets and coracles* (1974), p.34.

11 R. Lowe, 'Upmouths, cruckles and gillyns: notes on Wye fisheries between Ross and Monmouth', *Transactions of the Woolhope Naturalists Field Club*, 56 (2008), p.106.

12 Ibid., pp.99, 102, 108.

13 Jenkins, *Nets and coracles*, pp.83-4.

14 Waters, 'The salmon fisheries at Chepstow', p.24.

15 Jenkins, *Nets and coracles*, pp.98-9.

16 Ibid.

17 *Kilvert's Diary*, i, pp.333-4.

18 Lowe, 'Upmouths, cruckles and gillyns', p.107.

19 Jenkins, *Nets and coracles*, p.173, quoting *Travels in Great Britain*, ii (1805), pp.39-40.

20 J. Duncumb, *Collections towards the history and antiquities of the county of Hereford*, i (1804), pp.162-3.

21 National Library of Wales, Badminton collection, 11,808.

22 Waters, 'The salmon fisheries at Chepstow', p.22; W.C. Oulton, *The traveller's guide, or English itinerary* (1805), p.236.

23 Waters, 'The salmon fisheries at Chepstow', p.26; Jenkins, *Nets and coracles*, p.99.

24 H. Simpson, 'The salmon of the River Wye', in Harlan Walker (ed), *Fish: food from the waters* (1998), p.286.

25 *Kilvert's Diary*, ii (1939), p.221.

26 Waters, 'The salmon fisheries at Chepstow', p.27; Lowe, 'Upmouths, cruckles and gillyns', p.105.

27 *The Ancient Free Fishery in 7 miles of the River Wye between Hereford and Ross* (1911), *passim*.

28 *Kilvert's Diary*, iii, p.171.

29 Ibid., i, p.320.

30 Lowe, 'Upmouths, cruckles and gillyns', p.102; A. Gee & N. Milner, *Rod and net catch statistics for Atlantic salmon, Salmo salar, in the River Wye, 1905-77*. Unpublished report for UWIST Field Centre, Newbridge on Wye, p.21.

31 *Kilvert's Diary*, i, pp.316-17.

32 Hutton, 'The life history of Wye salmon', p.13.

33 Duncumb, *Collections towards the history and antiquities of the county of Hereford*, pp.161-2.

34 Gee & Milner, *Rod and net catch statistics*, pp.3, 9; Jenkins, *Nets and coracles*, p.17.

35 Simpson, 'The salmon of the River Wye', p.292.

Chapter 10 At home by the river

1 B. Burnham & J. Wacher, *The small towns of Roman Britain* (1990), p.71.

2 R. Shoesmith, *Hereford city excavations vol 2: excavations on and close to the defences* (1982), p.89.

3 W. Coxe, *An historical tour through Monmouthshire* (1801), p.303.

4 D. Defoe, *A Tour through the Whole Island of Great Britain* (1971), pp.374-5.

5 W. Wordsworth, 'Lines written a few miles above Tintern Abbey, on revisiting the banks of the Wye during a tour, July 13, 1798', lines 18-23.

6 S. Ireland, *Picturesque views on the River Wye* (1797), p.47.

7 R. Pococke, *The Travels through England of Dr Richard Pococke*, ii (1899), p.215.

8 T. Roscoe, *Wanderings and Excursions in South Wales* (1854), p.155.

9 W. Plomer (ed), *Kilvert's Diary*, iii (1940), p.202.

10 Ibid., i, p.104.

11 J. Eisel, 'The Castle Mills, Hereford', *Transactions of the Woolhope Naturalists Field Club*, 50.1 (2000), p.60.

12 T. Rammell, *Report to the General Board of Health on a preliminary enquiry into the sewerage, drainage, and supply of water, and the sanitary conditions of the inhabitants of the city of Hereford* (1853), pp.29, 31-2.

13 *Hereford Times*, 15/10/2015.

14 Roscoe, *Wanderings and Excursions in South Wales*, p.111.

15 J. Price, *An historical account of the city of Hereford* (1796), pp.74-6.

16 *Hereford Journal*, 29/9/1852, p.3.

17 *Hereford Times*, 18/6/1859, p.8; *Hereford Journal*, 11/7/1860, p.5; I. Cohen, *The Hereford Rowing Club: its history and development*, n.d.

18 *Hereford Times*, 26/4/1862; D. Chapman, *Hereford, Herefordshire and the Wye* (1880), p.99.

19 *Chepstow Weekley Advertiser*, 1/9/1860, p.1; *Hereford Times*, 14/9/1867, p.2.

20 Chapman, *Hereford, Herefordshire and the Wye*, p.82.

Chapter 11 Ice floes and inundations

1 T.H. Fielding, *A picturesque description of the River Wye* (1841), p.10.

2 J. Thelwall, 'The phenomena of the Wye, during the winter of 1797-8', *The Monthly Magazine*, 5 (1798), p.344.

3 Ibid., p.345.

4 *Hereford Times* 14/2/1852, p.8.

5 H. Southall, 'Records of meteorology on the variations of climate for this district of England', *Transactions of the Woolhope Naturalists Field Club* (1870), p.83; *South Wales Daily News*, 13/2/1899, p.5.

6 S. Ireland, *Picturesque views on the River Wye* (1797), p.103.

7 W. Plomer (ed), *Kilvert's Diary*, ii (1939), p.126.

8 Ibid., i, p.34; ii, p.95; iii, pp.436-8, 445, 450.

9 *Hereford Times* 14/2/1852, p.8.

10 *Gloucester Echo*, 29/3/1947; A. Vaughan, *The Great Western's Last Year* (2013), pp.58-9.

11 R. Pococke, *The Travels through England of Dr Richard Pococke*, ii (1899), pp.23-4.

12 J. Duncumb, *Collections towards the history and antiquities of the county of Hereford*, i (1804), p.160n.

13 J. Eisel, 'The great flood of 1795', *Transactions of the Woolhope Naturalists Field Club*, 58, (2010), pp.189-97.

14 Ireland, *Picturesque views on the River Wye*, p.29.

15 *Kilvert's Diary*, iii, p.431; *Hereford Times* 14/2/1852, p.8.

16 Eisel, 'The great flood of 1795', p.192; Southall, 'Records of meteorology', p.84.

17 *Kilvert's Diary*, iii, p.430.

18 Ibid.

19 *Hereford Times* 14/2/1852, p.8.

20 Ibid.

21 Thelwall, 'The phenomena of the Wye', p.345.

22 *Hereford Times* 14/2/1852, p.8.

23 Thelwall, 'The phenomena of the Wye', p.346.

24 Ibid.

25 *Hereford Times* 14/2/1852, p.8.

Chapter 12 The deceitful stream

1 I. Clayton, *Our Billie* (2010).

2 R. Bloomfield, *The Banks of Wye* (1811), pp.22-3n; C. Heath, *The excursion down the Wye* (1808).

3 *Gloucester Citizen*, 27 August 1898, p.4; *Gloucester Journal*, 16/9/1916, p.2.

4 W. Plomer (ed), *Kilvert's Diary*, i (1938), p.321.

5 *Hereford Journal*, 6 September 1862, p.3; *Gloucester Journal*, 17/11/1894, p.8.

6 H. Hurley, *Herefordshire's river trade* (2013), pp.25-6.

7 *Gentleman's Magazine* (1819), p.401.

8 *Gloucestershire Chronicle*, 27/6/1891, p.2; *Gloucester Citizen*, 22/6/1891, p.4; *Gloucester Citizen*, 10/8/1937.

9 *Hereford Journal*, 6/9/1862, p.3.

10 *Hereford Journal*, 27/6/1863, p.7; *Gloucester Citizen*, 10/4/1890, p.3.

11 *South Wales Daily News*, 8/10/1895, p.4; *Hereford Journal*, 3/8/1853, p.3.

12 *Gloucester Citizen*, 17/8/1895, p.3; 26/8/1895, p.4.

13 *South Wales Echo* 8/4/1886, p.4; *Western Times* 10/3/1921, p.4; *Gloucester Citizen* 6/12/1909, p.2.

14 *Gloucester Citizen*, 24/8/1899, p.4; *Gloucester Journal* 18/5/1901.

15 *Usk Observer, Raglan Herald, and Monmouthshire Central Advertiser*, 10/8/1861, p.1.

16 *Gloucestershire Chronicle*, 19/7/1902, p.6; *Monmouthshire Merlin* 18/4/1879, p.5.

17 *Gloucester Citizen* 27/6/1902; *Gloucester Journal*, 29/6/1901, p.8.

18 *Hereford Times* 24/10/1855, p.3; *Bell's Life in London and Sporting Chronicle*, 13/7/1856, p.6.

19 *Man of Ross & General Advertiser*, 9/8/1877, p.5; *Gloucester Citizen*, 31/5/1881, p.4; *Gloucester Citizen*, 26/9/1893, p.4.

20 *Kilvert's Diary*, i, p.50; *Gloucestershire Echo*, 1/8/1902, p.3.

Chapter 13 The Wye Tour

1 S. Ireland, *Picturesque views on the River Wye* (1797), pp.93-4; M. Thompson, *The journeys of Sir Richard Colt Hoare through England and Wales 1793-1810* (1983), pp.80-2.

2 W. Coxe, *An historical tour through Monmouthshire* (1801), p.314.

3 W. Gilpin, *Observations on the River Wye* (1782), p.16.

4 T. Roscoe, *Wanderings and Excursions in South Wales* (1854), p.130.

5 Thompson, *The journeys of Sir Richard Colt Hoare*, p.83.

6 Ireland, *Picturesque views on the River Wye*, p.97.

7 R. Warner, *A walk through Wales* (1798), p.220; Thompson, *The journeys of Sir Richard Colt Hoare*, p.64.

8 Warner, *A walk through Wales*, p.222.

9 R. Bloomfield, *The Banks of Wye* (1811), book i, lines 207-12.

10 Ibid., lines 497-500.
11 Ireland, *Picturesque views on the River Wye*, p.89.
12 Warner, *A walk through Wales*, p.230.
13 C. Heath, *The excursion down the Wye* (1808).
14 Warner, *A walk through Wales*, p.223.
15 Heath, *Excursion down the Wye*.
16 H.P. Wyndham, *A tour through Monmouthshire and Wales* (1781), p.5.
17 Ireland, *Picturesque views on the River Wye*, p.132.
18 Wyndham, *Tour through Monmouthshire and Wales*, p.4.
19 Ireland, *Picturesque views on the River Wye*, p.136.
20 Warner, *A walk through Wales*, p.231.
21 Thompson, *The journeys of Sir Richard Colt Hoare*, pp.83, 101.
22 Roscoe, *Wanderings and Excursions in South Wales*, p.152.
23 W. Plomer (ed), *Kilvert's Diary*, iii (1940), pp.203-4.
24 Ireland, *Picturesque views on the River Wye*, p.157.
25 Gilpin, *Observations on the River Wye*, p.8.
26 Ibid., p.14
27 Ibid., pp.6, 18, 32-3, 22.
28 Ibid., p.36.
29 quoted in J. Mitchell, *The Wye Tour and its artists* (2010), p.49.
30 Thompson, *The journeys of Sir Richard Colt Hoare*, p.80.

Chapter 14 For King and country men

1 M. Drayton, *Poly-Olbion*, song vi, lines 197-9.
2 Ibid., lines 335-7.
3 L. Booker, *The Springs of Plynlimmon*, 'Vaga', lines 44-51.
4 Ibid., lines 81-83.
5 Ibid., lines 239-40, 243-9.
6 Ibid., lines 373-6.
7 Ibid., lines 483-8.
8 R. Southey, 'From the apartment in Chepstow Castle where Henry Marten the regicide was imprisoned thirty years'.
9 W. Wordsworth, 'Lines written a few miles above Tintern Abbey, on revisiting the banks of the Wye during a tour, July 13, 1798', lines 6-8.
10 Ibid., lines 53-8.
11 Ibid., lines 123-4.

Chapter 15 Picturesque, various, and interesting in the extreme

1 W. Camden, *Britannia* (1695), p.586.
2 L. Ritchie, *The Wye and its associations* (1841), p.iii.

3 Ibid., p.23.
4 B. Malkin, *The Scenery, Antiquities and Biography of South Wales* (1804), p.272.
5 Ritchie, *The Wye*, p.22
6 Malkin, *Scenery, Antiquities and Biography of South Wales*, p.296.
7 Ritchie, *The Wye*, pp.26, 27
8 J. Thelwall, 'The phenomena of the Wye, during the winter of 1797-8', *The Monthly Magazine*, 5 (1798), p.344
9 T. Sherwood Smith, *The tourist's guide to the Wye* (1855), p.8.
10 S. Ireland, *Picturesque views on the River Wye* (1797), pp.3, 12.
11 T. Roscoe, *Wanderings and Excursions in South Wales* (1837), p.57; Ritchie, *The Wye*, p.11.
12 G. Borrow, *Wild Wales* (3rd edition 1872), p.271.
13 Ritchie, *The Wye*, p.11.
14 Roscoe, *Wanderings and Excursions in South Wales*, p.57.
15 Ibid., p.69.
16 Ritchie, *The Wye*, p.21.
17 T.H. Fielding, *A picturesque description of the River Wye* (1841), p.4.
18 Ibid.
19 R. Warner, *A walk through Wales* (1798), p.60.
20 M. Thompson, *The journeys of Sir Richard Colt Hoare through England and Wales 1793-1810* (1983), p.64.
21 Warner, *A walk through Wales*, p.57.
22 Ritchie, *The Wye*, p.21.
23 Camden, *Britannia*, p.586.
24 Warner, *A walk through Wales*, pp.52, 54.
25 Fielding, *picturesque description of the River Wye*, p.7.
26 Ritchie, *The Wye*, p.24.
27 Fielding, *picturesque description of the River Wye*, p.10.
28 W. Gilpin, *Observations on the River Wye* (2nd edition 1789), p.69.
29 Fielding, *picturesque description of the River Wye*, p.12.
30 J. Murray, *A handbook for travellers in South Wales* (1870), pp.102-3.
31 W. Plomer (ed), *Kilvert's Diary*, iii (1940), p.83.

✎ Select Bibliography ✑

Booker, Luke, *The Springs of Plynlimmon: A Poem*. William Parke, 1834.

Brooks, Alan, and Verey, David, *The Buildings of England, Gloucestershire: The Vale and the Forest of Dean*. Yale University Press, 2002.

Brooks, Alan, and Pevsner, Nikolaus, *The Buildings of England: Herefordshire*. Yale University Press, 2012.

Chandler, John (ed), *Travels through Stuart Britain: the adventures of John Taylor, the water poet*, Sutton Publishing, 1999.

Coxe, William, *An Historical Tour in Monmouthshire*, Cadell and Davies, 1801.

Crow, Alan, *Bridges on the River Wye*, Lapridge Publications, 1995.

Fletcher, H.L.V., *Portrait of the Wye valley*, Robert Hale, 1968.

Fairs, Geoffrey, *A history of the Hay: the story of Hay-on-Wye*, Phillimore, 1972.

Farr, Grahame, *Chepstow ships*, Chepstow Society, 1954.

Fielding, T.H., *A picturesque description of the River Wye*, Ackerman & Co, 1841.

Gilpin, William, *Observations on the River Wye*, R. Blamire, 1782.

Heath, Charles, *The Excursion down the Wye from Ross to Monmouth*, the author, 1808.

Hurley, Heather (ed), *Landscape origins of the Wye valley*. Logaston Press, 2008.

Hurley, Heather, *Herefordshire's River Trade: craft and cargo on the Wye and Lugg*. Logaston Press, 2013.

Ireland, Samuel, *Picturesque views on the River Wye*, R. Faulder, 1797.

Jenkins, Geraint, *Nets and Coracles*, Davis & Charles, 1974.

Kissack, Keith, *Monmouth: the making of a county town*. Phillimore, 1975.

Kissack, Keith, *The River Wye*. Terence Dalton, 1978.

Lewis, Colin and Richard, Andrew (eds), *The glaciations of Wales and adjacent areas*, Logaston Press, 2005.

Mitchell, Julian, *The Wye Tour and its artists*. Logaston Press, 2010.

Newman, John, *The Buildings of Wales: Gwent/Monmouthshire*, Penguin, 2000.

Plomer, William (ed), *Kilvert's Diary 1870-1879*. Pimlico, 1999.

Rowlands, M.L.J., *Monnow Bridge and Gate*. Alan Sutton, Stroud, 1994.

Scourfield, Robert and Haslam, Richard, *The Buildings of Wales: Powys*. Yale University Press, 2013.

Stockinger, Victor, *The Rivers Wye and Lugg Navigation: a documentary history 1555-1951*. Logaston Press, 1996.

Warner, Rev Richard, *A walk through Wales in 1797*, R. Crutwell, 1798.

Waters, Ivor, *About Chepstow*, Chepstow Society, 1952.

Waters, Ivor (ed), *Brunel's Tubular suspension bridge over the River Wye*, 1856, reprinted Moss Rose Press, 1976.

Waters, Ivor, *The port of Chepstow*, Chepstow Society, 1977.

Whitehead, David and Shoesmith, Ron, *James Wathen's Herefordshire, 1770-1820*, Logaston Press, 1994.

Willet, Mark, *An excursion from the source of the Wye*, 2nd edition, the author, 1820.

✌Index ✍

Italicized page numbers indicate illustrations

Also from Logaston Press   *www.logastonpress.co.uk*

Walking the Old Ways of Radnorshire:
the history in the landscape explored through 26 circular walks
by Andy and Karen Johnson

The walks explore Radnorshire's past, with each walk passing or visiting features about which some background information is given. These include churches, nonconformist chapels, castle sites, dykes, tumuli and other prehistoric remains, Roman forts, a battlefield, medieval houses, spas, upland farming systems, drovers' roads, squatter settlements, inns and a dismantled railway line. Several sites can only be reached on foot. Some walks follow river valleys whilst many more wander Radnorshire's rolling hills and provide expansive views. Others explore its towns and their nearby landscape. The walks range from 3½ to 10½ miles in length, with the majority being between 4 and 7½ miles. Each walk has a sketch map and detailed directions, together with background information about features en route.

Paperback (with flaps), 208 pages, over 200 colour photographs and 27 maps   Price £12.95

Walking the Old Ways of Herefordshire:
the history in the landscape explored through 52 circular walks
by Andy and Karen Johnson

Each walk passes or visits a number of features about which some background information is given. These include churches, castle sites, deserted medieval villages, landscaping activity, quarrying, battle sites, dovecotes, hillforts, Iron Age farmsteads, Saxon dykes and ditches, individual farms and buildings, squatter settlements, almshouses, sculpture, burial sites, canals, disused railway lines – to name but a few, and including some that can only be reached on foot. The walks have also been chosen to help you explore Herefordshire from south to north, west to east, from quiet river valleys to airy hilltops, from ancient woodland to meadows and fields, from remote moorland to the historic streets of the county's towns, and of course Hereford itself. The walks range from 2½ to 9½ miles in length.

Paperback (with flaps), 384 pages, over 450 colour photographs and 53 maps   Price £12.95

A Guide to Slow Travel in the Marches
by Les Lumsdon

The Guide is structured around eight towns – Welshpool, Oswestry, Shrewsbury, Church Stretton, Ludlow, Hereford, Llandrindod Wells and Abergavenny – which act as bases for exploration and for which there is a guided walk, with tours from each using trains and buses. There are also suggestions for cycle rides and walks. The guide also suggests places to eat and imbibe. The section for each location includes a list of extras such as farmers' markets, local activities and festivals, as well as a selection of useful local publications and websites. The book is also supported by its own website which will help keep information up to date.

Paperback, 240 pages, 30 colour & 100 b/w photos, 20 maps   Price £10

Herefordshire's River Trade; Craft & Cargo on the Wye & Lugg
by Heather Hurley

The story of the trade on the rivers Wye and Lugg in Herefordshire has never been told in its entirety – until now. The book covers the type of craft used, the cargoes carried, the families of boat owners, the masters and crew of the boats, accidents on the water, the development of wharves, the hiring of bowhauliers and the advent of the horse towing path. Perhaps most surprising is the extent of boat building along the banks of the Herefordshire Wye, with craft ranging from small ferries to barges and even steam-powered vessels. The book also covers the felling and transporting of timber to supply the shipyards building vessels for the Navy, the need to reduce the price of coal in Hereford, the trade in cider, wine and spirits, and the requirement of lime for agricultural and building purposes. There are also hints of the life-styles of some of those living near the Wye, indicated by the goods that were ordered and transported by boat.

Paperback, 208 pages, 190 illustrations, most in colour   Price £12.95

The Story of Hereford
Edited by Andy Johnson & Ron Shoesmith

This book tells the story of Hereford in breadth and depth, and includes the results of recent research and archaeological investigation. Alongside more familiar aspects of the city's history – how it fared in the Civil War, the foundation and history of the cathedral, the navigation of the Wye – there is new material on Saxon Hereford, medieval trade, Georgian Hereford and the activities of freehold land societies in the Victorian period. There is also information on less well known aspects of the city's past, including Hereford's prominence as a great centre of scientific and other learning at the end of the 12th century, and the use of the city as a base by Simon de Montfort, and also by Prince Henry in the wars with Owain Glyn Dwr. Whether you are familiar with Hereford's history or completely new to it, there is much here to interest, intrigue and surprise.

Paperback, 336 pages with over 160 colour and 50 mono illustrations   Price £15

Shadows in the Hay
Landscape, nature and the passage of time on a Herefordshire farm
by Colin Williams

The discovery of a batch of old photographs of a farm in Herefordshire that once belonged to his great-grandfather, and a conversation with his grandmother about her memories of life on the farm, inspired nature writer Colin Williams to go there on foot and walk the land his ancestors once tended. The journey prompted reflections: what is it about our relationship with where we live that gives us our understanding of 'home', and how has that changed over the generations since the days when his family worked the land of Wolf Point?

Hardback, 144 pages, with 40 b/w photos   Price £12.95